Nick and Zak's Adventures in Capitalism

$10.21
(12/31/13)

$1.00
(9/10/01)

Words of Wisdom from the Nomad Partnership Letters

Contents

PREFACE 5
PART I 8
INTRODUCTION 9
CHAPTER 1   ORIENTATION 13
CHAPTER 2   WHAT WE LOOK FOR 20
CHAPTER 3   MEASURING & EXPLAINING PERFORMANCE 32
CHAPTER 4   GREAT BUSINESSES & VALUE OF INACTIVITY 40
CHAPTER 5   SCALE ECONOMIES SHARED & OTHER INVESTMENT MODELS 50
CHAPTER 6   COMPETITIVE ADVANTAGE 58
CHAPTER 7   PSYCHOLOGY OF HUMAN MISJUDGEMENT 64
CHAPTER 8   LONG-TERM VIEW & DELAY OF GRATIFICATION 80
CHAPTER 9   CONCENTRATION 87
CHAPTER 10 SIMPLE, BUT NOT EASY 93
CHAPTER 11 ERRORS OF OMISSION 98
CHAPTER 12 HOLDING CASH 103
CHAPTER 13 LEVERAGE 105
CHAPTER 14 GROWTH VS. VALUE 107
CHAPTER 15 BUSINESS VALUES VS. STOCK PRICES 113
CHAPTER 16 THE ROBUSTNESS RATIO 118
CHAPTER 17 BUBBLES & ANTI-BUBBLES 126
CHAPTER 18 FOUNDER-LED, OWNER-OPERATORS & INSIDER BUYING 130
CHAPTER 19 INCENTIVES 135
CHAPTER 20 MISTAKES 142
CHAPTER 21 SLACK 155
CHAPTER 22 CONTRARIANISM & GOING AGAINST THE HERD 160

CHAPTER 23   INDEX THINKING 168

CHAPTER 24   INTERDISCIPLINARY THINKING & SCALING LAWS 171

CHAPTER 25   SHORT TERM VOLATILITY 181

CHAPTER 26   HARD & FAST RULES 183

CHAPTER 27   THE PRINCIPAL/AGENT PROBLEM 187

CHAPTER 28   PER SHARE DISCIPLINE & DILUTION RISK 190

CHAPTER 29   INVESTMENT HOLDING PERIODS 195

CHAPTER 30   MOMENTUM INVESTING 200

CHAPTER 31   THE QUIET APPROACH 202

CHAPTER 32   FUND SIZE & GOVERNANCE 206

CHAPTER 33   INFORMATION AS FOOD 218

CHAPTER 34   THINKING IN DECISION TREES 224

CHAPTER 35   SUPER HIGH-QUALITY THINKERS 227

CHAPTER 36   THE EQUITY YIELD CURVE 230

CHAPTER 37   INSTITUTIONAL DYSFUNCTIONALITY 233

CHAPTER 38   NON-TRANSITIVE DICE & INVESTING 236

CHAPTER 39   "SO, HOW DOES ZECKHAUSER PLAY BRIDGE?" 238

CHAPTER 40   DESTINATION ANALYSIS 255

PART II 257

CASE STUDY #1   INTERNATIONAL SPEEDWAY (2002) 258

CASE STUDY #2   MATICHON (2002) 261

CASE STUDY #3   XEROX (2002) 263

CASE STUDY #4   MONSANTO (2002) 267

CASE STUDY #5   STAGECOACH (2002) 269

CASE STUDY #6   COSTCO (2002) 273

CASE STUDY #7   WEETABIX (2003) 276

CASE STUDY #8   LUCENT TECHNOLOGIES (2003) 279

CASE STUDY #9   WEETABIX UPDATE (2003) 281

CASE STUDY #10	UNION CEMENT (2004)	284
CASE STUDY #11	COSTCO (2004)	286
CASE STUDY #12	ZIMBABWE (2005)	294
CASE STUDY #13	AIRASIA (2008)	300
CASE STUDY #14	GAMES WORKSHOP (2008)	303
CASE STUDY #17	BLACK ARROW PLC (2011)	311
CASE STUDY #18	AMAZON	312
THE POSTAMBLE		322

PREFACE

I don't remember exactly when Nick Sleep's letters came across my desk. I vaguely remember that it was either Mohnish Pabrai or Guy Spier who mentioned the letters, which intrigued me since I had never heard of Nick Sleep before during all my years. Even now, there are only two sources on Nick Sleep and Qais Zakaria's ideas I am currently aware of: the partnership letters[1] and Chapter 6 in William Green's **fantastic** *Richer, Wiser, Happier*.

Yet, as I am sure many readers of the letters can relate, I was blown away by the way these two men thought about investing and life. The letters are densely packed with ideas, case studies, and wisdom. They clearly loved what they did: analyzing companies, ruminating about investing and businesses, and accumulating worldly wisdom. Any investor, beginner or seasoned, will come away with new ideas and perspectives.

To be honest, I was slightly overwhelmed when I first started going through the letters (okay I admit, it was a bootleg copy). This "book" started out as a personal project of organizing, dissecting and re-organizing the lessons contained in the letters. I hope you find the lessons within as useful and delightful as I have.

---

[1] You can find the full collection of letters at Nick Sleep's charitable foundation (The International Geophysical Year (I.G.Y)): https://igyfoundation.org.uk/wp-content/uploads/2021/09/Nomad_Partnership_Letters_1-1.pdf

Similar to Jeremy Miller's *Warren Buffett's Ground Rules*[2], each chapter in this book centers around a single idea or theme from the letters and the format will be pretty consistent, starting with some summary points by the author and followed by excerpts from the letters themselves. I've tried to keep my points short, as I'm sure you would rather read the source directly than my interpretation of them. As Jeremy mentions, aggregating the commentary from all the letters on a single topic is pretty revealing, as it shows the revisiting of certain ideas over time and the progression of those ideas.

The book is outlined as followed:
- Part I consists of 40 chapters (or topics) ranging from incentives to scale economies shared to how to think about mistakes to competitive advantages.
- Part II consists of 18 case studies extracted from the letters discussing, among others, Costco, Amazon, and AirAsia.

One interesting thing to note is that many of the ideas presented within the letters aren't necessarily original ideas. Nick and Zak rationally cloned ideas from multiple disciplines and stood on the shoulder of giants (Warren Buffett, Charlie Munger, Bill Miller, Tom Russo, the Santa Fe Institute, etc.) and it is fascinating to see how they tied everything together into their thinking process and investments.

"As a young(ish) man there is something slightly depressing about thinking things through for a while, arriving at a somewhat reasoned conclusion only to find that others have been there before, and years earlier."

Happy cloning.

---

[2] *Warren Buffett's Ground Rules* (Harper Business 2016)

Sleep, Zakaria and Company, Ltd.

1a, Burnsall Street
London
England
SW3 3SR
T: +44 (0) 20 7101 1960
F: +44 (0) 20 7101 1965

Nomad Investment Partnership

Annual Letter

Cumulative returns for the period ended December 31st, 2013

To December 31st, 2013:	Nomad Investment Partnership	MSCI World Index (net) US$
Trailing:	%	%
One year	62.2	26.7
Two years	126.8	46.7
Three years	104.3	38.6
Four years	194.0	54.9
Five years	404.1	101.3
Six years	176.6	19.4
Seven years	235.3	30.2
Eight years	280.9	56.3
Nine years	316.5	71.1
Ten years	409.8	96.3
Eleven years	815.5	161.3
Twelve years	827.4	109.3
Since inception (September 10th, 2001)	921.1	116.9
Annualized since inception:	%	%
Before performance fees	20.8	6.5
After performance fees	18.4	
Value of a dollar invested at inception (pre-fees)	$10.21	$2.17

Part I

Chapter 0

INTRODUCTION

Investing is a wonderful, thoughtful, adventure but it can also be self-centered, a tendency that can be reinforced by the wealth that can follow.

We think it is true that, once past X-amount, real meaning comes with reinvesting in society through charitable giving, which can also be a thoughtful, challenging, wonderful adventure, but with the added bonus that it feels like the world working properly.

- SPRING 201

On September 10, 2001, Nick Sleep and Qais Zakaria launched their fund called the Nomad Investment Partnership. As William Green put it in his chapter on Nick & Zak in his book, Richer, Wiser, Happier[3] :

> *"In 2001, Sleep and his friend Qais "Zak" Zakaria created a fund called the Nomad Investment Partnership, which they viewed as a laboratory test for how to invest, think, and behave in the most "high-quality" way."*

---

[3] *Richer, Wiser Happier* (Scribner 2021)

From the onset, Nick and Zak viewed Nomad as investing for the long term and expected to beat the index handsomely over time. And indeed they did: over thirteen years, Nomad returned 921.1 percent versus 116.9 percent for the MSCI World Index[4]. The fund's annualized return before fees was 20.8 percent (after fees, 18.4 percent) versus 6.5 percent for the MSCI World Index. In other words, every dollar invested in Nomad became $10.21, compared to $2.17 in the index.

In a few of the early letters, Nomad laid out a few "ground rules"[5]:
1. We are investing for the long term in modestly valued firms run by management teams who may be making decisions the fruits of which may not be apparent for several years to come.
2. The near term results are likely to be as bad as they may be good, but we are confident that in the long run they will prove satisfactory.
3. Nomad's competitive advantage over its peers will come from the capital allocation skills of your manager (if any) and the patience of our investor base.
4. Only by looking further out than the short term crowd can we expect to beat them.
5. It is for this reason we named Nomad an Investment Partnership and not a fund. The relationship we seek is quite different.
6. One of Nomad's key advantages will be the aggregate patience of its investor base.

Over the next thirteen years, Nomad communicated to its investors through an annual and interim letter and luckily for us, the lessons contained in the letters offer timeless wisdom for investors of all markets, ages, and eras.

---

[4] *Richer, Wiser Happier* (pg. 141): These figures exclude Nomad's performance fees.
[5] The word choice here is on purpose because it is exactly how Warren Buffett described his philosophy about his Partnership: "These *ground rules* are the philosophy. If you are in tune with me, then let's go. If you aren't, I understand."

From the Partnership Letters: Introduction

Preamble

Below you will find a copy of the full collection of the Nomad Letters to Partners, our magnum opus, as it were. These letters were written every six months, from the end of 2001 to early 2014, and sent to Partners in the Nomad Investment Partnership. More recently, they have enjoyed a life of their own in the financial press and internet, quite without our knowledge or, in some cases, approval. Indeed, these bootleg copies were never intended for wide circulation, let alone involuntary publishing, and contain our personal details. We would ask that readers of those hooky letters please respect our privacy and preference to maintain our low profile (think deep-burrowing earthworms). The approved letters that follow have been lightly edited mainly for privacy purposes (and topped and tailed with this preamble and a postscript) but otherwise remain unchanged from the original. We hope that you enjoy the read and would ask only that we are attributed where required and that any web links used in reference are to the approved version found on the IGY Foundation website (not back to the bootleggers), please. Those that do wish to get in touch may do so through the "contact us" function on the IGY Foundation website.

The Nomad letters themselves have been reproduced here in chronological order to help the reader who has the stamina to make it through the next hundred and ten thousand words (what did we find to say?), understand our journey from cigar butt investing to near permanent holdings. With just a few months to go to the twentieth anniversary of the inception of Nomad, it is now all but inevitable that our annual performance will be around twenty percent for twenty years; evidence, perhaps, that investors don't have to go changing their holdings with their underwear and, forgive us if we continue the theme, they really can make their money sitting on their assets!

Our motivation for publishing the letters on Nick's charitable foundation website, is to raise the "and what then" issue: that is, if you are blessed with some success from investing, what then? Elsewhere on this website we have described our "what then" thinking in a drop down tab entitled "X-amount". But that is our journey and everyone is different. (As an aside, these may be the only investment letters published on a charity website, which asks the question, why aren't there more? And, if there were, might it help put the investment activity in the more productive psychic space?)

Investing is a wonderful, thoughtful, adventure but it can also be self-centered, a tendency that can be reinforced by the wealth that can follow. We think it is true that, once past X-amount, real meaning comes with reinvesting in society through charitable giving, which can also be a thoughtful, challenging, wonderful adventure, but with the added bonus that it feels like the world working properly. We hope that you can join us.

Nick Sleep and Qais Zakaria, Spring 2021.

JUNE 30th, 2002

A final word on the need for patience. We are aware that several investors are new to the fund since the beginning of the year and so it may be worth reiterating some ground rules so that we all know where we stand. One of Nomad's key advantages will be the aggregate patience of its investor base. We are genuinely investing for the long term (few are!), in modestly valued firms run by management teams who may be making decisions the fruits of which may not be apparent for several years to come. Mr. Buffett's comments notwithstanding, in the near term our results are likely to be as bad as they may be good, but we are confident that in the long run they will prove satisfactory. If Nomad is to have a competitive advantage over our peers this will come from the capital allocation skills of your manager (if any) and the patience of our investor base. Only by looking further out than the short-term crowd can we expect to beat them. It is for this reason we named Nomad an Investment Partnership and not a fund. The relationship we seek is quite different.

Chapter 1

ORIENTATION

The investment philosophy and methodology will be unchanged. All that changes is that Zak and I will be dedicating one hundred percent of our time to Nomad, rather than something less than one hundred percent, and that one hundred percent of our personal investments will be in Nomad, rather than something less than one hundred percent.

- JUNE 30th, 2004

From the onset, Sleep and Zakaria wanted to prove that there was another way of investing than whatever Wall Street was doing. They had no aspirations to build Nomad into a megafund that would collect an exorbitant amount of fees. Their fee scheme was abnormal: a tiny management fee just enough to cover costs (instead of the usual 1 or 2 percent of assets plus 20 percent of the fund's investment profits), but only *after* a 6 percent hurdle rate. Later on, they made it harder for themselves by setting aside their performance fees for a few years and if they fell short of the 6 percent hurdle, they would refund a portion of the previously earned fees to their investors.

They made it clear that they cared deeply about the quality of investors and would do anything to prevent the dilution of their partners (such as turning away unsuitable and annoying investors). They closed the fund to new money when ideas were scarce and opened up when opportunities presented themselves. They ignored get-rich-schemes used by hedge funds to pursue short-term results: they have never shorted a stock, never used leverage, never made a macroeconomic bet, never made a short-term bet, never touched exotic structures such as LYONs, PRIDEs, or MASTs.

Their goal was simple: absolute returns. They didn't care about how any index was doing or how their peers were performing. Specifically, they wanted to turn one dollar into ten dollars and they preferred to do it the old fashioned way: by buying a handful of thoroughly researched stocks and holding them for years.

From the Partnership Letters: Orientation

JUNE 30th, 2003

At Nomad we have as broad an investment mandate as possible, which has allowed us to make investments as diverse as the preferred shares of a US technology business (Lucent), the common equity of a Scandinavian newspaper business (Schibsted), unlisted UK equity (Weetabix), a small capitalisation Thai newspaper (Matichon), a South African casino (Kersaf), a Hong Kong mobile phone operator (Smartone) and even a large US discount retailer (Costco). This breadth of scope is why we named the Partnership "Nomad".

The point is that there are more tools in Nomad's box than are available to most fund managers and to help illustrate the point we would like to describe investments in Weetabix and Lucent 8% Redeemable Convertible Preferred stock. Nomad may be unique in the industry in having both investments in one portfolio.

DECEMBER 31st, 2003

Our aim is to make investments at prices we consider to be fifty cents on the dollar of what a typical firm is worth. Capital allocation by investee companies must be consistent with value creation and, if this is the case, we expect that the real value of the business (the 100 cents value) could grow at around 10% per annum. The effect over five years will be to compound US$1 of value into US$1.62, and companies that can build value like this are normally rewarded in the market with a fair valuation (i.e. are priced close to US$1.62). This happy outcome would imply a return from purchase price (50 cents) of around 26% per annum. So what happens when we are wrong? Our most common mistake is to misjudge capital allocation decisions by our companies: firms which articulate a share repurchase/debt repayment strategy and have incentives to reinforce that outcome, throw caution to the wind and make acquisitions instead. The Partnership's investment in Readers Digest falls into this category. Capital allocation mistakes such as these often prevent the compounding of value but to date have rarely resulted in a permanent decline in the share price to below our purchase price (50 cents). We have therefore tended to find that our mistakes atrophy (stay cheap) rather than collapse, although we can all name one collapse!

JUNE 30th, 2004

Job one, two and three for your manager is investment performance, not asset gathering. Few practice this approach. We work under the assumption that if performance is reasonable then the level of interest in what we are doing will increase and, if appropriate, the Partnership will grow in time. Common sense and simple maths dictate that it will be opportune if growth can be channeled to coincide with depressed prices, and not market tops. We must aim for this standard, even though it is contrary to common practice in the industry. Had we adopted the industry standard open-house approach the Partnership would be approximately three times its current size, but the results worse, and the quality of Partners meaningfully impaired. It is important to us that we all understand the investment process (a reminder is contained in the appendix, in the form of an interview published in the Outstanding Investor Digest), try hard to keep a healthy indifference to results achieved (certainly no extrapolation of annual results please) and maintain a patient temperament. Investment dollars work best when they occupy a different psychic space to almost any other form of savings you may have.

JUNE 30th, 2006

<u>Letter sent to Nomad Shareholders, April 2006</u>
As you may already know, Zak and I recently left Marathon to manage the Nomad Investment Partnership full time. In some respects, this does not represent much of a change from the status quo, as Nomad had come to dominate our time and thinking. However, some things will be new, and the purpose of this letter is to set out the philosophy of our new operations. This will give you time to think about their implications before we set out the methodology in a revised prospectus. The changes in the prospectus will require your vote, and of course, at any stage Zak and I will be free to answer any questions you may have and our contact details are at the bottom of this letter.

Between us, Zak and I have spent sixteen happy years at Marathon. It was a superb education, and in many important respects working with Jeremy has made us the investors we are today. We all remain close and indeed attended the Berkshire Hathaway AGM together last week. It is perhaps indicative of the friendship and out- of-the-box, non-consensual thinking that is typical of Marathon that an amicable, common sense arrangement, such as the spin of Nomad, has been proposed. Few institutions would behave so well.

Zak and I will only be in a position to manage Nomad once we have FSA authorisation to operate as a regulated fund management company. This largely administrative process is expected to take at least three months and along with the remaining duration of our employment contracts (until June 30th) means that, at soonest, we will be in a position to run Nomad from early July. In the meantime, Jeremy will be in charge and will liaise with Zak and me when appropriate. For the next two months we will be setting up a somewhat modest office (it appears that galactic headquarters is likely to be above a shop and opposite a Chinese restaurant in west London!), and configuring the necessary IT, legal and accounting systems. There will be time for research, and Jeremy has been kind enough to send on a formidable pile of annual reports! So, Nomad is being looked after in the meantime.

Our new company will be called Sleep, Zakaria and Company, Limited (catchy) and we will manage one fund, the Nomad Investment Partnership. I expect this statement to be as true in twenty-years' time, as it is today – Zak and I are not in the product diversification business. Indeed, we don't really see the new company as a business in the usual way: for example, we have asked our lawyers to structure the arrangement so that Zak and I could not sell Nomad to another fund manager – that way you will not wake up with someone else managing your money whilst your manager catches a plane to Hawaii! You can sack us, but we won't sell you. Perhaps an explanation of our proposed fee scale will make clear our orientation.

The Nomad Investment Partnership currently charges a management fee of 10 basis points per annum, a levy which leans somewhat on the in-place infrastructure at Marathon and which is insufficient to sustain a stand-alone operation. We would therefore like to propose a new management fee that will reimburse the operating company (Sleep, Zakaria and Company, Limited) for its costs incurred in running the operation (salary, rent, accounting, research, legal etc.). We guestimate this will be between 0.7% and 1% of the Partnership per annum at its current size, and we will cap the reimbursement at 1% of NAV and fund any deficit out of pocket if need be. Philosophically our position is that the management fee should not be a profits centre (although a small surplus float is prudent). This is not a blank cheque: Zak and I will take a salary cut to run Nomad, and a total remuneration cut that questions our sanity, but as I have said, this is not a traditional business. As the Partnership grows in size the management fee will decline as a percentage of assets and, that way, all investors share in the natural scale economics of the operation.

The performance fee also needs addressing, as there is an inconsistency between multi-year investments, multi-year orientation by investors and an annual payout for the manager! The performance fee should be appropriately calculated for the job, be at risk for subsequent poor performance and reflect the cost of capital. We will therefore propose that the existing six percent cost of capital hurdle remain (approximating five-year bond rates) and that the performance fee be deferred and subject to repayment in the event of subsequent underperformance.

There are several ways this could be achieved, the easiest of which may be to bank the performance fees, and for the bank to drip fees to us if performance remains reasonable, or drip reimbursements back to you to the extent we fail to maintain our advantage. One way our advantage may be compromised is if size becomes a meaningful drag on performance, as I said in the last letter to investors "our ability to expand and shrink will be an important tool sometime in the next twenty years. I guarantee it...". Our intention is that "the bus is always running at full speed with the number of passengers optimised to maintain maximum speed", and so we will also take powers to return cash to you should we find the opportunity set is small. I don't expect that we will return cash to you that much, and I would be delighted if we did not at all, but it seems silly to set off without the ability to do so. Again, the prospectus will elaborate.

The investment philosophy and methodology will be unchanged. All that changes is that Zak and I will be dedicating one hundred percent of our time to Nomad, rather than something less than one hundred percent, and that one hundred percent of our personal investments will be in Nomad, rather than something less than one hundred percent. Otherwise, it is business as usual and there will be no change in our fund administrator (Daiwa Securities Trust and Banking in Ireland) or auditor (Ernst and Young).

Zak and I are delighted that Marathon has allowed us to continue running Nomad; it is a generous gesture on their part. We are proud of what we have achieved at Nomad (as well as at Marathon) but no matter how noble Marathon's gesture is, it will mean nothing if it is not endorsed by you. Keeping existing investors has always been more important to us than acquiring new, and this transition will only be a success if you make it so. So, I encourage you to read through the Collection of Letter to Partners sent to you in January (Amanda Joss ajoss@marathon.co.uk can help you with reprints) and the prospectus you will receive shortly. And if anything is unclear then Zak and I await your call. You may also wish to contact Karl McEneff or Martin Byrne who are the independent directors of the Nomad Investment Company and Marathon (Cayman), which is the General Partner of the Nomad Investment Partnership. Karl and Martin are superb council and have your best interests at heart.

Zak and I are skipping happy about the new arrangements. We hope you will be too. Yours faithfully

Nicholas Sleep

DECEMBER 31st, 2013

This is the twenty-fifth letter to investors over fourteen calendar years. In these letters we have tried to cover the philosophy and methodology Zak and I use to approach the problem of investing. We keep our discussions to as high a level as we can manage in the belief that, in the long run, the high level is all that matters. In these letters we have therefore discussed business models, incentive compensation, capital allocation, mistakes, more mistakes, even more mistakes, lots on psychology and how to think, lots on attitude and so on. Whilst we may only write twice a year, we own shares for such long periods (if the current rate of portfolio activity should persist) that we write around twenty letters during the life of the average investment – that's a huge amount! In previous letters we have also discussed the psychological traps inherent in a more loquacious approach (been there, done that, don't want to do it again!). At its heart, investing is simple, and to make it seem anything but, with the frequent repartition of short-lived facts and data points, may be a conceit. Indeed, it could be argued that a running commentary obfuscates a discussion of the things that really matter. Whilst we have covered many of the topics relevant to long-term investing in these letters already, there is a topic that we have not discussed too much and that now affects the Partnership in a significant way. That is regulation (no moaning at the back).

Chapter 2

WHAT WE LOOK FOR

We are always on the lookout for companies with corporate character that are pursuing strategies designed to create sustainable value.

- JUNE 30th, 2003

Following in the footsteps of Benjamin Graham and Warren Buffett, Nomad viewed shares of stock as not just pieces of paper to be traded, but as partial ownership of a business. The underlying business can be analyzed, evaluated, and valued. Even better, the stock price would sometimes fall below the business' intrinsic value (the estimated value of what the company is worth) and when that happened, that would be the time to back up the truck.

As Joel Greenblatt puts it, *"Figure out what something is worth and pay a lot less."*[6]. Most people intuitively understand this concept and apply it in everyday life (think groceries, clothes, vacations, rent, etc.), but when it comes to stocks, this notion miraculously evaporates. Instead, they end up operating like heat-seeking missiles, chasing the latest fads and hottest stocks that everyone is talking about.

---

[6] *Richer, Wiser, Happier: pg 112*

Initially, Nomad operated true to the bedrock principles of Graham and Buffett, buying securities in reasonable businesses at discounted prices and holding for multi-year periods. Specifically, they looked for businesses:
1) Trading around half of their real business value (fifty cents on the dollar)
2) Run by owner-oriented management and
3) Employing capital allocation strategies consistent with long term shareholder wealth creation

Businesses that satisfy these three conditions are exceptionally rare.

However, it is also interesting to note Nomad's evolution from bargain hunting and cigar butts to a focus on quality compounders and a select group of high-quality business models. Specifically, Nomad found that the business model of scale-economies shared to be one of the best investment models ever; in short, companies with cost advantages that get shared with customers (we take a deeper look in Chapter 5: Scale Economies Shared).

In either scenario, searching for cigar butts or quality compounders, by having a long-term view and a holding period of multiple years, Nomad's success can be mostly attributed to the economics of the underlying business rather than short-term fluctuations of the share price. To quote a Graham cliche, "In the short term, the market is like a voting machine, but in the long term, it's more like a weighing machine."

This need to understand the underlying economics of a business echoes David Abrams, who wrote in *Security Analysis*,

> *"The success comes through really thinking about things, looking at the underlying economics, trying to understand those economics, and then looking at where you can buy those economics in the market."*

Mohnish Pabrai calls this understanding the DNA of a company: "*If you can find a great company with great genes trading below intrinsic value, back the truck up. Otherwise keep driving.*"[7]

At this point, the astute reader would probably mentally classify Nomad as a "value" fund since they prefer to buy stocks at half price. Yet, the same reader will realize later, many of Nomad's largest holdings are classified as "growth" stocks. How can this be? We'll dive in deeper into the debate in Chapter 14: Growth vs. Value, but in a nutshell, like Buffett, Nomad viewed growth as an inherent part of the value judgment and any distinction is quite unnecessary.

This difficulty to pigeon-hole Nomad into some checkbox is fitting, as Nomad had a broad investment mandate that allowed them to invest across the capital structure (common shares, preferred, debt or convertible bonds) as well across countries and industries. Nomad's portfolio featured companies that ranged from a Thai newspaper to a South African casino to an illiquid Philippines cement company. This willingness to scour the globe for value is why they named their partnership "Nomad".

To see just how far and wide Nomad searched:

> "*At Nomad we have as broad an investment mandate as possible, which has allowed us to make investments as diverse as the preferred shares of a US technology business (Lucent), the common equity of a Scandinavian newspaper business (Schibsted), unlisted UK equity (Weetabix), a small capitalisation Thai newspaper (Matichon), a South African casino (Kersaf), a Hong Kong mobile phone operator (Smartone) and even a large US discount retailer (Costco).*"

---

[7] https://acquirersmultiple.com/2016/12/mohnish-pabrai-spend-time-decoding-a-companys-dna/

From the Partnership Letters:
Buying Dollar Bills for Fifty Cents

JANUARY 18th 2002

When we evaluate potential investments we are looking for businesses trading at around half of their real business value, companies run by owner oriented management and employing capital allocation strategies consistent with long term shareholder wealth creation. Finding all three is rare, and that is why we think Nomad has a material advantage in being a global fund. We can look far and wide for candidates and simply are not required to invest in anything that does not fit. Chris Browne of Tweedy Browne has likened the research process to detective work or perhaps investigative journalism, and we could not agree more.

JUNE 30th, 2002

It is the first category [quality, difficult to copy, franchise operations such as newspapers, a TV station, motor racetracks, consumer brand names and casinos] that contains our current winners and the latter [discounted asset based businesses such as property, hotels, or conglomerates where fixed assets or cash makes up a large portion of appraised value] that contains our losers. In time both will contain winners. In aggregate we estimate our investments are currently priced by the market at 51% of their real worth, that is to say in our opinion we have bought dollar bills for 51 cents.

DECEMBER 31st, 2002

In aggregate these investments are priced in the market at around 50% of what we believe the businesses to be worth, that is to say we believe we have bought dollar bills for around fifty cents.

JUNE 30th, 2003

Indeed future results are almost certain to be different. The index is unlikely to continue to decline, and even though absolute returns may be favorable, our advantage over the index will in all likelihood erode somewhat. We are prepared for this and are recycling shares that have performed well (in aggregate the portfolio is valued at around 65c on the dollar of intrinsic value, up from 50 cents in December) into new fifty-cent dollars.

DECEMBER 31st, 2003

Our aim is to make investments at prices we consider to be fifty cents on the dollar of what a typical firm is worth. Capital allocation by investee companies must be consistent with value creation and, if this is the case, we expect that the real value of the business (the 100 cents value) could grow at around 10% per annum. The effect over five years will be to compound U$1 of value into U$1.62, and companies that can build value like this are normally rewarded in the market with a fair valuation (i.e. are priced close to U$1.62). This happy outcome would imply a return from purchase price (50 cents) of around 26% per annum.

If over five years our mistakes are on aggregate flat, and our mistakes total half of Partnership assets, then this implies a compounded annual return of 13% for the portfolio as a whole3. Not each year, and maybe not for several consecutive years, but over time this level of expectations appears reasonable to us. This model is daftly precise, a little too neat and the one thing we can almost guarantee is that returns will not be exactly 13%. It is important however that we all understand the investment process and time frames involved.

The prime determinants of outcome are price (sticking to 50 cents on the dollar) and capital allocation by management. The first is in our control, that is, it is in our control to be patient and wait for the right price. The second involves a subjective judgment about the quality of management, and an assessment about the sustainability of business returns in the long run. It is these factors that occupy almost all our time.

One Partner confessed to us that his wife viewed Nomad gains as jewelry in waiting and wanted to know what advice could we give him to delay the shopping spree? We offer no advice here but lay out some simple facts. Today, your manager's job is to reinvest the successful investments (dollar bills) back into more companies trading at half price. At the time of writing our internal calculation of the price to value ratio of the Partnership is 65 cents on the dollar, approximately the same as at the end of June despite fund performance. We have done this through investing incremental funding into new companies such as New World Development, Telewest, Midland Realty, and UnitedGlobal Communications, and through the sale of the Lucent Preferred shares (at above par value), the partial sale of Stagecoach and the pending sale of Weetabix (more later on this investment). Rest assured, nothing occupies your manager more than reducing the price to value ratio of the Partnership, as we believe this to be the best indicator of latent value and future performance. In the interests of fair disclosure Warren Buffett was asked a similar, jewelry-related question at the 2002 annual general meeting of shareholders of Berkshire Hathaway to which he replied with a grin that in his experience he had never been disappointed by what had happened after he bought the jewelry.

JUNE 30th, 2009

Return on capital in the portfolio is extremely high, as are endemic growth rates. We estimate that around three-quarters of the portfolio is invested in growth businesses, which have the potential to compound for many years, and the balance in more cigar butt like investments (we just could not help it!). In aggregate the portfolio is priced in the market at meaningfully less than half our appraisal of what our firms are really worth. The Partnership will remain open to incremental subscriptions whilst this is the case. Here ends the marketing pitch from the chief marketing officer, who now announces his retirement!

From the Partnership Letters: What We Look For

DECEMBER 31st, 2002

Nomad has as broad an investment mandate as we could imagine. We can, for example, buy common shares, preferred shares, debt or convertible bonds. In analysing a company, we assess the merits of investing in all levels of the capital structure but to date we have concluded that the common and preferred shares have been the more attractive investments. We have however attempted to buy the bonds of two companies which were trading at large, and in our opinion unwarranted, discounts to face value. How does one attempt, but fail, to buy a bond? One way is for the company to be more aggressive in bidding for the bonds than we were. Indeed, it appears in one case that the company, as part of a debt repurchase program, may have had a standing order with all the market makers on Wall Street to buy any of its bonds that were offered and to let none remain in the hands of third parties. This might seem unfair, but management score highly for gusto, and their equity holders, of which Nomad is one, should applaud such actions. In the light of the record credit spreads available in the US and widespread investor irrationality this is exactly how we want our company management to behave. A cool head under pressure once again.

JUNE 30th, 2003

We are always on the lookout for companies with corporate character that are pursuing strategies designed to create sustainable value. This is no mean feat, and we work hard reading annual reports and proxy statements and interviewing management trying to answer the questions: what are returns on incremental capital and the longevity of those returns, are management correctly incented to allocate capital appropriately, and what is discounted by prices? Once these businesses are found they can be multiyear winners provided capital allocation remains consistent with value creation. All too often however management become sidetracked and misallocate capital usually through diversification or in the words of Peter Lynch, "diworsification". The result of which is that aggregate returns on capital decline and the share price falls to discount poor performance. Quality of managerial character is therefore important to avoid capital misallocation and it is in the search for such character that we asked an investment bank to perform a simple company search earlier this year (the first search this manager has employed in twelve years).

The criterion was for companies with no increase or decrease in shares outstanding in the last ten years. This simple screen it was hoped would yield companies that had resisted the fashions for share repurchase, stock options and share issuance to fund growth. In short it was hoped that the search would lead us to firms that had not allowed the bubble to affect the way they operated their businesses. We knew of two companies that would make the list (Fastenal and Wesco Financial) but were amazed that there were just five others in the US with a market cap above US$50m. One of these was Erie Family Life, the life insurance subsidiary of the Erie Indemnity Company founded by H.O. Hirt in the 1920s. Management kindly obliged us with requests for an interview and when we explained why we thought the business may be of interest the response came,

"Hell, we have not issued a share since 1925!!!"

There are not many companies like that. In a similar vein we stumbled across Hershey Creamery, another business with reasonable economics, a low valuation and seemingly stubborn resistance to outside influence. So stubborn in fact that we found it difficult to obtain annual reports or proxy statements, and resorted to asking the CFO for a copy only to be told "these are mailed out to our shareholders". How then might a potential investor form a judgment whether they would like to become a shareholder without the benefit of an annual report?

"It's a common complaint", came the reply.

This analytical Catch 22 may not be helpful, but it does reveal that some firms remain resolutely independent of mind, despite the twenty-year bull market that has raged around them. As if to prove Groucho Marx right ("I do not care to belong to any club that would accept me as a member"), we have not given up on Hershey Creamery yet, if only to satisfy our curiosity.

DECEMBER 31st, 2006

How do we know we are taking a different view to the crowd? A clue can be gleaned from the period that other investors typically hold the shares of the companies in the Partnership. If Berkshire Hathaway (US), Jardine Matheson (Hong Kong) and Next Media (also Hong Kong) are excluded (these firms are in a class of their own due to either stock illiquidity or investor education) then other investors hold stocks in our portfolio for on average twenty weeks. We expect to own shares for around two hundred and sixty weeks! So, what is going on? It seems to us that most investors look at the accounting outputs of a company (the reported financial data) as a guide to near term price movements and play the market accordingly. As stated in the investment objective section of the Nomad prospectus our goal is to "pass custody (of your investment) over at the right price and to the right people". That's what investing is. Zak and I concentrate on a deeper reality: the inputs to future value moves. Our peers are trading shares at the short end of the equity yield curve where the competition is the greatest, and we are investing at the long end where competition is the least. We respond to completely different stimuli.

Take for example the current controversy at Amazon.com. Last year the company reported free cash flow of just over U$500m, indeed it has been around this number for the last few years. What is important is that the U$500m is after all investment spending on growth initiatives such as capital spending, but also research and development, shipping subsidy, marketing and advertising and price givebacks. The firm has been investing in these items today to grow the business in the future so that free cash flow in years to come will be meaningfully greater than it would be otherwise. By our estimates these discretionary investments, over and above that required to maintain the business, are in the region of a further U$500m, excluding the price givebacks. This is our subjective assessment of the discretionary investment spend and implies that management could, if so inclined, cancel the discretionary growth spending and instead return around US$800m per annum to investors after taxes. An operation that was able to produce cash flow on such a basis might be worth US$10bn or so, and along with Amazon's other assets would imply a share price of around US$26. In valuing the business at these prices, as occurred last summer, investors are saying to Amazon management "your growth spending has no value, you may as well turn yourself into a cash cow"! This is an odd statement to make for a business growing revenues in excess of twenty percent per annum.

How should we think about the price givebacks? Here is what Jeff Bezos, Amazon's founder, had to say in last year's annual report:

"As our shareholders know, we have made a decision to continuously and significantly lower prices for customers year after year as our efficiency and scale make it possible. This is an example of a very important decision that cannot be made in a math-based way. In fact, when we lower prices, we go against the math that we can do, which always says that the smart move is to raise prices. We have significant data related to price elasticity. With fair accuracy, we can predict that a price reduction of a certain percentage will result in an increase in units sold of a certain percentage. With rare exceptions, the volume increase in the short-term is never enough to pay for the price decease. However, our quantitative understanding of elasticity is short-term. We can estimate what a price reduction will do this week and this quarter. But we cannot numerically estimate the effect that consistently lowering prices will have on our business over five years or ten years. Our judgment is that relentlessly returning efficiency improvements and scale economies to customers in the form of lower prices creates a virtuous cycle that leads over the long-term to a much larger dollar amount of free cash flow, and thereby to a much more valuable Amazon.com. We have made similar judgments around Free Super Saver Shipping and Amazon Prime, both of which are expensive in the short term and – we believe – important and valuable in the long term."

This is a précis of the scale efficiencies shared model that we dealt with in some detail in our analysis of Costco (Nomad Letter to Investors, December 2004, please ask Amanda for reprints) and is deployed by companies which have now come to dominate Nomad: Costco, Dell, Amazon and Berkshire (Geico, Nebraska Furniture Mart). The controversy is in the first four words "As our shareholders know", judging by the share volumes - they don't! And that's the opportunity. If the share price is being set by those with an eye on the next data point, then they can't also be looking out for long-term value. There are few traders that disagree with Bezos' value creation process, but they don't think it will show up in the numbers just yet. And if you only own shares for a month or two then you may get away with several trades before Amazon's success becomes apparent. In short, the traders have many small ideas, and we have one big idea. Good luck to them. Picking up pennies in front of a juggernaut is just not how we behave.

Notice also that the decision to lower free cash flow this year through sharing scale benefits with customers through price givebacks is based on a subjective judgment of future returns and their timing. It is not a strictly maths based equation and there is no guarantee that investment spending will always work. Bezos again:

> *"Math-based decisions command wide agreement, whereas judgment-based decisions are rightly debated and often controversial, at least until put into practice and demonstrated. Any institution unwilling to endure controversy must limit itself to decisions of the first type. In our view, doing so would not only limit controversy – it would also significantly limit innovation and long-term value creation".* Amen.

I think Bezos would run a good investment fund: but that is the point, good investing and good business decisions are synonymous. Mr. Bezos does not control the timing of the payback, just as we do not control the timing of Nomad's performance but, in our judgment, the ever widening of the moat surrounding Amazon largely determines whether our investment will be a success. We must now have the patience to wait.

Today Nomad is close to fully invested and notably concentrated: the five largest holdings account for half the portfolio and the top ten around three quarters. The tail of around twenty other holdings includes baskets (such as Zimbabwe), several distressed turnarounds and rats and mice from the early days. The polarity of the portfolio, with several large, simple, high conviction holdings, and a tail of more complicated and less certain ideas (but which may have more upside) is likely to be a feature of Nomad for some time. There is a notable concentration in US stocks, a factor that also contributed to relative performance last year, while there are some interesting UK investments where we may have some influence on corporate development. The price to value ratio of the Partnership as a whole is in the upper 60 cents on the dollar, having risen from the low 60s in October.

DECEMBER 31st, 2012

Nomad's businesses, to generalise, are run by their founders and the businesses are blessed with cultures that see part of their identity in low operating costs: Costco Wholesale measures costs in basis points and at Amazon.com they take the light bulbs out of the vending machines to save money. In another sphere, the Olympic Team GB Cycling coach and Sky Tour de France Chief (now Sir) Dave Brailsford might refer to this type of behaviour as seeking "the aggregation of marginal gains". Just as it leads to gold medals and yellow jerseys, its effect is that AirAsia, for example, is the lowest cost airline in the world. Good things follow when you care about the pennies.

Chapter 3

MEASURING & EXPLAINING PERFORMANCE

Our preference is for results to be measured over a five-year time frame, and even this may be a little short compared to the average holding period of the underlying investments which is presently around ten years (inflated by a dearth of sales).
- JUNE 30th, 2003

In the Ground Rules that Buffett laid out for his Partnership investors in 1956, Buffett dedicated 2 Ground Rules on which active investment performance was to be judged.
- Ground Rule #4: "Whether we do a good job or a poor job is not to be measured by whether we are plus or minus for the year. It is instead to be measured against the general experience in securities as measured by the Dow Jones Industrial Average, leading investment companies, etc. If our record is better than that of these yardsticks, we consider it a good year whether we are plus or minus. If we do poorer, we deserve the tomatoes."
- Ground Rule #5: "While I much prefer a five-year test, I feel three years is an absolute minimum for judging performance. It is a certainty that we will have years when the partnership is poorer, perhaps substantially so, than the Dow. If any three-year or longer period produces poor results,

we all should start looking around for other places to have our money. An exception to the latter statement would be three years covering a speculative explosion in a bull market."

In a similar vein, Nomad also preferred to be measured over a five-year time frame, as five years should be enough time for capital allocation decisions to produce results. Although Nomad pursued absolute returns (as opposed to relative returns to the index), Nomad expected to beat the index by a wide margin over time. Nomad also expected to perform better than average in stable or declining markets and perhaps even poorer than average in rising markets. In short, they expected to do relatively well as a bubble collapses.

At the end of the day, most fund managers cannot afford to chronically underperform the index. Why bother spending so much effort if the result is just going to be poorer than just buying the index? As Miller put it, "If all the professional money managers adhered to his [Buffett's] standards, we'd witness a record number of early retirements on Wall Street."

From the Partnership Letters: Measuring Performance

JUNE 30th, 2002

Some insight into our performance can be gleaned from the early Buffett Partnership letters to investors which we were fortunate enough to be sent recently. In the 1960 letter Buffett writes:

"I have pointed out that any superior record which we might accomplish should not be expected to be evidenced by a relatively constant advantage in performance compared to the Average. Rather it is likely that if such an advantage is achieved, it will be through better-than-average performance in stable or declining markets and average, or perhaps even poorer-than-average performance in rising markets."

We had not explicitly thought of investment outcomes in this way, although it is axiomatic that results for value investors during booms will be poorer than average and results after booms, better than average. Marathon's long term track record demonstrates the same pattern, and Nomad's performance since inception is also in line with this phenomenon. You should therefore be expecting us to do relatively well as the bubble collapses.

JUNE 30th, 2003

Our preference is for results to be measured over a five-year time frame, and even this may be a little short compared to the average holding period of the underlying investments which is presently around ten years (inflated by a dearth of sales). In this context the short-term results remain just that, short-term, and you should be as indifferent toward results so far as the annual sequence in which they have occurred. A stoical disposition to short-term results is both the right way to think (never mark emotions to market) but it also prepares one for results that may be reasonable, but are unlikely to be an extrapolation of the last two years.

DECEMBER 31st, 2003

There are two ways to present results: either in discrete annual increments or on a compounded basis. The former is industry standard, useful in demonstrating consistency of results (which your manager makes no pretense of being able to achieve), and for helping to assess outcomes for those that invested part way through. Our preferred route however is to be assessed on a compounded, multi-year basis for the reason that the only event we control is whether we are right, not when we are right. It is quite possible that our annual results will be inferior to the market for a period, but this will only convey information about the timing of outcomes, whilst saying little about the end result itself. We would therefore encourage you to be indifferent to the results below.

JUNE 30th, 2004

Our preference is to be measured over a rolling five-year basis; consistent with time it takes for many large capital allocation decisions to bear fruit and the average period that we expect to own an investment.

JUNE 30th, 2006

The 1960 Buffett Partnership letter to investors included the following observation that we also carried in the June 2002 Nomad interim letter:

"I have pointed out that any superior record which we might accomplish should not be expected to be evidenced by a relatively constant advantage in performance compared to the Average. Rather it is likely that if such an advantage is achieved, it will be through better-than-average performance in stable or declining markets and average, or perhaps poorer-than-average performance in rising markets".

Our performance is following a similar path of superior results during market swoons and now reasonable absolute, if a little less than average, results during market booms. Indeed, the only time we have been ahead of the index year-to-date was during the market swoon in May and early June.

From the Partnership Letters: Explaining Performance

DECEMBER 31st, 2003

Accounting for Performance

In his autobiography Charles Darwin made an uncharacteristic error: as a young man at Cambridge he recalled that,

"...My time was sadly wasted there, and worse than wasted. From my passion for shooting and for hunting, and, when I failed, for riding across country, I got into a sporting set, including some dissipated low-minded young men. We used

often to dine together in the evening, though these dinners often included men of higher stamp, and we sometimes drank too much, with jolly singing and playing at cards afterwards. I know that I ought to feel ashamed of days and evenings thus spent, but as some of my friends were very pleasant, and we were all in the highest spirits, I cannot help looking back to these times with much pleasure".

However, in a footnote to the original text, Darwin's son, Francis, explains,

"I gather from some of my father's contemporaries that he has exaggerated the Bacchanalian nature of these parties".

Oh, dear! We all do that to some extent. It is at least comforting to know that even Darwin, a man whose great insights came from his ability not to fool himself, was capable of a little exaggeration. Perhaps he was just good at telling a story. At the inaugural Legg Mason Investor Conference Bill Miller, whose investment skills we much admire, confessed to analysing his mistakes more thoroughly than his successes. The latter he automatically presumed to have gone up for the very reason the shares were bought. As investors we all do this to some extent, winners flatter the ego regardless of the reason they went up, whilst we all feel bad about the losers. Several academic studies argue that mistakes hurt up to three times more than gains satisfy, a product of primordial environmental conditioning designed to prevent us from repeatedly eating poisonous food, apparently. For investors the implication of this asymmetry is great as it is often the favorable outcomes that drive performance more than losers destroy it. The Partnership's investment in Stagecoach has in effect paid for the failure of Conseco six times over and yet it was Conseco that we wrote to you about first. These biases are very ingrained.

So, in this letter we will take Bill Miller's advice and start by attempting to explain why the Partnership has performed well, whilst trying as best we can to avoid Darwin's error of fooling oneself. The reason, of which we are certain, is the decline in the level of fear felt by other investors. We can analyse and quantify this phenomenon. Take the interest rate that the market demanded from Stagecoach Plc, a relatively cash generative and asset rich business. At the peak the cost of debt reached 15% per annum and in the last annual letter we explained that the Partnership had made an investment in the common equity and attempted, but curiously failed, to make an investment in the firm's public bonds. (Readers may recall that we failed in this regard as the company had cornered the market in its own undervalued bonds). Thirteen months later the bonds trade above par (investors are paying more than 100c on the dollar to receive 100c at a pre-defined date in the future, and interest in the meantime). What has changed opinions of this firm in such a short period? The answer lies in the huge levels of free cash flow that has followed the decline in capital spending, restructuring and asset sales. By changing strategy and capital allocation on a six-pence the balance sheet has been repaired, the business shrunk to its cash cow operations and the market now anticipates, with almost 100% probability of outcome that the bonds will be repaid. Indeed the firm's standing is so good today as to be able to borrow money at a slight premium to the UK government and the share price at the time of writing has risen six fold from our original purchase price.

This sea change in company behaviour is not limited to Stagecoach. The Partnership's investments in Primedia, Xerox, New World Development, Schibsted, Lucent, Georgica, Hong Kong and Shanghai Hotels, Telewest, BIL International, Jardine Strategic and Kersaf can all be described in this way (even after the sale of Lucent Preferred shares, that's over 40% of Partnership assets). According to Empirical Research Partners, an independent research boutique in New York, in 2003 the ratio of capital spending to revenues at US companies was at its lowest level since at least 1965 and free cash flow the highest compared to market capitalisation. The predominance of free cash flow has allowed market interest rates charged to the most indebted businesses (the so called junk bond spread), the highest for a generation between the end of 1999 and 2003, to decline to more normalised levels and it is the shares of businesses perceived to be in the worst condition that have bounced the most. Nomad has been heavily concentrated in this category.

So performance to date has been a product of investments made in the most despised businesses, where temporary issues have depressed prices. We hope to be able to report that fact to you in most letters, although the names of the companies and circumstances will no doubt change. Over the coming years, although less so in the short term, it is possible that the other half of our portfolio, the higher quality portion, will contribute the most to performance. It is possible also that some of our successful turnarounds may find themselves in this higher quality category if current management behaviour is sustained. We travel hopefully in this regard.

DECEMBER 31st, 2006

There are two reasons for our relative performance this year – the first is that our companies, by and large, are reinvesting heavily in their businesses at a time when the market, taking its cue from the private equity buyers, have rewarded firms with high levels of current free cash flow. Second, it is also possible that the one-off workload associated with the transition of Nomad to SZ and Co, a very high proportion of which was bespoke work (notably the refundable performance fee), diverted attention from the day job. Zak and I consider non-investment distractions to be the single biggest risk to our operation and we are on to it. Amanda has the budget she needs to allow us to devolve duties but this process is new to us and we are learning as we go.

In 1948, Freddie Settrington (he rarely used the title Lord March) hosted his first motor racing event on the perimeter road of the airfield that lay in one corner of his Sussex estate. At first it was a modest affair, as the foreword to the first race card makes clear:

"We'll be quite frank with you from the start. This race meeting is an experiment. We cannot, on this occasion, offer you a seat in a grandstand – or even a seat at all. You'll be able to obtain some refreshments, and the loudspeaker people will do their best to make certain you hear the numbers of non-starters and of the winners.

"We think you will see some quite good racing and share our surprise if the programme keeps up to time. But if all the refinements of a fully developed

sporting arena are missing take our word for it, they will appear eventually-particularly if we have any success with the show today.

"*Meanwhile, months of negotiations have been necessary, just to make to-day's meeting possible. Government Departments have been involved – and you know what that means – but we've stuck manfully to the job, and here we are. To do justice to those with whom we have been called upon to negotiate, we must say that Government people have been more than helpful. Ministry of Works officials wear collars and ties, drink and eat just like you or I, and smoke cigarettes at 3s.6d. a packet. Sometimes, though, they do a little better with petrol.*

"*We've been greatly assisted, too, by local farmers, who do not subscribe to the view that dairy cows refuse to come across with the milk if they are within earshot of a racing car.*

"*Naturally, in the J.C.C. we are more than pleased to be staging our first race meeting in England since the war. As someone said the other day, we are a little lucky in having a President with an airfield in his back garden, but it's better to be born lucky than have to pay 19s. 6d. in the £.*"

Today, the Goodwood Revival is a unique, world-class motor racing event. In the last year we have also spent our fair share of time with the bureaucrats and, like Freddie, at times we would have struggled to offer you a seat (the office fit-out rumbles on). But, in time, we aim to produce something we can all be proud of and, we expect that at Nomad you will also see some quite good racing.

Chapter 4

GREAT BUSINESSES & VALUE OF INACTIVITY

> Nomad is overwhelmingly invested in businesses of great character.
> - DECEMBER 31st, 2009

Nomad's evolution from bargain hunting to focusing on a select group of high-quality business models is fascinating. In general, there are two ways for investors to invest:
1. Buy Cigar Butts: buy shares cheap, wait for the price to rise (the final puff), sell and repeat
2. Buy Quality Compounders and Hold: buy shares in a great business, let the business grow, and hold

It's fascinating to witness the transition because this was the path that Warren Buffett eventually took as well: "It's far better to buy a wonderful company at a fair price than a fair company at a wonderful price."

Nick and Zak also highlight their "drifting towards inactivity"; inactivity is something that can only be afforded if one holds quality businesses (no investor would argue that inactivity should be paired with low-quality businesses). On the surface, inactivity seems too simple, yet in reality, holding and doing nothing is fairly complicated (one, investors lack patience and two, not selling daily is also a series of decisions).

Owning a "portfolio of exceptional, iconoclastic businesses" is something Nomad deems as "investment heaven".

From the Partnership Letters: Great Businesses

DECEMBER 31st, 2009

Even though it may be tempting to flatter oneself, it is the businesses we invest in that do almost all the heavy lifting in the wealth creating process. If Zak and I bring something to the investment party, and I may be stretching things a little here, it is to be more rational than other investors. At least, we hope that is the case. Your trust, in turn, allows us to invest in firms that are misunderstood by many.

For example, we invest in firms that pay their employees 80% more than rival companies (Costco); firms that lower prices as an article of faith (Amazon.com); firms that force an equitable distribution of commissions in an industry dominated by an eat-what-you- kill culture (Michael Page); a low-cost airline for the masses in a region served by airlines for the rich (AirAsia); and a company that thinks table top figurine games are cool, really, (Games Workshop). Isn't it wonderful that these firms are behaving in this way despite being misunderstood by the outside world? All the social pressure will be to conform with industry norm but these companies have a deep keel that keeps them upright.

From the Partnership Letters:
Inactivity as a Source of Value Added

JUNE 30th, 2009

One common psychological trap that agents may fall into is that clients expect action, or to be more accurate, fund managers expect their clients to expect action! The investor Seth Klarman was once challenged on whether Buffett's track record was statistically significant as he traded so little? To which Klarman answered that each day Buffett chose not to do anything was a decision taken too. It is quite possible that we may not change the companies in which we have invested very much over the next few years. Indeed, that is our preference. Zak and I expect that we have built a portfolio not just for the recovery out of recession but for many years after that too. At least, we aim for such a Zen-like state.

JUNE 30th, 2013

Our portfolio inaction continues and we are delighted to report that purchase and sale transactions have all but ground to a halt. Our expectation is that this is a considerable source of value added! At the time of our initial investments in Nomad's investee businesses, the firms were, on average, around fifteen years old. Take out the two grandparents (Berkshire Hathaway and Costco) and the average falls to twelve years. It is hard to know how this compares to businesses at large (what is the average age of a listed company?), but we do know that the average time S&P500 constituent stocks have been included in that index is twenty-five years. One could guestimate that those firms might have been say, twenty years old on inclusion? At any rate, the statistic helps to illustrate how youthful Nomad's firms are. The runway ahead for our businesses may be very long indeed. In action on our part is counter- cultural and deliberate and is easier said than done. Really. For those used to a more industry- standard level of trading activity, we hope to update you in real time on our level of inaction through our planned "Nomad Inactivity App.", available only in the Amazon

App. store, of course. As Berkshire Hathaway Vice-Chairman, Charlie Munger, says, you make your real money sitting on your assets!

From the Partnership Letters: Great Businesses + Value of Inactivity + Character as a Way of Reducing Reinvestment Risk

DECEMBER 31st, 2009

Judging by our hit rate with companies interviewed, Zak and I would guestimate that fewer than five percent of publicly listed firms do what they think is right, rather than what they think plays well with the outside world (media, Wall Street, investors). Even so, the vast majority of Nomad's firms do what is right long term. But I suspect we have a predilection for such people. Which brings us on to an important characteristic of Nomad today that we hope will affect results for years to come.

There are, broadly, two ways to behave as an investor. First, buy something cheap in anticipation of a rise in price, sell at a profit, and repeat. Almost everybody does this to some extent. And for some fund managers it requires, depending upon the number of shares in a portfolio and the time they are held, perhaps many hundred decisions a year. Alternatively, the second way to invest is to buy shares in a great business at a reasonable price and let the business grow. This appears to require just one decision (to buy the shares) but, in reality, it requires daily decisions not to sell the shares as well! Almost no one does this, in part because it requires patience - and the locker room set does not do patience - but also because inactivity is the enemy of high fees.

Regardless of how it may appear, Zak and I are drifting toward inactivity, at least as judged by our industry. As we have set out in earlier letters, in part this is because we realise through vicarious, and not so vicarious (!), experience that we do not know that much. We certainly do not have an opinion on many hundred shares, at least, not an opinion in which we would invest money. Second, we have learned or, rather, come to appreciate, that the character of a firm - call it the ability to resist locker room temptation - is far more important than first we realised. This is an important insight. In the long run it may be all that matters. And note,

Nomad is overwhelmingly invested in businesses of great character.

Third, if our firms can successfully grow, and we can resist the temptation to fiddle, then we can meaningfully reduce the reinvestment risk embedded in lots of share buying and selling. Finally, great businesses have been "on sale" and were, in our opinion, the investment opportunity of the credit crisis period. When we wrote to you a year ago, we said, "It may not feel like it but for a long term investor this is the best of times not the worst… Take heart and look to the horizon." Today we have a portfolio of exceptional, iconoclastic businesses that we could own for many years.

This is investment heaven.

From the Partnership Letters:
Value of Inactivity & Activities Outside of Investing

DECEMBER 31st, 2012

"Don't just do something, stand there!"
The White Rabbit, Alice in Wonderland

All is quiet at Galactic HQ.

Each day Zak and I shuffle in, swop trainers for slippers, pull up a pile of annual reports and set about analysing and re-analysing our investments. Routinely we try to kill our companies (they can be killed!), and we sift prospective investments. This week: a Glaswegian office property (in administration) – running yield 22%, we kid you not; a Thai big box retailer – scaling laws work in

Thailand just as they do in Seattle; and a large pharmaceutical business (whose Chief Executive does not think it worth mentioning a multi-billion dollar acquisition a year after it was made!). The research continues but, as far as purchase or sale transactions in Nomad are concerned, we are inactive. Inactive except, perhaps, for the observation, seldom made, that the decision not to do something is still an active decision; it is just that the accountants don't capture it. We have, broadly, the businesses we want in Nomad and see little advantage to fiddling.

And so it should be. If you did not buy the companies you always wished you had owned when they were on fire sale over the last few years then, when exactly are you going to buy them?

Nomad's businesses, to generalise, are run by their founders and the businesses are blessed with cultures that see part of their identity in low operating costs: Costco Wholesale measures costs in basis points and at Amazon.com they take the light bulbs out of the vending machines to save money. In another sphere, the Olympic Team GB Cycling coach and Sky Tour de France Chief (now Sir) Dave Brailsford might refer to this type of behaviour as seeking "the aggregation of marginal gains". Just as it leads to gold medals and yellow jerseys, its effect is that AirAsia, for example, is the lowest cost airline in the world. Good things follow when you care about the pennies.

Zak and I have come to appreciate the value in retreating a little from endless stock analysis. From time to time we swap slippers for brogues and head out into the world with the expectation that what we learn through investing helps us in other activities outside the office, and what we learn doing other activities helps us as investors. I have my school turnaround project, Zak has various charity projects and, together with members of his family, has set up a children's activity center. In this letter I thought I might describe some of these activities.

When we visited Carpetright, a UK carpet retailer, a few years ago we spent the morning with its founder, Lord Harris, discussing his firm and the industry. Lord Harris is a great advocate of watching the pennies. One of his store managers told us that his boss had baulked at the cost of new price tags whenever the shops had a sale. To begin with he made the store managers use both sides of the old price tags, at least this would halve the tag budget, but the real saving came from using the same card with replaceable, reusable numbers. It may seem trivial, but the saving has been in the tens of thousands of pounds. Lord Harris is a wealthy, successful man who does not need to work and so, over lunch, we asked him what still gets him motivated, at the age of 66, "Oh", he said "you should see the academies".

When schools fail in the UK, and the definition of failure is appallingly low exam results sustained through three annual warnings, oversight of the school is taken away from the local education authority and given to an independent body, in this case Lord Harris' Federation of Academies. Once inside the Federation the school (now called an academy) is free to hire a new head, new governors and set its own employment contracts. In the case of the school I became involved with, all three were necessary, the result being an almost complete turnover in staff and governors. It is brutal, but necessary, in order to change the culture. Gone are protected, high salaried employment, a clock watching mentality, and indifference to the pupils' education, and instead teachers are provided with bonuses for attendance and improved exam results.

Not that there is a lot of money to go around. The school does not receive the additional funding that may come with a location in inner London (the school is just over the border and classified, unlike some other local schools, as outer London), and the catchment area is not sufficiently poor to warrant aid, but then it is not wealthy either. The effect is that funding per pupil is one of the lowest in South London and, to put the figure in perspective, funding per child is around one third of the school fees paid for private education at nearby London day schools. The comparison is not quite apples to apples as private schools have to fund their property, but quite how the school runs inside its budget is extraordinary. Every penny is watched, and resources are spent on the right things such as rewarding good practice in teachers and funding extra-curricular activities. It is amazing to see the result: after five years - and with no more funding than the predecessor school - an exam failure rate of around 85% will in the near future, become an 85% pass rate (fingers crossed!). It is quite something to witness.

Zak's family's activity centre is an interesting tale. The centre is located in a light industrial building and consists of climbing structures and slides set in a three story netted frame, a restaurant for the parents and separate entertainment rooms for birthday parties. There is little endemically proprietary about the business, real estate is relatively cheap, the climbing frames are easily purchased and catering is catering. The operation has relatively high fixed costs, which means that incremental revenues appear disproportionately valuable and so centres usually compete on price in the hope of attracting customers. The problem is the supply-side, which periodically gets out of control, as a hopeful newcomer sets up another operation in the same catchment area.

It is tempting in managing such an operation to pay the minimum wage. However, after a short while the family found that the quality of staff improved noticeably if, Costco–like, they paid a bit more. Instead of employing relatively young, unskilled (shop) assistants, the centre began attracting people with experience of working with young children, such as nursery school assistants, who cared about the children. The centre polled customers to find out who had made the decision to visit. Contrary to expectations it wasn't child nagging that forced a decision, but parents wanting something to do with (out!) the kids. What parents care about is cleanliness, new fittings and a decent cup of coffee, so money was spent on these items, not on wowing the children with the newest slide. The activities were keenly priced but the centre found that customers responded more to relative prices and so rates were kept just under those of the competition, rather than ruinously low.

At the end of the first year the centre was running at a loss, but one of the competing centres had closed down. Last year the business was breakeven and, just recently, after the demise of a second competitor (with sizeable debts and which had, interestingly, been run by hired hands and not the proprietor) revenues have jumped by a quarter and the activity centre is now earning proper profits.

It is tempting for Zak's relatives to think the battle has been won and, in line with many a business school case study, now gently raise prices to earn a monopolist's rent. However, Zak's advice to his relatives is counter-intuitive: take prices down (he is a hard man to have on your board). The risk with super-normal profitability is that the profits are an incentive for a new competitor: far better, Zak argues, to earn less, but for a much longer time. This is tough advice for the family members who have been cleaning loos and hoovering floors at eight o'clock at night, but the long-term logic is undeniable. To their very great credit the family are once again lowering prices just a little.

Zak's family's activity centre beat the competition because they understood the difference between good costs (nice staff, clean loos, good coffee) and bad costs (a whizzo new slide) and invested appropriately. They were smart enough to poll customers and observe the influence of pricing (there was no need to over-discount). The operation was equity funded and did not include a third party in the capital structure (bank debt). But most of all it was founder managed and they cared. Watching the pennies and investing carefully has led to the "aggregation of marginal gains" and financial success, and as such it has much in common with the investments that populate Nomad. It has been fun for Zak and me to practice in the real world, what we preach in investing.

Not that we get it right all the time. The agent behind the high yielding Glaswegian office property told us that he had just re-let his first building, twenty-five years later.

"The rent then was £4.26 per foot; it was never going to sell for a round number because both parties cared about the pennies. I have just re-let it for £42 per foot, a round number. You only ever deal in round numbers these days. People don't care about the pennies anymore, that's why no one has got any money," he told us.

Zak and I spend all our time thinking about good business practices and we greatly admire firms that watch the pennies but we looked at our shoes as we were told this story - the rent at Galactic HQ is...ahem...I will whisper this...a round number.

We still have much to learn.

Chapter 5

SCALE ECONOMIES SHARED & OTHER INVESTMENT MODELS

> Scale economics shared operations are quite different. As the firm grows in size, scale savings are given back to the customer in the form of lower prices. The customer then reciprocates by purchasing more goods, which provides greater scale for the retailer who passes on the new savings as well. Yippee.
>
> - DECEMBER 31st, 2008

Scales economies shared was one of the investment models Nomad uncovered and settled on to pick good investments.

In short, scale economies shared was a business model that creates sustainable wealth over long periods of time and was accomplished by:
1. Keeping costs low, which allowed them to
2. Pass on most of the savings back to the customers in the form of lower prices
3. Who reciprocated by doing more business with them,
4. Which allowed them to grow and continually lower costs

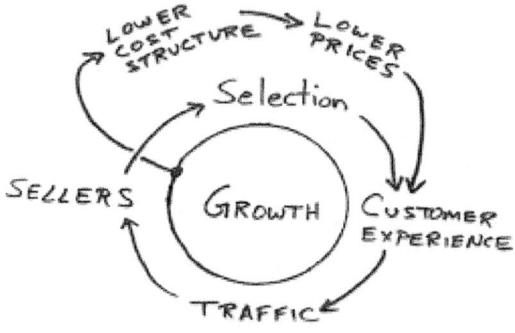

As Sleep puts it: "*Increased revenues begets scale savings begets lower costs begets lower prices begets increased revenues.*"

This virtuous cycle, which requires discipline and self-restraint to maintain, enables these firms to keep and extend its advantage over rivals. Very few founders have the vision or desire to pursue such a path.

However, companies and founders that did follow this path were all durable winners: Costco, Amazon, Wal-Mart, Southwest Airlines, AirAsia, GEICO, Nebraska Furniture Mart, and Ford.

As William Green writes,

> *Once Sleep and Zakaria understood the magic of this one business model, they made it the overriding focus of their fund. The attraction of cigar butts waned and they concentrated instead on a handful of companies that shared their economies of scale with customers. They were acutely aware of how little in life we ever truly know. But they knew that they had uncovered a deep truth.*

---

[8] Figure from Scale Economies Shared

From the Partnership Letters: Scale Economies Shared

DECEMBER 31st, 2004

In the office we have a white board on which we have listed the (very few) investment models that work and that we can understand. Costco is the best example we can find of one of them: scale efficiencies shared. Most companies pursue scale efficiencies, but few share them. It's the sharing that makes the model so powerful. But in the center of the model is a paradox: the company grows through giving more back. We often ask companies what they would do with windfall profits, and most spend it on something or other, or return the cash to shareholders. Almost no one replies give it back to customers – how would that go down with Wall Street? That is why competing with Costco is so hard to do. The firm is not interested in today's static assessment of performance. It is managing the business as if to raise the probability of long- term success.

JUNE 30th, 2005

So far, we have only discussed one model we use to pick good investments which we call "scale efficiencies shared" as evidenced by Costco (and to a lesser extent Amazon.com). We have little more than a handful of distinct investment models, which overlap to some extent, and Zimcem is a good example of a second model namely, "deep discount to replacement cost with latent pricing power". Indeed, these two models combined can be used to describe around 45% of total Partnership assets. It was this model that led to many investments during the Asian crisis (such as Siam Cement which has risen twenty-fold from the trough in eight years) and to neighbouring South Africa where Pretoria Portland Cement could be bought at a price of US$20 per ton of capacity in 1998 and is now valued at US$180 per ton. The model is premised upon the observation that the business needs to replace its assets and will require prices which 1. fund the capex, and 2. economically justify the spending. Either that or Zimbabwe will have to go without cement or import from abroad (tricky for this land locked country). In any event, provided discretionary capital is not invested to exacerbate the situation, the supply side remains muted (industry capex is zero) and the business is not nationalised, then the shares ought to do well, in time.

This last point, along with other confiscation events, does not have a zero probability, and is the main reason our investments in the country will be modest in size. Even if we were able to secure all the shares we desire (which we seem incapable of doing) it is unlikely that the total investment would be much more than a few percent of the Partnership at cost. There is no a priori reason why Zimbabwean businesses should not trade at a premium to replacement cost. Just over the northern border Zambia's dominant cement company is now valued at a premium to replacement cost following recovery in the economy after years of mismanagement. In Zimbabwe this may require "regime change", or even regime changes. Perhaps the investment case rests in your manager being fifty years younger than Bob Mugabe.

JUNE 30th, 2007

It seems to us that the basic building block of internet retailing, its skeletal structure, is far more robust, scalable and cheaper than the high street equivalent. In other words, its power law is very high, and implies that businesses with the simplicity of operation as say, Amazon.com, have a shot at being far bigger, quicker and more profitable than their high street equivalents. Nomad has an investment in Amazon for more reasons than the firm's simplicity of operations. But when this basic building block is combined with the scale efficiencies shared model (which increases the moat as the firm grows), customer centric orientation of the firm's founder, as well as his healthy disdain for Wall Street, this combination makes us think that we may have a mouse that can turn into an elephant. To those who argue Amazon is large already we ask two questions: what do you think e-commerce will be as a proportion of US retailing in ten-years' time, and what do you think it was last year? Write both numbers down and turn to the end of this letter***[9] for the answer to the second question.

JUNE 30th, 2008

AirAsia is an example of scale-economics shared, which like Amazon, Costco, Carpetright and elements of other businesses in the portfolio (Geico, Nebraska Furniture Mart) have come to dominate Nomad (around 45% of the portfolio). AirAsia is the first sizeable, professional, entrepreneur owned and run low-cost airline to operate in Asia and as the firm began operations in 2002 these are pioneering days. For example, we do not know how big the market for low-cost travel is in Asia, although U$22 to Bangkok strikes us as market stimulating. Joint venture operations in Thailand and Indonesia offer a population base seven times the domestic Malaysian market and it is for this reason that the firm has 175 A320 aircraft on order. The negotiated price of the A320s is, as far as we can tell, the lowest price paid by anybody for A320s and the firm has secured a guaranteed lowest price for an Asian carrier from Airbus for its planes. On paper then, AirAsia could be the most fantastic business.

DECEMBER 31st, 2008

Scale economics shared operations are quite different. As the firm grows in size, scale savings are given back to the customer in the form of lower prices. The customer then reciprocates by purchasing more goods, which provides greater scale for the retailer who passes on the new savings as well. Yippee. This is why firms such as Costco enjoy sales per foot of retailing space four times greater than run-of-the-mill supermarkets. Scale economics shared incentivises customer reciprocation, and customer reciprocation is a super-factor in business performance.

---

[9] The US Census Bureau estimates that e-commerce sales grew from 2.7% to 3.1% of all retail sales in the United States during the quarters of 2006. The source document can be found at www.census.gov/mrts/www/data/html/07Q1table1.html.

Scale economics shared works across industries too with the effect that load factors at the low-price Malaysian airline, AirAsia, are superior to high-low flag carrying airlines. And it works online: Amazon have deployed it so well that Amazon's operating costs (per dollar of sales) plus its operating margin are less than some of its high street peers' costs (per dollar of sales). This offers the prospect that, in theory, Amazon's high street peers could price their products at net income breakeven and still not undercut Amazon's prices or profitability. For these high street competitors the game is over. They will leak revenues to more efficient rivals as customers respond to the incentive of consistently low prices and convenience. Over time high street rivals, and less successful online rivals, will need to restructure, change their product, or go out of business. We estimate Amazon's immediate hinterland of high street rivals have combined revenues of US$150bn in the US alone. If these firms go away over the next ten years, as Circuit City, Woolworths, Zavvi and others have recently, and Amazon picks up one dollar in ten of their sales, then this alone would be enough to quadruple Amazon's US revenues over the next decade.

Scale economics works well in bad economic times as well as good. On the busiest day in the run up to Christmas this year, order volumes at Amazon were 16% higher than the previous year and note this compares to industry-wide US retail sales which declined nearly ten percent in December, according to the commerce department! And at AirAsia revenues per seat per kilometer flown rose 33%, whilst costs per seat per kilometer flown excluding fuel declined 10% in the latest quarterly period. Our businesses are surging ahead, even if, in some cases, their share prices are half what they were twelve months ago. In the last few months Amazon has been priced in the market as if it would not grow in the future, despite some of the best growth prospects we can imagine. That is a very rare combination and, combined with other similarly cheap stocks in the partnership, was the basis for Nomad's reopening at the end of last year.

JUNE 30th, 2009
Seeing, but Not Understanding

How might corporate success be predictable? There are some clues in the world around us. Zak and I observe several business models that work in the long run, and scale economics shared is one of these, witness Ryanair, Wal-Mart, Geico, Southeast Airlines, Tesco, Nebraska Furniture Mart, Direct Line et al. And that is why companies that share scale with the customer such as Carpetright, Costco, Berkshire Hathaway, Amazon and AirAsia make up around sixty percent of the Partnership. It works because it turns size, normally an anchor to growth and returns, into an asset. But I also don't think this is a great secret.

There are very few business models where growth begets growth. Scale economics turns size into an asset. Companies that follow this path are at a huge advantage compared to those, for example, that suffer from Barbie syndrome. Put simply: average companies do not do scale economics shared. Average companies do not have a healthy culture. After all, average companies are more like GM than Wal-Mart! The removal of a portion of failure risk from the investment equation creates a huge opportunity for those investors that can see the company in its true perspective and act with a bit of patience. It is a huge anomaly that investors recognize success incrementally when the factors that lead to success, such as scale economics shared reinforced by a strong culture, may be constant. If the early investors in Wal-Mart had understood this, they may have retained their holding along with the, now billionaire, Walton family.

Some facts and figures may help paint a useful aggregate picture of the Partnership. Zak and I think of the Partnership in terms of business models deployed by our investee firms. The names we use to describe these models are not that catchy but please bear with us. The largest group making up over half the Partnership are, no drum roll required, scale-economics-shared; next comes discounts-to-replacement- cost-with-pricing-power (I warned you) at around fifteen percent; hated-agencies fifteen percent; super-high-quality-thinkers just under ten percent. The Partnership has twenty investments but a noticeable concentration in ten, which make up around eighty percent of the portfolio, and for those with sharp eyes around thirty percent of the Partnership in one investment. Although the bulk of the Partnership is listed in the United States, look-through revenues are far more diversified: US dollar revenues forty- seven percent, Euro and Swiss Franc revenues twenty-one percent, South East Asian currencies sixteen percent, Sterling ten percent, Yen three percent and others three percent. There are perhaps six main industry groups and their weightings are as follows: internet thirty percent, consumer staples sixteen percent, consumer discretionary fourteen, business services thirteen, insurance and finance eleven, and airlines eight percent, with a tail of smaller groupings.

JUNE 30th, 2010

Take Costco Wholesale: Costco's advantage is its very low-cost base, but where does that come from? Not from low-cost land, or cheap wages or any one big thing but from a thousand daily decisions to save money where it need not be spent. This saving is then returned to customers in the form of lower prices, the customer reciprocates and purchases more goods and so begins a virtuous feedback loop. The firm's advantage starts with 147,000 employees at 566 warehouses making multiple daily decisions regarding U$68bn worth of annual costs. It's thousands of people caring about thousands of things a little more, perhaps, than may occur at other retailers. No fig leaf here. When Zak and I met Jim Sinegal, Costco's CEO, Jim suddenly stopped in mid-sentence, his face lit up, "I must show you this" he said and disappeared into a filling cabinet. He emerged with a memo from 1967 written by Sol Price, Fed-Mart's founder (the predecessor firm to Costco), "here you can have a copy of this" he said, and that copy is framed on our office wall. The memo says this,

> *"Although we are all interested in margin, it must never be done at the expense of our philosophy. Margin must be obtained by better buying, emphasis on selling the kind of goods we want to sell, operating efficiencies, lower markdowns, greater turnover, etc. Increasing the retail prices and justifying it on the basis that we are still "competitive" could lead to a rude awakening as it has with so many. Let us concentrate on how cheap we can bring things to the people, rather than how much the traffic will bear, and when the race is over Fed-Mart will be there".* [The best summary of the business case for scale economics shared we have come across].

Chapter 6

COMPETITIVE ADVANTAGE

One of Nomad's key competitive advantages will be the aggregate patience of its investors.
- DECEMBER 31st, 2002

Main Points
- As an investor, one of the most important questions to answer is, "What is your competitive advantage in investing?"
- The answer to the question requires both a thorough understanding of yourself AND the ability to be brutally honest with yourself: two things that are incredibly difficult to achieve.
- Bill Miller posed the exact question in a speech to students at the Columbia Business School and provided an elegant answer:
    1. **Informational Advantage:** you know something nobody else knows
    2. **Analytical Advantage:** you can analyze public information to come up with a superior conclusion
    3. **Psychological Advantage:** you have a behavioral edge
- A long-term sustainable advantage usually consists of both an analytical and or psychological advantage. In Nomad's case, their advantage was the combination of (1) the patience of the investor base and (2) the analytical and psychological traits of Nick and Zak.

- These two traits allowed Nomad to be patient, let expensive businesses fly by them, and wait for the fat pitches without the pressure from investors to always be invested.

From the Partnership Letters: Competitive Advantage

DECEMBER 31st, 2002 / JUNE 30th, 2003 / JUNE 30th, 2004

One of Nomad's key competitive advantages will be the aggregate patience of its investors. We are genuinely investing for the long term (few are!), in undervalued firms run by management teams who may be making decisions the fruits of which may not be apparent for several years to come. In the near term our results are as likely to be bad as good, but we are confident that in the long run they will prove satisfactory. If Nomad is to have a competitive advantage over our peers this will come from the capital allocation skills of your manager and the patience of our investors. In the latter we have started well, with no investor turnover since we began and almost no enquires into performance despite the general decline in market prices. This is very unusual and a huge credit to our investors, and implies a similar long term outlook. Only by looking further out than the short term crowd can we expect to beat them. It is for this reason we named Nomad an Investment Partnership and not a fund. The relationship we seek is quite different.

JUNE 30th, 2005

Competitive Advantage

As a young(ish) man there is something slightly depressing about thinking things through for a while, arriving at a somewhat reasoned conclusion only to find that others have been there before, and years earlier. In some respects we are fifty years behind Buffett, but that's ok so long as the average investor is at least fifty-one years behind! I would estimate we were some way behind Bill Miller as well, as evidenced by his recent speech to students of the Columbia Business School in which he posed the question – what is your competitive advantage in investing? It was the elegance of the answer that grabbed us. Broadly Bill Miller argued that there are three competitive advantages in investing: informational (I know a meaningful fact nobody else does); analytical (I have cut up the public information to arrive at a superior conclusion) and psychological (that is to say, behavioural).

Sustainable competitive advantages are usually a product of analytical and or psychological factors, and the overwhelming advantage with regard to Nomad is the patience of the investor base and the alignment of that disposition with the analytical and psychological traits of your manager. It simply would not work otherwise. In the investment objective section of the Nomad prospectus we say that our job is to "pass custody [of your investment] over at the right price and to the right people"... and that "the approach will require patience". That's what investing is, at least for us. But let me return to the speech for a moment.

> *"Think of how the future will be different from the past. Most people default to the directions and trends that they are currently observing...The important thing is that most things change. In longer term projections, Peter Bernstein tells us, that cone of uncertainty gets wider as time goes out. What are the chances that IBM will be bankrupt tomorrow morning? Probably none. A year from now? Five years from now? What about one hundred years from now? The point being that the possibilities increase as time goes out. So what you are trying to do as an investor is exploit the fact that fewer things will happen than can happen. So you are trying to figure out how that probability distribution works and stay in the middle of what will happen. The market has to worry about all the things that can happen."*

To repeat: "what you are trying to do as an investor is exploit the fact that fewer things will happen than can happen". That is exactly what we are trying to do. We spend a considerable portion of our waking hours thinking about how company behaviour can make the future more predictable, and lower the risk of investment. Costco's obsession with sharing scale benefits with the customer makes that company's future much more predictable and less risky than the average business and that is why it is our largest holding. Our smaller holdings are less predictable but in certain circumstances could do much better as investments. We are just not sure that they will as their "cone of uncertainty" has a much greater radius than at Costco. Bill Miller got there years ago. We are just getting there today.

DECEMBER 31st, 2005

<u>Comparative Advantage Revisited</u>
It is an interesting psychological phenomenon to observe that if our annual results were reordered, we might feel differently about them. For example, place the results in descending order (+80%, +22%, +10%, +9%, +1%) and one is depressed by the decline; place them in ascending order (+1%...+80%), and we tend to think of them more favourably, even though the end result (the destination) is identical. Recent success feels better than distant success, as the brain perceives recent rewards more vividly. Psychologists call this the "availability heuristic" and it is this phenomenon that has sold a thousand mediocre mutual funds that appear, momentarily, to have a pulse! But that is not the way to invest. Annual results will bounce around all over the place, and for Nomad more so than more diversified funds. But does that matter if the destination is secure? Indeed, if we could turn US$1 into US$16, does it matter if it takes 18 years or 22 years? There is a difference in the annual compound rate of appreciation (over 3% per annum, and I do not wish to make light of that), but securing the destination is also important.

And securing the destination is much harder to do if you are trying to beat the index in annual increments at the same time. Nassim Nicholas Taleb (author of "Fooled by Randomness") published an interesting paper (free, on the internet) which also linked the sequence in which returns occurred to how they made investors feel. He argued that investors often accept the risk of an occasional large loss for a steady small profit as the recurrence of the gains made them feel better. This occurred even when an opposite strategy, of steady small losses followed by a large gain, generated superior end results. Travelling comfortably dominates people's thinking when they should be thinking about destinations.

To our way of thinking the question is, what good habits and techniques ensure that the destination is secure (even if the ride is bumpy), and that U$16 will be realised? This comes down to the sustainability of an investor's comparative advantage. In the last letter we discussed the comparative advantages an investor may have. To recall, "there are three competitive advantages in investing: informational (I know a meaningful fact nobody else does); analytical (I have cut up the public information to arrive at a superior conclusion) and psychological (that is to say, behavioural)." We concluded that the enduring advantages are mainly psychological. In this letter I thought I might describe some of the largest, common psychological causes of investor mis-judgement, and apply these to some of our investments

JUNE 30th, 2010

Some Observations on the Nature of Comparative Advantages
There are, perhaps, few things finer than the pleasure of finding out something new. Discovery is one of the joys of life and, in our opinion, is one of the real thrills of the investment process. The cumulative learning that results leads to what Berkshire Hathaway Vice-Chairman Charlie Munger calls "worldly wisdom". Worldly wisdom is a good phrase for the intellectual capital with which investment decisions are made and, at the end of the day, it is the source of any superior investment results we may enjoy. So, when analysing a firm, one just knows one is on to a good thing when one learns something new and the penny finally drops. And many times more fortunate if that insight can be applied more generally across businesses.

Take, for example, a recent research trip to a Welsh insurance company. The firm's products are nothing special, primary auto insurance sold to customers who buy mainly due to the legal requirement to be insured on the public roads. There is little product differentiation across the industry and the customer purchase decision is usually driven by price. This is a soul-less relationship: it is near on impossible to get customers to love their insurance companies and, for their part, insurance companies don't give the impression they love their customers much either. Be that as it may, the firm we visited has a wonderful track record of financial results going back decades. Not just good by insurance industry standards (a low hurdle to jump if ever there was one), but good by any standards. So, what is going on?

It is tempting when analysing such situations to look for the big thing the firm does right. In effect, one is looking for the smoking gun that explains the firm's success. A smoking gun may be a vivid image, but the world does not always work like that. I should have known better when I asked what big idea had led to the firm's success: "No, no, Nick, there is no secret sauce here", one senior executive explained, "we don't do one thing brilliantly, we do many, many things slightly better than others". I have heard this line frequently over the last twenty or so years, and I have always dismissed it as a fig leaf covering the lack of any real corporate advantage. And I think that all this time I may have been wrong.

Chapter 7

PSYCHOLOGY OF HUMAN MISJUDGEMENT

> I have long been very interested in standard thinking errors.
> - Charlie Munger

The *Psychology of Human Misjudgment*[10] is a speech that Charlie Munger gave to an audience at Harvard University in 1995 (he actually gave a revised version of it in 2005). In it, Munger discusses how behavioral psychology can be applied to decision-making and how to avoid "standard thinking errors".

Specifically, he outlines 25 psychological tendencies that cause humans to make poor decisions. For example, one tendency is the "Authority-Misinfluence Tendency", or that humans tend to obey authority without question, even if the actions are against their own better judgment (e.g., Milgram Experiment).

Nick and Zak consider Munger's speech the "finest investment speech ever given" and also discuss a few of the biggest common psychological causes of investor misjudgment in their letters.

---

[10] The Revised Psychology of Human Misjudgment, by Charlie Munger (Farnam Street)

(1) Social Proof/Group Psychology

In 1968, Stanley Milgram conducted the Street Corner Experiment.

First, they put a single person on a street corner and had him look up at the sky for 60 seconds. A small number of people walking by stopped and also looked up, but most just walked by.

Next, they put 5 men to look up at the sky. Four times as many people stopped to look up.

Last, they put 15 men. Now, an extra 80% of people walking by looked up.

So what does this teach us? That people have a tendency to assume that if lots of people are doing something (or believe something), there must be a good reason why.... So you assume the crowd knows best and follow along. This tendency is known as "social proof".

In markets, the exact same thing occurs and this is evidenced by waves of overinvestments in various sectors in history: Thai cement industry in the mid 1990s and the US telecom, technology companies in the late 1990s. Once one company starts building, all the other companies pile in over the fear of missing out (FOMO). Combining social proof + envy + financial incentives available in the markets is a recipe for disaster.

(2) Availability

Availability is the tendency to over-weight vivid or easily obtained evidence. In other words, we tend to over-value what is easily available to us and under-value what is not.

For example, as investors we might over-value financial statements or earnings call transcripts and completely under-value less visible items, such as the product life cycles or management incentives.

(3) Lack of Probability-Based Thinking

Humans tend to have an inability to think probabilistically. Charlie Munger has said that "the right way to think is the way Zeckhauser plays bridge, it's that simple."

Zeckhauser? Well, Robert Zeckhauser was the world bridge champion in '66 and (among other things) a professor at the Kennedy School of Government at Harvard. He thinks in terms of decision trees and attaches probabilities to the various branches. And of course, when facts change, so do the probabilities.

However, people don't think rationally when it comes to probabilities. For example, take the following problem: assume one person in a thousand suffers from a disease and the test for that disease is 99% accurate. If you test positive for that disease, what is the probability that you have the disease? (Hint: use Bayes' Theorem)

Most would assume 1%, but the answer is ~9% (one in eleven).

As investors, properly valuing a company requires estimating the likely outcomes given many factors (management behavior, competitive forces, etc.) and weighing the probable outcomes. Most investors fail to properly arrange the outcomes in probabilities, which is a source of error in decision-making and valuation.

(4) Lack of Patience

At the beginning of the annual meeting for Berkshire Hathaway they show a video of Buffett being asked what the main difference between him and the average investor is, to which he replies "patience". Who doesn't want to get rich fast? But it is that exact mentality that heavily distorts one's decision-making and gets people in trouble.

At the root of the problem is that most investors crowd into positions that have an expected payout within the year (if they even think that far out!) and the majority of these investors are fund managers, since they are evaluated by their year-end performance. As a result, the prices get pushed up which diminishes the return; this is around the time you or I hear about it.

In short, there are more opportunities if you are willing to look out past a year as the field of competition has thinned out. A lot. Some have called this "time arbitrage" and we discuss it more in the Equity Yield Curve chapter.

(5) Mental Shortcuts

Through our experiences, we humans have picked up a lot of learned biases, shortcuts, fears, habits and associations which may hinder us from making rational decisions. This is exactly what Charlie Munger meant by "the human mind is a lot like the human egg": once one sperm has entered an egg, the egg shuts down and all other sperm are locked out. Similarly, when an idea has taken root in a mind, the mind shuts down to other ideas.

In the letters, Nomad outlines two examples:
1. Zimbabwe: At a panel hosted for investment professionals, Richard Zeckhauser passed a note to a fellow panelist that read, "One of our participants is buying Zimbabwean securities, which are priced at a small percentage of Net Asset Value. Would you try to invest with him?" And the panelist replied, "No!". As soon as the panelist saw the word Zimbabwe, his mind blocked out the idea and ignored the fact that a gain could actually be made from low prices.
2. Slow-Growing Internet Retailers: in 2011, Nomad posed the question of: why were internet retailers growing so slowly? They were essentially growing at the same rate as a physically constrained retailer (e.g. Wal-Mart) was growing at a similar stage in its development.
    a. In comparison to traditional retailing, internet retailers are not bound by the physical constraints of a building's size, location and opening hours. Nomad postulated that the slow growth rate in online retailing was a function of our incumbent habits and associations. In short, our own psychological biases prevented us from adopting internet retailing (even though it would have been the more rational choice).

(6) Commitment Bias

Commitment bias occurs when we publicly disclose our intentions and thoughts and we feel the need to commit to those past behaviors. As Munger says, "if you make public disclosure of your conclusions, you're pounding into your own head." In short, the more public you make your conclusions, the deeper you drive that conclusion back into your own mind.

In investing, commitment bias occurs when we publicly disclose our positions, which most definitely affects our objectivity towards the position. Fund managers deal with this problem all the time, as they must both market the fund (by disclosing their process and stock picks) and be objective in their thinking (which entails admitting when they are wrong and close a position). Warren Buffet seemed to solve this problem a long time ago when he was running Buffett Partnership, as he was very secretive about his holdings and didn't talk much about what the Partnership was doing:

"For Buffett, the Generals were a highly secretive, highly concentrated portfolio of undervalued common stocks that produced the majority of the Partnership's overall gains."
            -Jeremy Miller, *Warren Buffet's Ground Rules*

For example, it is interesting that two of the best performing funds of all time did not disclose their holdings to investors. These were the Buffett Partnership and Walter Schloss Associates. (December 31st, 2007)

From the Partnership Letters:
Social Proof/Group Psychology

DECEMBER 31st, 2005

We all know that social decisions can be suboptimal, but even so, that is how most decisions are made. In the last letter we reproduced one of our favourite Punch cartoons and make no apologies for doing so again here.

Look at the angel in the last frame: think of her as a metaphor for the investment management industry. We sit at the top of the capitalist pyramid, collecting our rent from the layers below, and we should be thinking differently from the crowd. We should behave with some integrity. But what is the angel doing? Stanley Milgram performed an experiment very similar to the Punch cartoon and found that as the size of the crowd increased, so the proportion of passers-by that stopped and looked up increased too. I have not seen the study but I bet the relationship wasn't linear, that instead it had these step functions to it. No one stops if there's just one guy standing there, but perhaps a group of three would get some passers by looking up, and by the time it's a big group almost everyone is stopping: that's the way it works in the markets. Witness the waves of massive overinvestment such as occurred in the Thai cement industry in the mid 1990s, and the US telecom and technology companies in the late 1990s. It appears to us that once one company starts building they all do through fear of missing out. Once Siam Cement had built all the capacity Thailand could need there was no need for Siam City Cement to join in. Let alone TPI Polene. But they all went mad. Combine social proof with envy and the financial incentives available in the stock market and that's a recipe for a sizeable mistake.

From the Partnership Letters: Availability

DECEMBER 31st, 2005

A second source of misjudgement is availability, or the tendency to over-weight the vivid evidence or the evidence easily obtained. We discussed this somewhat above in relation to annual performance. We all do this to some extent, as the tendency is to concentrate at the task in hand, and miss the bigger picture. Looking around you is the most important skill, and is largely innate, although Professor John Stilgoe at Harvard is trying to teach it and wrote an interesting book recently entitled "Outside Lies Magic". In the markets investors tend to latch on to what can be measured, aided by the accountants and to some extent by their own laziness. But there is a wealth of information in items expensed by accountants, such as advertising, marketing and research and development, or in items auditors ignore entirely such as product integrity, product life cycles, market share and management character (this is not an exhaustive list!).

From the Partnership Letters: Probability Based Thinking

DECEMBER 31st, 2005

Third is an inability to perform probability based thinking. In one of Charlie Munger's talks he makes the statement "the right way to think is the way Zeckhauser plays bridge, it's just that simple". Well, to a young man in London that is a very infuriating statement as it took me about a year to track down Richard Zeckhauser. He was world bridge champion in '66 and, amongst other things, now runs a brilliant Behavioural Finance course at the Kennedy School of Government at Harvard. So, how does he play bridge? He thinks via decision trees and attaches probabilities to the various branches. And as the facts change, change the probabilities. And when you are comfortable dealing with probabilities, and the vast expanse of opportunities such as the global stock and bond markets, you don't have to be too conservative with your bets.

But people don't think clearly when faced with probability trees. Take the following example, one person in a thousand suffers from a particular disease. The test for that disease is 99% accurate. What is the chance that your friend, who has tested positive for the disease, actually has the disease? The answer is one in eleven. However many people mistakenly think the answer is one in a hundred (hint for the confused: one in a hundred is the accuracy of the test). As the tests aren't as accurate as they sound, and many doctors miscalculate the probabilities of disease, the General Medical Council (in the UK) requires that doctors test for dreadful diseases like HIV twice! Understanding the value of a company involves assessing the likely outcomes given management behaviour and competitive forces, and weighing the probable outcomes in a valuation. So an inability to arrange outcomes in probabilities is a considerable error causing bias in investors decision making processes and is behind many mis- valuations.

From the Partnership Letters: Patience

DECEMBER 31st, 2005

Finally, patience, or the lack thereof. At the beginning of the annual general meeting of the Berkshire Hathaway Company they show a video in which Buffett is asked what is the main difference between himself and the average investor, and he answers "patience". There is so little of it about these days: has anyone heard of getting rich slowly? Jack Bogle, founder of the Vanguard Group, claims that the holding period for stocks is down to 10 months and the average mutual fund is held for 2 years. What's that all about? And this behaviour feeds back into how managers report to their clients, to the extent that quarterly reporting borders on an obsessive compulsive disorder. And how did we get to this state of affairs?

I think the problem is that two agents, the fund manager and his immediate client, try to eek out some value added in the mind of their clients, and it creates these counter productive consequences. Few people honestly believe this is the right way to behave, but they think that is what is expected of them by others, and so a spiral of dysfunctional behaviour is established. You would never get this level of reporting nonsense if it was on a principal to principal basis! And who is to blame? I side against the investment institutions. These are largely rich organisations and should behave with integrity, not bow to dysfunctional requests. And it is so unnecessary: as investors we own the only permanent capital in a company's capital structure, everything else in the company: management, assets, board, employees, can change but, absent bankruptcy, our equity will still be there! Institutional investors have never really reconciled their ability to trade daily with the permanence of equity. Are they long-term or short-term?

From the Partnership Letters: Observations on Mental Shortcuts

JUNE 30th, 2011

At Professor Richard Zeckhauser's Behavioural Finance course at the JFK School of Government at Harvard University, the following note was scribbled by Professor Zeckhauser and passed to a fellow panelist, whilst both men hosted a discussion group with an audience of investment professionals.

Zeckhauser: *One of our participants is buying Zimbabwean securities, which are priced at a small percentage of Net Asset Value. Would you try to invest with him?*

Other panelist: *No! (the exclamation mark is original)*

Oh dear! We suspect that the other panelist made up his mind the moment he saw the word Zimbabwe and that blocked his thinking of the gain that could be made from such low prices. We all do this to some extent. It is so easy to screen out a good idea because of a bad association. As Charlie Munger quipped at a speech given at the same course a few years earlier "*the human mind is a lot like the human egg*": once one sperm has entered then all the other sperm are locked out. A market research company we visited recently told us that most car advertising is read after the purchase decision for the car has already been made! And it was read only then to gather information to convince other people the purchase decision was rational ("*no, no it wasn't the car's sexy shape – this car has twelve airbags and emits 170g of carbon per mile!*") We have all done it. The human mind has these learnt biases, short cuts, fears, habits, and associations and, in the case of the panelist above, they can stop us from making rational decisions.

An odd question popped into our heads the other day: why are internet retailers growing so slowly? Unlike traditional retailing, where growth is bounded by the physical constraints of a building's size, location, and opening hours, internet retailing has no such constraints. We could all, for the sake of argument, decide to do all our shopping online next week, and Amazon et al would take the orders. Odd, then, that the growth rate in revenues at the main internet-based retailers is, very broadly, comparable to that enjoyed by a physically constrained retailer, say, Wal-Mart, at a similar stage in its development. So, what is going on?

If Frank Capra is right that "*a hunch is creativity trying to tell you something*" then our hunch is that the growth rate in online retailing is held back by consumers' psychological biases. We are all creatures of habit, and most of us give up comfort blankets quite reluctantly. It therefore takes time for a new regime to be adopted and, for instance, to buy books online instead of buying them at the local store. Perhaps then, after we have become comfortable with buying books online, we may experiment with something else, trainers say, or magazine subscriptions, or plant pots, or bike saddles or grocery. The process requires a good retail experience (price, convenience, selection etc.), the building of trust, and is often fanned with personal recommendations (social proof) and even bragging rights for the early adopters. The process is more of a drift than epiphany. Our hunch is that the growth rate in online retailing is regulated, not by physical capacity, although that can be a limiting factor, but more by the rate at which our own incumbent habits and associations are replaced with more rational behaviour.

The models we use may not be the right ones
In high street retailing we can estimate, broadly, what revenue growth for each firm will be next year: it is a product of same store sales growth plus any new stores. We might not be precisely correct about either number, but the range is bounded and so we can make a reasonable, "generally-right" (as opposed to "precisely wrong") estimate. When investors think about the future of a business, they often have in mind the assumption that growth rates slow with time, as competition ekes away advantages and market places become saturated. Predicted revenue growth rates (used in valuation models) therefore start high and end low. This is especially true for firms that are quite large already.

However, if the rate of growth in internet retailing is a product of attitude, rather than assets, then, the fact that a firm is quite large already does not necessarily tell you that its growth rate is set to slow. The widely held presumption that regression to the mean begins the moment the analyst picks up their pen, risks being wrong footed as a result. Two years of forty percent revenue growth, for example, will result in revenues doubling in twenty-four months and regression to the mean based estimates would be out by almost a factor of two! That did not take long. In other words, although some online retailing firms may be quite large, they may also be quite young. In our opinion, it is this realisation that has partially driven the revaluation of internet retailers these last few years.

From the Partnership Letters: Commitment Bias

DECEMBER 31st, 2004
(Appendix: Introduction to the Global Investment Review, September 2004)

"...this is a superpower in error-causing psychological tendency: bias from consistency and commitment tendency, including the tendency to avoid or promptly resolve cognitive dissonance. Includes the self-confirmatory tendency of all conclusions, particularly expressed conclusions, and with a special persistence for conclusions that are hard-won".

- Charles T. Munger, speech at Harvard Law School, estimated date June 1995

It is not uncommon for plan sponsors and other clients to ask their fund managers to discuss their latest stock purchases. Perhaps the supposition is that these are the investments on which the manager is most bullish. Perhaps it is a test of conviction. Perhaps the client is looking for a tip, who knows? No matter how good the relationship between fund manager and client there is inevitably a bias at least to defend and at worse promote the purchase decision. We have all done this to some extent. It's only natural; the manager has made the decision to invest and is talking to the client, how can he not be upbeat? Promotion is one thing, and we can all adjust more or less for its effects, decades of company visits have honed that particular skill, but that is not the issue at hand. The issue is whether, in trying to convince the client of the merits of the case, the manager convinces himself. The danger is highlighted by Munger in the passage below:

"And of course, if you make public disclosure of your conclusions, you're pounding into your own head. Many of these students that are screaming at us, they aren't convincing us, but they are forming mental chains for themselves, because what they are shouting out, they are pounding in. And I think that educational institutions that create a climate where too much of that goes on are...in a fundamental sense, they are irresponsible institutions".

It is for this reason that in its purest form a fund management company's sales function (whose basic technique is to "shout out and pound in") can be counter-productive. And it is why the most successful salesmen (as measured by commissions earned over the short-term) are frequently void of rooted-in-reality objective thinking, such as is vital for good long-term investment performance. Either fund management companies are investment companies or marketing companies. Not both. At Marathon we think we understand this conflict but even we struggle, and we make no claim to maximise both functions. The fact is that sales and size are the two main detractors of long-term performance, after inability. To paraphrase Mr. Buffett, should you come across individuals suggesting otherwise our advice is watch their noses, for signs of abnormal growth.

This is not to say that investors do not have the right to question their managers about stock picking – far from it. But both parties must be aware of what they are doing. Our thinking is that fund managers should have absolute conviction on the philosophy and methodology of their investment principles, providing of course that those principles reflect reality. But they should be circumspect about expressing these tenets as they relate to individual stocks. Evangelism is not healthy. The reason is that, whilst fund managers have it in their powers to control the way they think, they are unable to control how their companies behave. Businesses evolve, companies make mistakes, business managers change their minds, share prices depart from reality – the investment manager can control none of these factors but needs to assess objectively each one for the risk of misanalysis. The issue is: in publicly disclosing his stock picking commitments, does the investment manager subtly and no doubt subconsciously rob himself of his objectivity and the option to change his mind? To deny this takes place seems foolhardy. The question is, how many recognise the risk of dysfunctionality, and adjust their behaviour? Certainly, those consultants and plan sponsors that insist upon frequent, detailed, blow-by-blow reporting may be surprised to learn that their seemingly reasonable request risks being counterproductive. Consultant meetings, which aggressively bear down on the microeconomics of an individual business, seem designed to form mental chains that neither side needs to bear. But where does that leave monthly reporting, quarterly reporting, annual reporting, and even this publication?

Fund management errors are not the only ones that result from over-promotion activity. Quarterly, or even monthly, client reporting routinely marks fund management performance to market and these result snapshots acquire an extra validity, simply by virtue of their being reported. At Marathon a full holding cycle can exceed 5 years, so any quarter individually considered could be poor without affecting long-term outcomes. For those keen on monthly results there will be 60 such data points in a full holding cycle. These data points, in the hands of an inexperienced investment committee, could be misconstrued or worse. After all, most of Marathon's client termination events occurred after, rather than before, a period of underperformance. According to Munger, it is a common psychological tendency that people overweigh the vivid evidence (or recent experiences). This is clearly what can happen via the mark-to-market effects of quarterly reporting. The "Pavlovian" association of poor short-term results with long-term incompetence and confusion between the two can lead to disastrous decisions. Today this risk is greater than ever because, relative to history, consistency of investment performance is an attribute prized almost above all others in some parts of our industry.

At a New York cocktail party populated by investment professionals this author clumsily asked one fund manager what his largest holding was. My acquaintance's response was to decline to answer for reasons that this essay makes plain. His response seemed rude in a social setting, at least to this author, but having thought about the issues for about a year, it was perhaps the highest quality answer he could have made. He certainly understood elementary psychology.

From the Partnership Letters: Final Note on Psychology

DECEMBER 31st 2013

It is almost ten years since Barry Schwartz published his popular psychology book "The Paradox of Choice". To précis part of the book: Schwartz observed that western society tends to view choice as a good thing, and more choice as better still. In his local supermarket Schwartz counted one hundred and thirty or so different salad dressings, excluding the dozen olive oils and balsamic vinegars should the pre-made salad dressings not offer enough choice! In his local electronics store he found over six million possible combinations of hi-fi components. Even though consumers were being offered what seemed to Schwartz to be an ever-increasing plethora of choice to meet their needs, he could find no correlation with increased happiness. Instead, he hypothesised, that with all the choice came the (subconscious) expectation that the outcome ought to be perfect, and this expectation rendered the actual choice made as disappointing in comparison. It was as if too much choice was making us unhappy.

Schwartz does not make mention of it directly, but the problem is not confined to consumer decision-making. The public stock markets have many tens of thousands of potential investments, and the price of each of those changes almost constantly. The number of possible profit or loss combinations would make Schwartz's hi-fi store look like a multiple-choice test. It is very easy, therefore, to feel unhappy about one's investments. Indeed, on any one day, month, year it is highly likely, indeed statistically almost certain, that one's chosen combination of investments will lag alternatives – there will always be someone who did better.

In a recent Nomad letter (June 2010) we wrote...

"Readers that make it to the end of our letters (we may be flattering ourselves), including the footnotes (we may be deluding ourselves!), may recall the story we retold of the Ferrari 250 GTO bought by a collector in the 1960s for the effective

price of £750. The beauty of the story is that although the car is one of the most valuable in the world, the collector still has his car today. A different 250 GTO has recently changed hands, and the price...US$20m!"

..Stop Press: a Ferrari 250 GTO changed hands recently for U$52m! That represents an annual return of over twenty percent for around fifty years. There is always something going on that makes Nomad's performance look a bit weedy! Before you show your disappointment and reach for the rotten fruit to throw our way, I think it is time we got back to dealing with the regulations (x4).

Chapter 8

LONG-TERM VIEW & DELAY OF GRATIFICATION

> In a world that's increasingly geared toward short-termism and instant gratification, a tremendous advantage can be gained by those who move consistently in the opposite direction.
> - William Green in *Richer, Wiser, Happier*

Main Points
- This is a fairly simple and well-known idea: focus on having a long-term view.
- Most people are too focused on the short-term and receiving instant gratification; if you are able to move in the opposite direction, you can gain a tremendous edge.
- In investing, people tend to trade too frequently, make decisions based on the most recent news, chase the latest fads, and sell too early before allowing investments to compound over the years.
- "It's all about deferred gratification", says Sleep. "When you look at all the mistakes you make in life, private and professional, it's almost because you reached for some short-term fix or some short-term high… And that's the overwhelming habit of people in the stock market."

From the Partnership Letters: Long-Term View

JUNE 30th, 2002

The fund has a profit on eighteen of its twenty-one investments compared to average purchase price. For those shares that have fallen we have bought more. This reminds us of *"A Little Wonderful Advice"* Fred Schwed gives in his book *"Where are the customers yachts?"* (recommended reading for those with a healthy disdain for Wall Street and its practices as well as an interest in post-boom psychology).

"When there is a stock-market boom, and everyone is scrambling for common stocks, take all your common stocks and sell them. Take the proceeds and buy conservative bonds. No doubt the stocks you sold will go higher. Pay no attention to this – just wait for the depression which will come sooner or later. When this depression – or panic – becomes a national catastrophe, sell out the bonds (perhaps at a loss) and buy back the stocks. No doubt the stocks will go lower still. Again pay no attention. Wait for the next boom. Continue to repeat this operation as long as you live, and you'll have the pleasure of dying rich".

The operative phrase here is "pay no attention". This is not easily done. Many investors are professionally required to "pay attention" to the latest trend for fear of missing out (pay attention and be invested!). The dysfunctionality of the short term investor was neatly described to us recently by a fellow long term value investor. Imagine, he said, that you knew with 100% certainty of outcome, that on JANUARY 1st next year a company would come by some good fortune, perhaps a government contract or license award, which would result in the price of the share quickly rising tenfold. You and I would buy the shares today and wait. However, to the short term investor the utility of this piece of information would be nought until after this year is ended. This is because he feels he is required to perform this quarter, next and by year end through fear that sub-par performance might cost him his job. A share which may be flat for the balance of the year is therefore of no use to him. This tale illustrates the dominant dynamic in the markets today: investment time frames are very compressed, and few investors it seems bother to assess the real value of a business but instead respond to the latest data point to determine share price direction. This is momentum investing and is the mechanism by which expensive shares become very expensive, just as cheap shares may become very cheap. In the above example both sets of investors may even have privately agreed that the share in question was an outstanding investment, but only one would have bought. You can bank on us being the buyer.

This is not a wholly theoretical discussion. Only this week Estée Lauder, a company which we much admire and would consider owning if only someone would sell it to us at a reasonable price, announced that earnings would decline as the firm had decided to invest in brand building instead. Such investment could be expected to raise long term revenue growth and pricing power but even so the share price declined 15% on the news. The reason was that short term investors responded to the warning about next quarter's profits and missed the long term outlook. As Fred Schwed would say "pay no attention to this". In effect the company had been punished by the markets for being sensible. It is this behaviour that gets us excited and sets up investment opportunities.

JUNE 30th, 2003

In December's annual letter to Partners we wrote:

"During the late summer and autumn, when investors were at their most depressed, we made several new investments and, in some cases, added to existing holdings. Although time will tell, this period may mark the end of investors' mood swing from euphoric at the turn of the millennium to manic depressive almost three years later...We also feel that there are many undervalued investments available to us, to which we could put incremental capital to work. You can expect us to caution you when the opposite is true, and we find little available at reasonable prices. But for now, for those with a long-time horizon, we think it is a good time to be making investments".

That seems to have been the case, but for the record, and in case there is any misunderstanding, we do not have the faintest idea what share prices will do in the short term - nor do we think it is important for the long-term investor. All that we observed in the autumn was that barring a catastrophe, indeed in some cases perhaps even including a catastrophe, prices were so low that long-term success was almost inevitable. Even though these are still early days, the Partnership now enjoys a 52% advantage over the investment averages, as presented by the MSCI World Index (for mathematicians the calculation is $(((1+0.406)/(1-0.078))-1) \times 100$)! This is a reasonable absolute gain, and large relative gain over a short period of time, so may we provide some simple philosophy and maths as guidance in how to think about results so far?

DECEMBER 31st, 2005

Our work for the next period
We are very conscious of the destination (U$16 after twenty years) and raising the probability of reaching the destination involves understanding the psychological mistakes mentioned above and thinking in evolutionary terms to stay ahead of the crowd. If people learn and the economy is adaptive one would expect that over time price anomalies may diminish. You might have thought people would notice! But it is also true that some of the behavioural mistakes listed above are as old as the stars and were as valid when Graham wrote the first edition of Security Analysis in 1934 as they are today. Indeed, it is quite possible, in our opinion, that today's business-oriented investment world is leading to a widening of the principal agent conflict and this may increase the psychological mistakes investors make. If so, the opportunity set should be increasing. This may be conjecture on our part, but that seems to be the way the industry is going. Know of any hedge funds that own stocks long- term? That want to own illiquid stock? That don't price gouge? And we are told these guys are the future! At its heart we are trying to be people of good judgement and do intelligent things with money and this necessitates that our stock picks are contrarian. This approach has served us well in the first five years. But we regard it as only a start, and if we are to turn U$1 into U$16 over 20 years, which would

be stunning, then sitting at just below U$3, as we do today, is not much to crow about. There is still much to do.

Matichon is one of six Nomad investments that have been bid for in the last eighteen months! By number that is one quarter of the portfolio. And whilst most of these have either failed (Brierley and Matichon), are pending (Telewest) or remain somewhat inconclusive (Thornton's and Holcim Philippines which is in dispute in the high court) there is likely to be some recycling of investments in the coming period and we remain vigilant for stocks that others despise. It was put to us recently that we have a *"told you so"* portfolio (stocks which others will be dying to point out the idiocy thereof) and that pretty much sums it up. The task in hand is to find some more *"everybody knows that's a bad idea"* stocks.

JUNE 30th, 2007

The circa forty percent annualized gain for Nomad since September last year is quite normal in the sense of being within an expected distribution of short-term results, but even so it is ahead of our averaged-out, multiyear return, which has been in the order of half as great. As ever, a stoic indifference to these short-term steps, both up and down, is the right way to think, and Zak and I would encourage you to mentally reallocate recent excess to leaner periods. Make that, future leaner periods! As Mrs. Zakaria and Mrs. Sleep remind us, we are no cleverer today than we were last year, although our results recently have been far superior.

The lag that often exists between investment decision and eventual reward is a problem for long-term investors, as the brain is wired to learn from immediate feedback. The biological presumption (and, as mentioned in the last Nomad letter, the academic presumption too) is that cause and effect sit chronologically on top of each other – after all, you would want to know that the plant you have just eaten is poisonous now (so you can stop eating it) rather than in a week's time, when it would be too late. Stock traders benefit from the same immediate feedback, but not so long-term investors who run the investment equivalent risk of continuing to eat the hemlock. The real world is messy, and moves in a messy sort of way, and means that long term investors probably have to work harder at intellectual honesty so as not to mis-analyse cause and effect. We all fool ourselves to some extent and so this hair-shirted attitude is hard work. Perhaps it is the biggest investment challenge of them all!

JUNE 30th, 2009

Weighting the Information

Investors see the information (on conference calls they cheer "great quarter, Wal-Mart") but, in our opinion, they incorrectly weigh the information. It could be argued that lots of things had to go right for Wal-Mart to grow for forty years. That is certainly true but, at its heart, a very few simple things really mattered. In our opinion, the central engine of success at Wal-Mart was a thrift orientation fueling growth with the savings shared with the customer. The culture of the firm celebrated this orientation and reinforced the good behaviour. This is the deep reality of the business. This should have had the greatest weighting in the minds of long-term investors even if other things looked more important at the time. Instead, investors may place too much emphasis on valuation heuristics, or margin trends, or incremental growth rates in revenues or any of the list above, but these items are transitory and anecdotal in nature.

DECEMBER 31st, 2011

Keep Your Eyes On the Horizon

It is not the easiest time to be an equity investor. The factors that have led to the devaluation of equities relative to almost all other investment possibilities (perhaps with the exception of housing) have little to do with how well companies have been managed. Be that as it may, Nomad's firms are, on average, so cost advantaged compared to many of their competitors that the worse it gets for the economy, the better it gets for our firms from a competitive position. The trick to being a good investor, over the long-term, is to maintain your long-term oriented discipline. Bezos again:

"Our first shareholder letter, in 1997, was entitled, "It's all about the long-term". If everything you do needs to work on a three-year time horizon, then you're competing against a lot of people. But if you are willing to invest on a seven-year time horizon, you're now competing against a fraction of those people, because very few companies are willing to do that. Just by lengthening the time horizon, you can engage in endeavours that you could never otherwise pursue. At Amazon we like things to work in five to seven years. We're willing to plant seeds, let them grow – and we're very stubborn. We say we are stubborn on the vision and flexible on the details".

The uniqueness of Nomad's ecosystem is the look-through consistency of approach of its participants, from Mr. Bezos and the good folks that run Nomad's other businesses, to Zak and me and on to our investing partners. We are all choosing to see the world in the same way. It is very simple and, because it is the road-less-travelled, it is also very valuable, but it is not always easy. Please, never underestimate the importance of your role in the ecosystem. It is for that reason we named Nomad a Partnership, not a fund.

Chapter 9

CONCENTRATION

Sam Walton did not make his money through diversifying his holdings. Nor did Gates, Carnegie, McMurtry, Rockefeller, Slim, Li Ka-shing or Buffett. Great businesses are not built that way. Indeed, the portfolios of these men were, more or less, one hundred percent in one company and they did not consider it risky!

- JUNE 30th, 2009

Main Points
- Nomad ran a fairly concentrated partnership, which averaged around 10 positions.
- For example, as of June 2009, Nomad had around 20 positions, but 10 positions accounted for 80% of the portfolio (and one accounted for ~30%).
- In a sense, this concentration actually reduced risk, as they understood exactly how these businesses functioned and operated.

… rtnership Letters: Concentration

JUNE 30th, 2004
… p Investments

Growth in the Partnership and disparate performance of individual holdings means that the distribution of Partnership investments is a little more diffuse than would normally be the case. Ten holdings still make up almost half of the Partnership, but there is a tail of smaller investments from the early days, which were sizeable at one time, and now bring the total number of holdings to just over thirty. In effect, we are building a new portfolio (the ten large holdings) within the old portfolio (the tail). Around one third of Partnership assets are invested in companies in South East Asia, one fifth each in the UK and the US and one-tenth in Europe. Approximately seventy percent of the Partnership is invested in common shares, ten percent in corporate bonds (distressed) and the balance held in cash on deposit. The estimated price to value ratio of the Partnership is 61c on the dollar, down slightly from the end of the year due to the new investments.

Our Thoughts on Portfolio Concentration

As the cash is invested, portfolio concentration will rise. In theory, if we could find fifty ideas at equal discounts to value, with equal probability (conviction) of value being realized, then they could all be equally weighted in the Partnership. We could all then look forward to a nice smooth rise in the value of our shares in Nomad, free from the swings a more concentrated portfolio might create. But life is not like that. In reality opportunities in which we are comfortable to deploy capital are rare, and the highest conviction ideas the rarest of them all. The issue then is how much to invest in each idea? Bill Miller, who has run the Legg Mason Value Trust so brilliantly for many years, suggests the use of a system devised in 1956 by J. L. Kelly. A simplified version of the Kelly criterion is that investors should bet a proportion of the portfolio equal to $2.1 \times p - 1.1$, where p is the probability of being right. The common sense outcome of this equation is that if one is certain of being right, one should invest the entire portfolio in that idea. Even if one is say 75% certain of being right the correct weighting remains high at 47.5% ((2.1 x 0.75) – 1.1). But does anyone do that? As far as we are aware, only the early Buffett Partnership portfolios had anywhere near this level of concentration, and then mainly in companies in which Buffett was a controlling shareholder. But is this not the right way to think? If you know you are right, why would you not bet a high proportion of the portfolio in that idea? The logical extension of this line of thought is that Nomad's portfolio concentration has at times been too low. And if it has been too low at Nomad, what has been going on at the large mutual fund complexes with many hundred stocks in a single country portfolio? Apply the Kelly criterion, and the average fund manager would appear to have almost no clue as to the likely success of any one idea. In our opinion, the massive over-diversification that is commonplace in the industry has more to do with marketing, making the clients feel comfortable, and the smoothing of results than it does with investment excellence. At Nomad we would rather results were more volatile year to year, but maximized our rolling five-year outcome. If you do not share this view, think long and hard about your investment in Nomad.

One of the Consequences of Industry-Wise Over-Diversification
Parents will understand when I say that when children are born, they seem to bring their own love with them. However, stocks are not like children. The more stocks you own the less you care about each one individually. Attention paid to corporate governance, capital allocation, incentive compensation, accounting, and strategy has to be diluted as the number of stocks rises. Alternatively, armies of analysts are drafted in, risking a decline into committee-based decision-making. When over- diversification becomes the industry norm then in aggregate investors risk failing to police bad corporate behavior. Would fund managers be so liberal with dysfunctional management if the holding was 20% of the portfolio rather than 0.2%? Of course not. Perhaps some of the scandals of the last few years would have been averted if fund managers had been more proprietorial about their holdings.

However, there are some glimmers of hope. We have been inclined to think of the largest shareholders in publicly listed companies as general partners. This works better with some fund management organizations than others, but the influence that a large properly oriented outside shareholder can have over corporate behavior should not be under-estimated. At Jardine Matheson, Brandes Investment Partners (the largest outside shareholder) proposed, and Marathon seconded, a motion to reorganize the firm. Although this proposal failed as management voted against via their shares in sister company Jardine Strategic, a watered down version of the Brandes strategy has been pursued ever since and with wonderful results. At Kersaf, Allan Gray Limited and Marathon combined votes to propose an about-turn in company strategy. The strategy (all Allan Gray's work, not ours!) has proved to be excellent, and the share price of Kersaf has doubled in rand (and risen almost four fold in dollars). At Hollinger International, Tweedy, Browne Company have professionally and selflessly pursued former Chairman Conrad Black to recover funds paid to him, and in the process have realized the private market value of the newspaper properties resulting in a doubling of the shares from Nomad's purchase. Our input has been limited to private correspondence with Lord Black, which is framed and may be viewed at Marathon's offices. Should you meet representatives from any of these fine investment-oriented fund management organizations buy them a drink. They have added greatly to your returns.

JUNE 30th, 2009

<u>The Investment Industry and Over-Diversification, again.</u>
In business, thoughtful whispering works, which makes it all the more remarkable that the investment industry, as well as many economic commentators, spend so much time shouting. So much commentary espouses certainty on a multitude of issues, and so little of what is said is, at least in our opinion, knowable. The absolute certainty in the voice of the proponent so often seeks to mask the weakness of the argument. If Zak and I spot this, we metaphorically tune out. In our opinion, just a few big things in life are knowable. And it is because just a few things are knowable that Nomad has just a few investments. The church of diversification, in whose pews the professional fund management industry sits, proposes many holdings. They do this not because managers have so many insights, but so few! Diversity, in this context,

is seen as insurance against any one idea being wrong. Like Darwin, we find ourselves disagreeing with the theocracy. We would propose that if knowledge is a source of value added, and few things can be known for sure, then it logically follows that owning more stocks does not lower risk but raises it! Real diversification is offered by index funds at a fraction of the price of active management. Sam Walton did not make his money through diversifying his holdings. Nor did Gates, Carnegie, McMurtry, Rockefeller, Slim, Li Ka-shing or Buffett. Great businesses are not built that way. Indeed, the portfolios of these men were, more or less, one hundred percent in one company and they did not consider it risky! Suggest that to your average mutual fund manager. And it is interesting to note that none of the great fund management organizations got rich on the back of the most successful companies of the modern era either! This failure goes largely unrecognized, and certainly ignored, perhaps because it is the elephant in the room. (Quick, change the subject). It is ignored because some fund managers are not trying to make clients rich per se, but instead their goal is to beat their peers or a benchmark. Fine, but what strikes us about such a disposition is that, somewhere in that frame of mind, one ceases to be an investor and starts to be a business manager and, to borrow a phrase from a popular UK TV advert, "that's not what is says on the tin". When investment skills share a seat with business management, in time, it's the commercial genes that tend to thrive, and investment skills that are not used end up atrophying. Is that why the fund management industry finds itself, like GM, relying so heavily on marketing?

JUNE 30th, 2009

Some facts and figures may help paint a useful aggregate picture of the Partnership. Zak and I think of the Partnership in terms of business models deployed by our investee firms. The names we use to describe these models are not that catchy but please bear with us. The largest group making up over half the Partnership are, no drum roll required, scale-economics-shared; next comes discounts-to-replacement- cost-with-pricing-power (I warned you) at around fifteen percent; hated-agencies fifteen percent; super-high-quality-thinkers just under ten percent.

The Partnership has twenty investments but a noticeable concentration in ten, which make up around eighty percent of the portfolio, and for those with sharp eyes around thirty percent of the Partnership in one investment. Although the bulk of the Partnership is listed in the United States, look-through revenues are far more diversified: US dollar revenues forty- seven percent, Euro and Swiss Franc revenues twenty-one percent, South East Asian currencies sixteen percent, Sterling ten percent, Yen three percent and others three percent. There are perhaps six main industry groups and their weightings are as follows: internet thirty percent, consumer staples sixteen percent, consumer discretionary fourteen, business services thirteen, insurance and finance eleven, and airlines eight percent, with a tail of smaller groupings.

Chapter 10

SIMPLE, BUT NOT EASY

Investing is, at its heart, a very simple discipline. Simple, perhaps, but not easy. And judging by my efforts, certainly hard to communicate. The truth is that there is not that much to say, at least, not much that hasn't been said before.

- Nick Sleep i*n Richer, Wiser, Happier*

Main Points
- Honest, simple, long-term investing is un-exciting.
- There are four choices when deciding to invest: add to existing holdings, invest in new firms, invest in growth businesses, invest in cigar butts.
- Prefer to add to existing holdings.
- Nomad should do well if their existing companies grow from acorns to oaks.
- Simple, but not easy. Why?
    - They have to reject industry dogma. It is a blessing that the crowd has rejected investing at its simplest.
    - There is almost no competition for long-term investors who have done their homework.
    - The road less traveled is hard, since there is a lot of heavy lifting done while doing the homework.

From the Partnership Letters: Simple, But Not Easy

JUNE 30th, 2009

Simple, but Not Easy

When Zak and I trawled through the detritus of the stock market these last eighteen months (around a thousand annual reports read and three hundred companies interviewed) we had four main choices: add to existing holdings, invest in new firms, invest in growth businesses, invest in cigar butts. Overwhelmingly we have preferred our existing businesses to the alternatives. Of course, such a conclusion will only make sense if the businesses in which we have invested have great prospects and the shares are cheap. Like Darwin, perhaps, we are well aware that we live in an ambiguous world. And we are not saying, for example, that Amazon is the next Wal-Mart. Time will tell on this front. But we are asking the question, what if? The portfolio weightings are sizeable in the firms we consider to be the pick of the bunch, and Nomad should do well if our firms grow from acorns to oaks. It is this rational will to believe and be patient that perhaps marks Nomad out from its peers.

What we are doing is investing at its most honest and most simple. But it is not easy. It is hard because one first has to reject industry dogma. The non-thought of received wisdom is shouted from the rooftops and it is safe and comfortable, glamorous, exciting even, being part of the crowd. The road less travelled is hard as there is lots of heavy lifting involved in the homework, although we happen to rather like the workout. As Darwin found, it is hard to let the facts speak for themselves, reject the established way of thinking and to do so in good conscience. And it is a blessing for us that the crowd have rejected something so obviously right as investing at its simplest. Phew, that was just as well! Indeed, such is the lure of, what might be called, professional fund management techniques (!) that we find there is, albeit with a few notable exceptions, almost no competition for the long-term investor who has done his homework. Isn't it exciting that honest, simple, long-term investing is so, well, un-exciting.

DECEMBER 31st, 2011

As a young(er) investment analyst, I once met with the CFO of a large US West Coast bank. I was anxious beforehand, it is not easy for a young man to hold his own with a senior executive of any business, let alone one as opaque as a bank. I forget which question I asked, no doubt it was cloaked in the latest management buzzwords of the day but, at any rate, it was so overly complicated that it elicited the following response,

"Look, son, at the end of the day it is all about cash-in, and cash-out".

Oh dear! Well, the put down could have been worse, and probably deserved to be worse. That was a lesson learnt: keep it simple, it is all about cash-in, and cash-out.

Zak and I run a single partnership that has long-term investments in the shares of, for all that matters, ten companies, all paid for with cash. We own the investment advisor that manages the partnership and, ordinarily, we are closed to incremental subscriptions and so free of marketing obligations. That's it. It is terribly, terribly simple, but it is not easy. It is not easy because there are so many distractions: news items, the soap opera of the stock market, macro-economic events, politics, currencies, interest rates, principal/agent temptations, regulation, compliance, administration and so on - this list is not exhaustive! It is all too easy to make things more complicated than they need to be or, to invert, it is not easy to maintain discipline. One trick that Zak and I use when sieving the data that passes over our desks is to ask the question: does any of this make a meaningful difference to the relationship our businesses have with their customers? This bond (or not!) between customers and companies is one of the most important factors in determining long-term business success. Recognising this can be very helpful to the long-term investor.

For example, what investors needed to understand, and attribute sufficient weight to, in order to hold Colgate-Palmolive shares for the last thirty years, and so enjoy the fifty-fold uplift in share price, was the economics of incremental products (often referred to as "line extensions", from the first "Winterfresh" blue minty gel in 1981 to "Total Advanced Whitening" today) and the psychology of advertising. Other items were important too, discipline in capital spending in particular, and there were lots of other things that seemed important along the way (stock market crises, country crises, management crises and so on) but it was the success and economics of line extensions and advertising that, in our opinion, was what the long-term investor really needed to embrace. A similar story can be told at Nike and Coca-Cola (manufacturing savings funneled into dominant advertising) or Wal-Mart and Costco (scale savings shared with the customer). Recognising and correctly weighing this information in-spite of the latest news flow is a matter of discipline, and it is that discipline that is so richly rewarded in the end.

The simple deep reality for many of our firms is the virtuous spiral established when companies keep costs down, margins low and in doing so share their growing scale with their customers. In the long run this will be more important in determining the destination for our firms than the distractions of the day. Jeff Bezos, founder of Amazon, made the following point in a recent interview in Wired magazine:

> *"There are two ways to build a successful company. One is to work very, very hard to convince customers to pay high margins [the Colgate, Nike, Coca-Cola model alluded to above]. The other is to work very, very hard to be able to offer customers low margins [the Wal-Mart, Costco, AirAsia, Amazon, Asos model]. They both work. We're firmly in the second camp. It's difficult – you have to eliminate defects and be very efficient. But it's also a point of view. We'd rather have a very large customer base and low margins than a small customer base and higher margins."*

Although Mr. Bezos does not mention it, one reason he prefers Amazon to be a large company with small margins is that if he shares the efficiency benefits that come with growth with his customers, he turns size, frequently an anchor on business performance, into an asset. In other words, the moat surrounding the firm deepens as the firm grows. So, having shared low costs with their customers, how are our firms' relationships with their customers going? One way to look at this is revenue growth. The weighted average revenue growth of Nomad's firms is currently over thirty percent per annum. Note: this is organic growth with, if anything, falling prices and no acquisitions in a time of austerity and little economic growth. It would appear to us that the company – customer relationship is in rude health. That's the cash-in. And the cash-out? Keeping it simple again: return on capital at Nomad's firms is over twice that of competing businesses.

Chapter 11

ERRORS OF OMISSION

The trick, it seems to us, if one is to be a successful long-term investor, is to recognize the sources of enduring business success, get in early and own enough to make a difference. Which raises two questions: what are the sources of success and second, if these are so readily recognized up front why are they not discounted in prices already?

- JUNE 30th, 2009

Main Points
- Errors of omission are mistakes where we failed to act when we should have.
- Errors of commission are those where we chose to do something—we acted and we were wrong.
- In investing, errors in omission actually can cost us more; for example, by not owning Wal-Mart or IBM. Nomad gives the example of a large fund in the 1970s realizing that their sale of IBM thirty years ago was a huge error of omission; if they had just kept it, that stake alone would have been larger than their total assets under management.
- Around the same time, the same fund also sold their Wal-Mart, which thirty years later, would be worth more than their future assets under management.

- Nomad then goes into some potential reasons for making these errors of omission:
    1. Misanalysis: using heuristics for valuing a business rather than assessing the real value of the business
    2. Structural or Behavioral: fund managers have to look active
    3. Incorrectly Weighing the Bet: investors tend not to believe in "longevity of compound"; in short, investors believe that good things do not last (but sometimes they do)

From the Partnership Letters: Errors of Omission

JUNE 30th, 2009

Back to real investing! The trick, it seems to us, if one is to be a successful long-term investor, is to recognize the sources of enduring business success, get in early and own enough to make a difference. Which raises two questions: what are the sources of success and second, if these are so readily recognized up front why are they not discounted in prices already? We will spend the balance of this letter answering these two questions.

How might corporate success be predictable? There are some clues in the world around us. Zak and I observe several business models that work in the long run, and scale economics shared is one of these, witness Ryanair, Wal-Mart, Geico, Southeast Airlines, Tesco, Nebraska Furniture Mart, Direct Line et al. And that is why companies that share scale with the customer such as Carpetright, Costco, Berkshire Hathaway, Amazon and AirAsia make up around sixty percent of the Partnership. It works because it turns size, normally an anchor to growth and returns, into an asset. But I also don't think this is a great secret. Investors are broadly rational people (they all knew that Wal-Mart was a wonderful business) and fund managers operate under healthy profit incentives that ought to foster good outcomes, so why is it that no one but the founding Walton family-owned Wal-Mart all the way through?

Zak and I were told a story by one of the industry's most senior fund managers which we enjoyed enormously and might help illustrate the point. In the early 1970s a then, and still today, large successful fund management company analysed its portfolio and discovered that their sale of IBM thirty years earlier had been a huge error of omission. If they had instead kept their IBM shares for the last thirty years, that stake alone would have been larger than total funds under management. No doubt they all agreed to learn from that particular mistake and, as so often happens, went back to their desks and got on with life as before, as if nothing had happened. It is fun to note that, at about the same time, they also made the decision to sell their stake in Wal-Mart, which, thirty years later, would be worth more than their then-to-be funds under management! In terms of dollars of opportunity lost, it is likely to be the biggest single error this firm will make. We offer the following reasons for this mistake:

1. Misanalysis, or using the wrong mental model: Investors are used to firms which have one good idea, such as a new product, but then struggle to replicate success and end up diluting returns (Zak and I call this the Barbie problem, as Mattel has struggled to replicate the economics of its famous doll). Taking this model and applying it to Wal-Mart would miss the company's source of success entirely as the strategy of price givebacks did not change from year to year; culture plays a part in the continuity of a successful price giveback strategy and factors such as culture, because they are hard to quantify, often go undervalued by investors; investors presume regression to the mean starts at the time of their analysis or, as CFA students may recognize, in year three or five of a DCF analysis! Investors use valuation heuristics rather than assess the real value of the business.

2. Structural or behavioral: Active fund managers have to look active. One way to do this is to sell Wal-Mart, which appeared expensive (but actually wasn't), to buy something that appeared cheaper (but err, also wasn't); investors are not long-term and did not look further than the next few years or, more recently, few quarters. Evidence for this can be gleaned from the average holding periods for shares which stands at just a few months; fund managers wish to keep their jobs and espousing a ten-year view on a firm risks being a hostage to fortune;

marketing folks require new stories to tell and new stocks in the portfolio provide new stories; fund managers sell their winners in order to appear diversified in the eyes of their clients.

3. Odds or incorrectly weighing the bet: In the words of my first boss, investors tend not to believe in "longevity of compound". Conventional thinking has it that good things do not last, and indeed, on average that's right! Empirical Research Partners, an investment research boutique, discovered that the chance of a growth stock keeping its status as a growth stock for five years is one in five, and for ten years just one in ten. On average, companies fail.

The list above is far from exhaustive and we can all pick our favorites. No doubt some combination of these, plus others, acted in the minds of sellers. It matters not particularly. What matters is the effect of this collective mis-cognition. Investors know that in time average companies fail, and so stocks are discounted for that risk.

However, this discount is applied to all stocks even those that, in the end, do not fail. The shares of great companies can therefore be cheap, in some cases, for decades. To illustrate the point, consider the graph below. The blue line represents the share price of Wal-Mart and the red line the price that one could have paid at any time since 1972 (the firm's initial public offering) and then earned a return of ten percent (a proxy for a reasonable equity return) through to today. The red line can be thought of as what the firm was really worth.

Chart 2: Cheap for Decades. Share price of Wal-Mart (blue) and the price one could have paid and still earned a ten percent return (red).

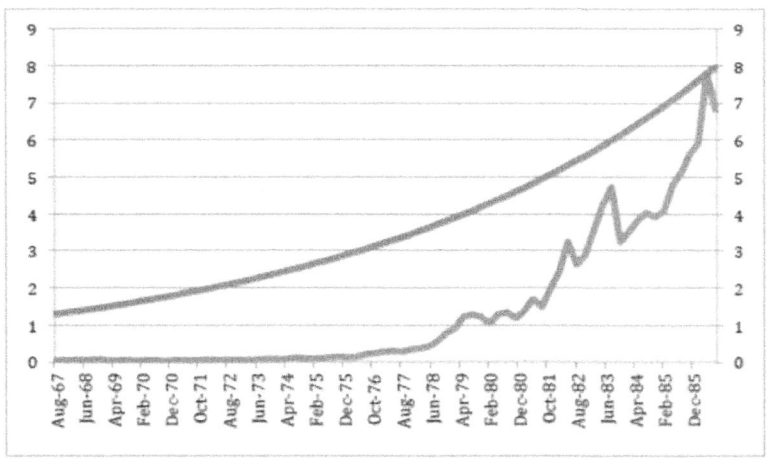

Source: Company accounts, Bloomberg, Sleep, Zakaria and Company, Ltd.

Just look how long the undervaluation persisted! If, in 1972, upon reading that year's twelve page annual report (!) an investor chose to make a purchase of shares, he could have paid over one hundred and fifty times the prevailing share price (a price to earnings ratio of over fifteen-hundred times, a ratio far in excess of what professional fund managers would consider prudent. They would be mistaken, as it turns out) and he would have still earned a ten percent return on his investment through to today. If, instead, the investor thought about it for a while and decided to purchase shares ten years later he could still have paid over two hundred times earnings for his shares (beware heuristics) and still earned ten percent on his investment. And ten years after that could also have paid a premium over the prevailing Wal-Mart share price and done well subsequently. The market struggled to appreciate the magnitude and longevity of the business' success. But why?

Chapter 12

HOLDING CASH

Whilst we are conscious that holding cash does not meet our long term investment goals (to say little of earning our incentive fees) we are in no hurry to invest the money in companies that do not meet our criteria.
- JANUARY, 18th 2002

Main Points
- Nomad didn't actively hold cash because they were predicting a downturn or calamity.
- It was rather a function of whether or not there were enough companies that met their criteria.

From the Partnership Letters: Holding Cash

DECEMBER 31st, 2002

The result of our recent purchases is that cash as a proportion of the overall fund has been reduced from over 20% during the summer to around 5%, with much of the remaining balance ear-marked for an investment we would like to describe in our next letter, that is when we have finished acquiring our shares. (Discretion whilst investing is normally an advantage.) This means that in effect we are close to fully invested. We also feel that there are many undervalued investments available to us, to which we could put incremental capital to work. You can expect us to caution you when the opposite is true, and we find little available at reasonable prices. But for now, for those with a long-time horizon, we think it is a good time to be making investments.

JANUARY, 18th 2002

So, nearly four months since inception where are we now? Our investments are presently priced in the markets at considerable discounts to our assessment of their real worth, performance is satisfactory and we remain with substantial cash holdings of approximately 28% of the fund at year end, although you can expect this to decline markedly. Whilst we are conscious that holding cash does not meet our long term investment goals (to say little of earning our incentive fees) we are in no hurry to invest the money in companies that do not meet our criteria. The markets are very volatile, and we expect to operate with some cash or bond holdings as a matter of course. We also have many ideas that we are working through. You can also be assured that Marathon insiders are the largest group of investors in Nomad.

Chapter 13

LEVERAGE

It is worth noting also that the Partnership results have been achieved without leverage, shorting or financial derivatives of any kind, nor do we wish to employ such techniques.
- DECEMBER 31st, 2002

Main Points
- No leverage.
- Results have been achieved the old fashioned way, by buying securities in reasonable businesses at discounted prices.

From the Partnership Letters: Leverage

DECEMBER 31st, 2002

It is worth noting also that the Partnership results have been achieved without leverage, shorting or financial derivatives of any kind, nor do we wish to employ such techniques. Rather our results have been achieved the old fashioned way, through buying securities in reasonable businesses at discounted prices. It may be instructive perhaps that these old techniques, though deeply unfashionable in modern financial circles, work just fine. For example our results include the demise of Conseco, which filed for Chapter 11 bankruptcy protection in

December. We have retained our shares in the company and you will find them included in the statement of investments at the end of this letter although we expect them to be all but worthless. Investment mistakes are inevitable and indeed to some extent desirable, and we have no interest in hiding them from you (or in portfolio window dressing) - as they say, it is what it is. A full Conseco mea culpa was published in September's Global Investment Review (Volume 16, No.6). All that said, we derive little pleasure, to say nothing of performance fees, from earning the equivalent of money market rates whilst investing in the equity market. It is absolute returns that we are after, and on this score our results since inception are only fair.

DECEMBER 31st, 2003

It may also be worth reiterating that the results have been achieved without leverage, shorting, contracts for difference, options, synthetic structures (LYONs, PRIDEs, LEAPs, MASTs - we are not making these names up) or financial exotica of any sort. If we ever write to you asking for permission to invest in any of the above, sell your shares. And call us to sell ours. Nomad is not a hedge fund, it is an Investment Partnership, and the results below have been achieved without the investment Viagras that have become so popular with the get-rich-quick-crowd. The results have been earned the old fashioned way, through contrarian stock picking.

Chapter 14

GROWTH VS. VALUE

We won't end the debate here but, so that we all understand, our definition is that a business is worth the free cash flow that it can be expected to generate between now and judgment day, discounted back at a reasonable rate. Period. Growth is therefore inherently part of the value judgment, not a separate discipline.
- DECEMBER 31st, 2004

Main Points
- The perennial debate. Nomad agrees with Buffett that the debate is fairly pointless and that the valuation metrics (e.g. EV/EBITDA, price/book, price/sales, etc.) used by the investment industry to classify "growth" and "value" are just heuristics and serve as a poor proxy for value.
- Such metrics don't tell us what a business is truly worth, which Nomad defines as the "amount of free cash flow that can be expected to generate between now and judgment day, discounted back at a reasonable rate".
- Nomad is a "value" investor in that they sought to buy businesses at half price, but their largest holdings would be described by most as "growth" stocks.
- My main takeaway is that in order to truly value and understand a business, investors must dig down into the underlying reality of the company and view the business as an evolving, compounding machine (and not just as a static metric).

From the Partnership Letters: Growth vs. Value

DECEMBER 31st, 2004

There has been much comment in the press of the recent success of so called "value investors". In general the commentary has described the last few years as suiting "value investors", just as the last few years of the previous decade are described as suiting "growth investors". We will discuss growth and value some more in this letter. Certainly it is fair to say that our results indicate they have been fruitful for contrarian investors. But now with prices higher it is a little harder. A word of warning: the current market is not like the end of the 1990s when a bubble in high priced mainly technology stocks was balanced with Zen like symmetry by an anti-bubble of cheap, slower growth business. Today, prices are evenly high across the various opportunity sets, and there are few readily apparent pockets of under-valuation of size. We particularly enjoyed an editorial in the Investor's Business Daily carried in December, which captures the mood of the markets quite well,

> "The Fed tightens, stocks go up.
> The dollar falls, stocks go up.
> Oil soars, stocks go up.
> Retail sales wobble, stocks go up.
> Is this a great country or what?"

Growth and Value

The debate over growth and value is perennial, and quite unnecessary. Warren Buffett got it right years ago:

> "Whether appropriate or not, the term "value investing" is widely used. Typically, it connotes the purchase of stocks having attributes such as a low ratio of price to book value, a low price-earnings ratio, or a high dividend yield. Unfortunately, such characteristics, even if they appear in combination, are far from determinative as to whether an investor is indeed buying something for what it is worth and is therefore truly operating on the principle of obtaining

> *value in his investments. Correspondingly, opposite characteristics – a high ratio of price to book value, a high price-earnings ratio, a low dividend yield – are in no way inconsistent with a "value" purchase."*
>
> Source: Berkshire Hathaway 1992 Annual Report.

We won't end the debate here but, so that we all understand, our definition is that a business is worth the free cash flow that it can be expected to generate between now and judgment day, discounted back at a reasonable rate. Period. Growth is therefore inherently part of the value judgment, not a separate discipline. If it is that simple, and it is, (at least, the definition is simple) then how has the industry got in such a muddle, and why do commentators continue to use price to book ratios, price to earnings ratios or their modern equivalents such as EV to Ebitda, as a proxy for value. We all know that it does not mean a thing. So why do we do it?

Psychologists refer to simple rules of thumb as heuristics. In normal life heuristics generally work. We do not consciously process all the possible combinations of clothes in our wardrobe when dressing in the morning, instead we subconsciously use heuristics to narrow the options. However, in the stock market, doing half the work (only observing a portion of the wardrobe) is of limited benefit if successful investment requires more work. Price to book, price to cash flow etc, cannot be an accurate substitute for the definition we provided above. The wide use of valuation heuristics in the industry is quite bizarre. Their informational value, leaving aside inaccuracy for a moment, can be limited if only because successful investing is a minority sport. Their survival can probably be attributed to intellectual laziness on the part of the investment professional, and spin on the part of the industry's marketing departments. It certainly has little to do with investment excellence. So when commentators suggest that "value" has beaten "growth", or "growth" has beaten "value", please note that little of real substance is being imparted. It certainly has little to do with our Partnership's results.

Why We Think What We Think

It is only in such a topsy-turvy world that a common sense Investment Partnership, such as Nomad, can be seen as lunatic fringe – trust me, we are. The industry has a dreadful time pigeon-holing our Partnership. Not that we mind one jot. Nomad is a value investor in the sense that we like to buy stocks at half price. But the largest holdings would be described by most of our peers as growth stocks. We have the ability to invest globally, but 40% of Partnership assets are in South East Asia. We are concentrated (the top ten holdings make up around 65% of Partnership assets), but we have investments as small as 0.5% of assets. This year we held company meetings in California, Johannesburg and Hong Kong, where we have investments, but also in Zimbabwe, where we have none, just because we were curious. We asked the London office of Rio Tinto plc., a large global mining business, if they could help arrange a meeting with their Zimbabwe subsidiary quoted on the Harare Stock Exchange, only for their investor relations officer to ask "is it listed?"! We can own listed and unlisted equity and bonds, like a hedge fund, but we can't go short. We have a performance fee that is equitable, not egregious, in an era when egregious is the norm. It is so equitable that a famed US investor told us "you won't make money like that", meaning the management fee is too low. But we have made money, we have earned it through performance, not asset gathering. But most important of all, we do not resort to "belief" statements to justify our actions (look out for the use of that particular word when discussing investments, particularly when "belief" is attached to a heuristic). Ayn Rand had it about right when she wrote John Galt's famous speech in Atlas Shrugged that "no substitute can do your thinking". Watch out, this industry is full of the non-thought of received ideas, starting with the value, growth debate and valuation heuristics. We think we try harder than most to be rational and creative. The combination of the two is important. It is nearly seventy years since John Maynard Keynes wrote his "General Theory". Surprisingly little has changed:

> *"Finally it is the long term investor, he who most promotes the public interest, who will in practice come in for the most criticism, wherever investment funds are managed by committees or boards or banks. For it is in the essence of his behavior that he should be eccentric, unconventional and rash in the eyes of average opinion. If he is successful, that will only confirm the general belief in*

his rashness; and if in the short run he is unsuccessful, which is very likely, he will not receive much mercy. Worldly wisdom teaches that it is better for reputation to fail conventionally than to succeed unconventionally."

> Source: The General Theory of Employment, Interest and Money
> John Maynard Keynes.

Among the best performing stocks of the 1990s were EMC, Dell, PMC Sierra and Microsoft. These were the cheapest stocks a decade ago, but no value investor owned them. But then again, none of the large growth investors (excluding insiders) owned the shares all the way through the decade either. Why is this? Why weren't value investors, those who claim to be good at pricing a business, invested in Dell in 1990?
Why is no one doing a really good job?

No, we weren't invested in Dell either. Worse still, we weren't looking. Although Dell was not expensive at the time, I am sure we would have concluded that its probability of failure over the next decade would have been high, or at least high enough to stop us owning the shares. A study by Michael Goldstein at Empirical Research, a research boutique, claims that the probability of growth stock failure (company growth slowing) is as high as four in five over five years and nine out of ten over ten years. And in the case of Dell we would have been wrong. We take no comfort from the fact that not seeing success is a perennial investment mistake: in the 1950s a large Baltimore based fund management company sold their clients' shares in IBM only for the shares to appreciate to the point that the value of the shares sold would become bigger than the whole fund management company itself. What we are trying to do today is avoid the Baltimore company's second mistake, which was to sell an equally big stake in Wal-Mart in the 1970s!

When investors describe themselves as growth or value it might be helpful to have two questions in mind. To the value investor ask, "what is it about your approach that would have stopped you owning K-Mart for much of the last twenty years?" (K-Mart was a "cheap" stock, as measured by say price to book value – but a dreadful investment, recent performance notwithstanding), and to the growth investor ask "what is it about your approach that would have stopped you selling Wal-Mart?". So how does one avoid these mistakes? The answer lies in analyzing not the effects and outputs of a business, but digging down to the underlying reality of the company, the engine of its success. That is, one must see an investment not as a static balance sheet but as an evolving, compounding machine.

Chapter 15

BUSINESS VALUES VS. STOCK PRICES

Whether business values rise faster than share prices, or share prices fall faster than business values, either way the effect is the same: a growing differential between the price of a business in the stock market and its real value.

- DECEMBER 31st, 2008

Main Points
- Like Benjamin Graham and Warren Buffett, Nomad viewed stocks as not just pieces of paper to be traded back and forth, but as claims on an underlying business that can be analyzed and valued.
- Sometimes Mr. Market becomes so depressed, that he gives away the shares at a price far below what the business is worth; that's the moment that you want to put your money to work.

From the Partnership Letters: Business Values vs. Stock Prices

DECEMBER 31st, 2002

During the late summer and autumn, when investors were at their most depressed we made several new investments and in some cases added to existing holdings. Although time will tell, this period may mark the end of investors' mood swing from euphoric at the turn of the millennium to manic depressive almost three years later. Anecdotal evidence suggests that investors are not thinking straight. Take for example recent events at one of our UK investments, Georgica Plc. One day in early November the company issued a press release which began as follows:

> "Georgica Plc has today noted that an administrator has been appointed to Riley Leisure Limited. Georgica wishes to emphasize that Riley Leisure limited is not a member of the Georgica group although Georgica's Cue Sports businesses do trade under the name Riley's".

That announcement did not stop the share price from declining over 6% that day. Presumably somebody, somewhere had decided that the company now in administration was owned by Georgica and without checking, hurriedly sold their shares. Nervous investors tend to shoot first and ask questions later. As the saying goes, act in haste - repent at leisure. We were particularly heartened that Georgica resumed its share repurchase program the following week. A cool head under pressure is what is required.

JUNE 30th, 2004

We can all observe that stock prices, set in an auction market, are more volatile than business values. Several studies and casual observation reveal that individual prices oscillate widely around a central price year in year out, and for no apparent reason. Certainly, business values don't do this. Over time, this offers the prospect that any business, indeed all businesses, will be meaningfully mispriced. Even the mighty Berkshire Hathaway with its stalwart long-term shareholder base was demonstrably half priced in early 2000. And Marathon bought shares (unfortunately pre-Nomad inception). It is just a matter of time. Those that chase high prices today, leave less gunpowder for the future. In effect, they value future opportunities close to nil. So opportunity cost is partly behind our decision as well. Today, we have made two investments in wonderful compounding machines, and only one of those is meaningfully represented in the portfolio (Costco Wholesale). What is the probability that say, over the next ten years, a good portion of these "super high quality thinkers" will be priced at 50c? Our betting is that the odds are reasonable. Even though prices are generally high, the trick is to do the work today, so that we are ready.

DECEMBER 31st, 2004

<u>A Short Word on thinking about Business Values as opposed to Stock Prices</u>
We go through this analytical process with each investment and have expressed our thoughts on Costco here to help illustrate that transient stock price quotations mean little to us (except as an opportunity set for incremental capital). And they should mean little to you. Ignore Nomad's performance so far. We own shares for multi-year periods and so our continued investment success has far more to do with the economics of the underlying businesses than it has to do with their last share price quote. In the last year or three, share price quotes happen to have been in our favour and they flatter your manager's input. You should not always expect this to be the case. There is no reason why business values and share prices should move hand in glove. You should expect that there will be a time when prices, and Nomad's performance, significantly lags the performance of our underlying businesses. It is then that we will ask you to be contrarian, and invest more.

DECEMBER 31st, 2008

Thinking about Inputs: The Price to Value Ratio

It is quite something to arrive at the end of a five-year period and for Nomad's returns to be all but zero, and precious little better than the index to boot. This is a very interesting statistic. All that work and effort! Quite what are we doing with our lives, and with other people's money? Please don't answer that just yet! One could compare market trough to market trough, broadly equivalent to our performance since inception (suspend judgement if you will and call today a trough) in which case returns are in the order of 10% per annum, and 9% per annum superior at Nomad compared to the average share or broadly a doubling in Nomad's share price whilst the index did nothing. That is more like it. And it could be argued that, since inception the price to value ratio of the partnership has been meaningfully lowered, implying healthy deferred returns to come. Even so, bear markets are tough and make you test the most basic assumptions. When moments like these arise grace under pressure all- round is the order of the day.

The following excerpt is taken from the June 2005 Nomad letter to Partners:

"Zak and I concentrate on the price to value ratio of the Partnership and ignore its performance as much as is practical, and we would encourage you to do the same. In our opinion you should be more pleased with the improvement in the price to value ratio of the Partnership than the gain in the price of the Partnership this year. That's easy to say when results have been reasonable. But it would feel quite different if the Partnership had declined in price instead. Unfortunately nature does not always help us to think rationally. Psychologists (McClure, Laibson, Loewenstein and Cohen 2004) have found that the brain perceives immediate rewards differently to deferred rewards because two different parts of the brain are involved. Immediate gains are perceived positively compared to larger deferred gains as the limbic (survival) system has the ability to over-ride the fronto-parietal (analytical) system. Interestingly, stress induces this over-ride, and of course, money induces stress. So, the more stressed we are, the more we value short-term outcomes! This is not without

reason, for if starving is a real possibility, a meal today is more important than a feast in a week's time, and the brain's wiring reflects that survival bias. Such notions are embedded in popular phrases such as "a bird in the hand is worth two in the bush". But at Nomad we try to be more analytical: it is the two birds in the bush we are concerned with and how they compare to the bird in the hand...It is price to value that's important."

Whether business values rise faster than share prices, or share prices fall faster than business values, either way the effect is the same: a growing differential between the price of a business in the stock market and its real value. It does indeed "feel different" when performance has been as poor as it was in 2008, but the rational mind will anchor on the notion that today the birds in the bush are very large indeed. It may not feel like it but, in many respects, these are the best of times for an investor, and we shall lay out why in this letter. The reason opportunity abounds and there are so few takers (indeed the two are necessary bedfellows) is the headline to every newspaper, leads every news channel, is on the lips of every politician and we have all been subjected to so much economic prognostication that we will spare you its repetition here. Crises such as these do not reveal mankind at its best, far too much limbic thinking for our liking, and the sooner we can learn and move on the better. It does not feel like it, but crises like these are a force for good, and we will discuss this point too later in this letter. First, what can we learn?

Chapter 16

THE ROBUSTNESS RATIO

The robustness ratio is a framework we use to help think about the size of the moat around a company. It is the amount of money a customer saves compared to the amount earned by shareholders.

- JUNE 30th, 2005

Main Points
- The robustness ratio is a fascinating lens Nomad viewed the moat of a company. In short, it's a ratio that measures how much a customer saves vs. the amount earned by shareholders.

    $ Customers Save vs. $ Earned by Shareholders

- One could argue that a business with a higher ratio means that it would be harder to compete with them (higher ratio → higher moat).
- Nomad estimated that Costco's ratio is around 5:1 (it saves $5 for their customers for every $1 they keep!). And Geico is around 1:1.

From the Partnership Letters: Robustness Ratio

JUNE 30th, 2005

The Robustness Ratio

At the risk of mildly boring some readers, it may be worth completing the analysis of Costco here by introducing the robustness ratio. (Avid readers will recognise that this ratio was introduced in a Global Investment Review, contained in the appendix to this letter). The robustness ratio is a framework we use to help think about the size of the moat around a company. It is the amount of money a customer saves compared to the amount earned by shareholders. This ratio is more appropriate for some companies than others, the prime criteria being that the customer proposition is based on price, such as exists at Costco, as opposed to an advertising-reinforced purchase such as Nike trainers. In the Berkshire Hathaway annual report this year, the Chairman tells us that Geico policyholders saved U$1bn on their policies compared to the next cheapest carrier. It also turns out that Geico earned around U$1bn as well. So that's one dollar saving to the customers and one dollar retained for shareholders. At Costco we think the customer saving is around five-dollars, compared to shopping at most supermarkets, for every dollar retained by the company.

So what? Well, it is probably fair to argue that the higher the ratio, the harder it would be to compete against Costco on a like for like basis. Also, a higher ratio may imply a somewhat inequitable distribution of system rewards between customer and shareholder than a lower ratio. There is a tension here between the size of the moat on the one hand and the distribution of rewards on the other. In the last few years the pendulum has swung in favour of the customer, with the result that the stock is cheap enough to be vulnerable to a leveraged buy out (completely unobserved by Wall Street where only one in five analysts rate the stock a buy, which solves for the shares being cheap enough to fund a buy out in the first place – the two are of course linked). This is a huge source of risk for current shareholders since being taken out at a low price amounts to theft. It's that serious, and you can rely upon us to see it that way. We think the board understands this, and the way to bet is that the pendulum will swing back in favour of the shareholders over the next few years. Look around you. How many companies save five dollars for their customers for every one dollar they keep?

It does not happen in the investment industry were fees can be levied regardless of performance – that's not much of a robustness ratio and does not take into account the asymmetry of the risks involved. You can't lose money shopping at Costco, but you can investing. This would argue that robustness ratios needs to be much higher in the investment industry than for normal businesses to compensate for the risks involved. We have tried to some extent to account for this asymmetry through Nomad's six percent performance hurdle. It is not perfect, there is no science behind the number, although it is meant to represent a generous proxy for deposit rates. And besides having a hurdle rate helps us sleep at night.

JUNE 30th, 2005 (Appendix I)

Measuring the Moat. Global Investment Review, May 2005
The phrase "business moat" is often banded around when discussing the absolute or comparative strength of a franchise. That there are businesses with defendable positions is of little doubt; but what these discussions often lack is any empirical method by which moat size or longevity can be measured, compared or monitored over time. In addition, stock investors (particularly those who, for their sins, have been labelled growth investors) face an important task, namely, how can one recognise the creation of a business moat well in advance of its value being discounted in the stock market? While reading the 2005 Berkshire Hathaway Annual Report, one paragraph stood out for us as Warren Buffett referred in passing to the division of operating and underwriting cost savings at motor insurer GEICO. These "benefits" were divided between shareholders, policy holders and employees and the statistics spelt out in some detail. This simple breakdown struck a chord with our continuing analysis of Costco, a significant Marathon shareholding in the United States. What is becoming clearer in our minds is that one can empirically measure the strength of a

business franchise through such an analysis of the division of benefits, what we have come to call its "robustness ratio".

First, a brief recap of Buffett's comments with respect to GEICO.

> *"Indeed, GEICO delivers all of its constituents major benefits: In 2004 its customers saved $1 billion or so compared to what they would otherwise have paid for coverage, its associates earned a $191 million profit- sharing bonus that averaged 24.3% of salary, and its owner – that's us – enjoyed excellent financial returns."*

Source: Berkshire Hathaway, 2005 Annual Report

These financial returns, measured in terms of an underwriting profit, were close to US$1 billion pre-tax last year but this excludes the investment returns earned on the US$5-6 billion of float generated by GEICO throughout the year (on which we may want to assign subjectively a return of 5%). These benefits, of course, only accrue to the three groups as a result of scale (if one assumes that underwriting skill can be developed or acquired). This allows us to construct a pie chart (Figure 1) representing how these scale economies are shared. The robustness ratio, defined as the combined distribution to customers and employees (through a profit share or the like) divided by the distribution to shareholders, is in GEICO's case about 1:1.

Figure 1: GEICO: A fair division of spoils

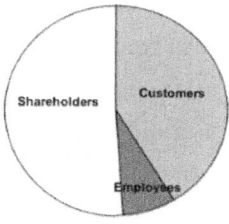

Source: Marathon

This picture, of course, represents a snapshot; just as important is how this division of benefits develops over time, a subject we will touch on later. Tracking back to Costco, we are able to construct a similar pie chart using the following facts and figures. On average, a Costco cardholder (as opposed to household; on average each household holds 2 cards) spends US$1,100 per year in the store. Costco spends US$980 at cost to supply these goods which, if one assumes similar buying power and a comparable basket make up, would cost US$1,300 at a competing supermarket such as Kroger or US$1,250 at Wal-Mart (gross margins of 26% and 23% respectively, compared with 11% at Costco). Now these comparisons are not quite so straightforward as Costco's members must "pay to play", currently US$23 per cardholder on average, and this annual fee is fixed whatever a cardholder spends (this implies the distribution of customer savings is not even across the membership base, a fascinating influence on customer behaviour and itself worthy of analysis). But we can estimate that, on average, a Costco cardholder saves somewhere in the region of US$175 per year by shopping at Costco in return for an annual fee investment of US$23, or a net gain in the region of US$150 per cardholder per year.

Now we turn to employees. From recent management meetings, we have gained some clarity on the difference between Costco's wage/benefit scales and those available from competitors (this difference being the functional equivalent of GEICO's profit related bonus). If we assume that 70% of Costco's SG&A is made up of wages/benefits and that Costco's wage/benefit scales are 55% higher than the competition, then Costco, in a sense, "overpays" its employees to the tune of US$1.1bn per year, or US$26 per cardholder per year. Finally, shareholders. On Wall Street, there has been a suspicion that the return to shareholders has been a "residual" after customers and employees have been well cared for. And at US$32 per cardholder pre-tax, or 15% of the distributable pie, the shareholders' share is not in the same league as at GEICO. In any case, Costco's pie chart (Figure 2) looks something like this, and its robustness ratio is of the order of 5:1.

Figure 2: Happiness is... being a Costco customer.

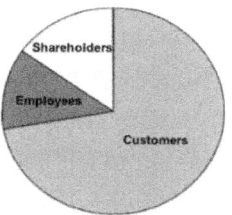

Source: Marathon

While the standard Wall Street view is that such a picture is retailing's equivalent of collectivism, in our view it represents an excitingly wide and unassailable moat. While "unassailable" may seem like a bold assertion, an analysis of the limited disclosure of financials at Sam's Club suggests that the size of the distribution to Costco customers is so large that any attempt to match its prices would cost Sam's somewhere in the region of US$1.4 billion annually while matching Costco's pay scales would set them back another US$750million. Such numbers are not insignificant even to Wal-Mart which last year earned net profits of US$9 billion. Such a chasm of competitiveness is, of course, difficult to capture using traditional analytical tools. After all, both Costco and Sam's Club generate thin profit margins, both are growing revenues, and both are placing enormous pressure on traditional supermarkets and smaller wholesale clubs. But it seems inevitable that the long-term outcome for the two businesses will be significantly different particularly as measured by the growth of revenue per unit of selling space over the long-term. And Costco's business model dictates that this competitive gap should expand over time as a fall in Costco's relative asset intensity and increasing buying power will lead to greater scale efficiencies, which in turn are handed back to the customer in the form of lower prices. Game over.

Having come to such a robust conclusion we should offer a word of warning. Both Costco and GEICO have strong corporate cultures, embedded in which is the inspirational thought that the rational (and equitable?) division of benefits is the only appropriate way of ensuring these businesses will grow in strength as they grow in size. And while culture slippage at GEICO is hard to envisage, courtesy of its place in the Berkshire Hathaway corporate museum, the same may not be true of Costco. An unpleasant output of this apparent disregard for shareholder returns is that the Costco share price is broadly unchanged on levels reached six years ago. And Wall Street is, by all accounts, not happy. Even a culture built up over forty years is not immune to this pressure and Costco's senior management team are beginning to feel the heat. Indications are that the company is gently tinkering with the division of benefits in favour of shareholders in part to satisfy the quarterly EPS junkies but also in recognition that an asset-rich Costco represents an attractive target for private equity buyers. Long-term shareholders should view such slippage as worrying and unnecessary. In our view, the correct response to a six-year share price famine is for the company to use its balance sheet to buy back shares at prevailing prices and allow the long-term growth in free cash flow per share (an inescapable function of steady margins, falling asset intensity, growing revenues and a shrinking base of shares outstanding) to translate into a higher share price over time. The argument for allowing the robustness ratio to drift gently ignores the impact on future generations of managers who will have been presented with a precedent for tweaking the model when expedient. We do not presume to lecture the remarkable managers at Costco on what the appropriate robustness ratio should be, just that any changes to the division of benefits should be made for purely competitive reasons and not driven by a wish to pander to investors.

We wouldn't wish readers to come away with the view that robustness ratios are a numerical magic bullet to measure moats. They are plainly not. There are numerous reasons why Costco's 5:1 and GEICO's 1:1 ratios may be equally powerful barriers to competition and why a ratio even finer than that at GEICO may be perfectly sufficient to repel competitive marauders. Also, falling ratios are not necessarily a sign of shrinking moats, just that moats are not being made as wide as they could be. Where robustness comes into its own is in identifying companies, such as Costco, which may be under-earning when compared to their potential. This generates super long-term investment opportunities for those willing to look beyond reported earnings.

Early in a firm's development it makes sense to reward customers disproportionately as customer referrals and repeat business are so essential to the development of a valuable franchise. With maturity this bias can be reduced, and shareholders can reasonably take a greater slice of the pie. Too much, however, and the moat is drained with negative consequences for longevity. The temptations are enormous because capital markets will reward profiteering. There are many examples of companies which "harvest" excessively, when perhaps they should focus on longevity. This may have been what happened at Coca Cola which has leant excessively on bottlers, or Gillette where advertising has been cut, or even at Home Depot which has boosted gross margins in recent years. Shareholders often suffer a double whammy as highly rated companies enter "growth purgatory", because growth slows just at the time when shareholders spot their misanalysis of reported profitability.

Chapter 17

BUBBLES & ANTI-BUBBLES

When there is a frenzy of activity in one area of the market there is very often an anti- bubble of discarded companies. In the dot com era these were companies with steady cash flow. Where is today's anti-bubble?

- JUNE 30th, 2006

Main Points
- Nomad was acutely aware of the current bubbles and frenzy in the markets and was careful to sidestep them.
- On the flip side, Nomad was also aware of the anti-bubbles, or the sectors and companies that were left behind and discarded.
- It reminds me of one of my favorite quotes from Marc Faber's *Tomorrow's Gold*[11]:
  - *I would therefore want readers to be extremely cautious when investing in a widely accepted and highly popular major investment theme, because, once it is known to just about every investor around the world, the market is likely to enter its most speculative - and final - phase.*
  - *When the investment community is fascinated by a major investment theme, outstanding opportunities arise elsewhere.*

---
[11] Faber's *Tomorrow's Gold* (CLSA Ltd 2002)

From the Partnership Letters: Bubbles and Anti-Bubbles

JUNE 30th, 2006

The stock market is booming, perhaps more than is apparent in the indices as the action is taking place in lowly represented sectors and the privatisation of smaller companies (as the cycle develops this is sure to end is a truly big privatisation). There has been much market commentary offering evidence for a bubble in commodity prices and the valuation of commodity stocks. The evidence, as such, has centered on the high price of commodities compared to history, the resurgence of investment banking activity in the sector, media column inches devoted to the subject, the price of real estate in northern Alberta and so on. New Era theorists argue that China and India offer a here- to- unexperienced demand boost, whilst protagonists throw up their hands in disbelieve at commentary referring to a New Era so soon after the last ended in collapse.

What strikes us was the evidence for stock market excess: in short, something is up in the global capital markets when investors' average holding period for Phelps Dodge stock, a relatively sober copper mining company, is three months. This is not normal for any business let alone one whose assets last for decades. Investors typically hold stock for around two years, although the average mutual fund manager holds shares for around eleven months according to Vanguard founder, Jack Bogle. However, frenzied trading is not uncommon, witness six week holding periods for Yahoo in 1999, or in the Malaysian Second Section in 1997, but it is frequently associated with investor uncertainty, and speculation.

Prices are a language, and the US$20bn equity market valuation of Phelps Dodge states that, with no margin for error, the business will earn record levels of free cash flow for the best part of the next decade and with no decline (in nominal terms) in terminal value. Maybe so, but the frequency with which investors change their mind implies this is hardly a stable statement of fact. Let's be more blunt. There is an inconsistency between the multi-decade New Era-like prediction embedded in the share price, and the lack of will to see that prediction through. It is almost as if investors know it's a lie. This is not an isolated event, according to the research boutique, Empirical Research Partners, oil service companies holding periods are equally truncated and the firms are valued three or four times more highly than their customers (shades of Cisco circa 1999?).

In a traditional capital cycle framework, the high valuation of these businesses encourages a supply side response, which eventually undermines the economics discounted in the stock price. The operative word here is "eventually", so how long is eventually? Company reports this year show an expected increase in capital spending of around forty percent compared to 2005. However, in our opinion, managements tend to low-ball forward capital spending plans for fear of upsetting investors, and so it may be reasonable to expect that spending will surprise on the upside. One Wall Street guru used an American football analogy "management used to be blocking and tackling for us, now they see themselves in the glamorous receiver position". Indeed, human nature being as it is, we can almost guarantee that capital spending will continue to grow until share prices decline.

We cannot be certain when the tipping point will come. For such stocks to be a viable investment for Nomad we would have to feel confident that sector economics are not discounted in prices several years out and, given the rise in capital spending plans, that is not the way to bet. And this is Nomad's great strength. By looking out five years we do not have to invest in shorter-term phenomena in order to look good this year. And in our opinion that is at the heart of what is driving the frenzied trading in Phelps Dodge – the desire to look good this year, quarter, month, week, or just today.

JUNE 30th, 2006

When there is a frenzy of activity in one area of the market there is very often an anti- bubble of discarded companies. In the dot com era these were companies with steady cash flow. Where is today's anti-bubble? Perhaps in large high quality growth businesses that appear cheaper to us than for many years. It is for this reason that Nomad's largest holdings are dominated by traditional growth stocks, in contrast to five years ago when we owned the detritus of the New Era boom. It is interesting to note that five years ago although the most despised stocks were extremely cheap, each individual opportunity was relatively small (our investments in Stagecoach and Midland Realty were seven-baggers but the opportunity size was perhaps U$20m each). Today the discount to fair value of the most despised stocks would appear to be much less (doubles over five years are more likely than spectacular multi-baggers) but the dollar size of each opportunity may be greater. The case for a Nomad reopening rests on this observation, and our job over the next few months will be to analyse this proposition.

Chapter 18

FOUNDER-LED, OWNER-OPERATORS & INSIDER BUYING

Almost ninety percent of the portfolio is invested in firms run by founders or the largest shareholder, and their average investment in the firms they run is just over twenty percent of the shares outstanding.

- JUNE 30th, 2008

Main Points
- Nomad had an attraction towards companies that were run by the founder or the largest shareholder. In addition, they also kept track of the amount of insider buying at the various companies they held in the portfolio.
- Why founder-led companies? Because they don't reward themselves with exorbitant compensations and prefer to build wealth through the appreciation of the company' stock price.
- As a result, they act in the interests of their shareholders (because they are one) and make decisions based on a long-term investment horizon.

- Horizon Kinetics also figured this out, as owner-operator companies[12] is one of their "predictive attributes":

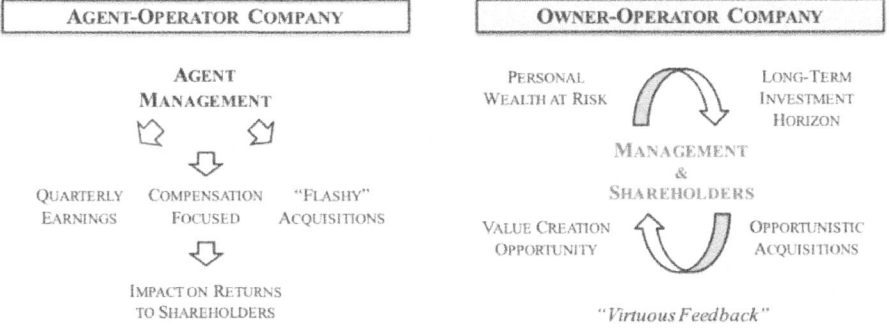

From the Partnership Letters: Founder-Led / Owner-Operators

JUNE 30th, 2007

The Deep Reality of Markets

It was recently reported that oil had been found, not in the far flung reaches of the globe, but under the headquarters of the Exxon Mobil Corporation in Irving, Texas, and not by Exxon! Sometimes, what you are looking for is right in front

---

[12] https://kineticsfunds.com/wp-content/uploads/2014/08/Owner_Operator_Two-Pager.pdf

of you. If Exxon can make this mistake, we all can. Investors are often guilty of chasing the new-new thing far from home sometimes in the name of diversification, or higher returns, or both. To our way of thinking such activity often has more to do with marketing than it does with underlying investment reality. Selling the new thing in order to buy the new-new thing is a common human habit (as a society we trade houses, cars, wives rather than try to fix roofs, gearboxes, marriages) and it almost always raises the question, why are people dissatisfied with what they have? In the spirit of trying not to make Exxon's mistake, we suspect that Nomad portfolio turnover will be particularly low going forward: we are quite happy with what we are currently sitting on. One reason for this is that the fund is <u>over-whelmingly (over eighty-five percent) invested in firms run by their founders or first generation management</u>. Just as interesting is that Zak and I did not plan for this! We have ended up with a portfolio of owner-managed businesses as a by-product of our assessment of the quality of the people involved. In other words, these managers earned their way into the portfolio. We feel slightly foolish for not recognizing this trait in advance, but, of course, we would have a bias toward founder-managed businesses (duh!).

By the standards of the industry we do not own very many shares (ten stocks account for over eighty percent of the Partnership) and we own them for long periods. If the existing portfolio is to be successful then our results will come from the mismatch between the orientation of the founders and the mark to market mentality of the quarterly holding period investors that set the price of the companies on the stock market. This principal (founder) agent (trading oriented fund manager) conflict is the deep reality of the markets and probably the dominant characteristic of our careers. I also think we understand it far better than our peers.

JUNE 30th, 2008

Almost ninety percent of the portfolio is invested in firms run by founders or the largest shareholder, and their average investment in the firms they run is just over twenty percent of the shares outstanding. Fifty-five percent of portfolio companies are either repurchasing shares or have had meaningful insider buying. There is huge growth embedded in the portfolio and normalized profitability is high. Despite these attractive prospects the average investor rents shares in our firms for fifty-one days. They simply cannot be looking at what we are looking at. Our shares are cheap because investors prefer to chase the new booms surrounding Chinese urbanization and associated natural resources demand. We have no idea whether purchases of resource stocks at current prices will prove profitable for these investors. However we do know that our stocks are selling at bargain prices. Since September 2001 the Nomad share price has risen from U\$1000 to around U\$3000 today. Zak and I see our job as getting it to U\$10,000 in time, and the current portfolio should get us substantially there.

JUNE 30th, 2013

The best entrepreneurs we know don't particularly care about the terms of their compensation packages, and some, such as Jeff Bezos (Amazon) and Warren Buffett (Berkshire Hathaway) have substantially and permanently waived their salaries, bonuses, or option packages. We would surmise that the founders of the firms Nomad has invested in are not particularly motivated by the incremental dollar of personal wealth. When we asked Nick Robertson, the founder of Asos, whose paper net worth has increased hugely since we have known him, whether, now he is a rich man, he has thoughts of leaving, his face lights up with the future possibilities of his firm and says he is having more fun now than ever before. In this aspect of his life he has moved on from monetary rewards driving his behaviour, and we are sure the business will be better for it.

The same is probably true for Jim Sinegal before his retirement (Costco), Lord Harris (Carpetright) and some of the other founders of the firms in which Nomad has invested. These people derive meaning from the challenge, identity, creativity, ethos (this list is not exhaustive) of their work, and not from the incentive packages their compensation committees have devised for them. The point is that financial incentives may be necessary, but they may also not be sufficient in themselves to bring out the best in people. In its own little way, this is why Zak and I are quite relaxed about six percent not being six percent. It was an arbitrary number in the first place, and we derive a great deal of value from the meaning of the work we do (challenge, sense of job well done, identity, creativity and so on) not just from the financial rewards (although we will learn to live with those too!). By having an attitude that is somewhat independent of financial rewards, we are sure that Nomad's performance in the long run will be far better too.

Chapter 19

INCENTIVES

"Show me the incentives and I will show you the outcome."
                                                Charlie Munger

Main Points
- Incentives are an underrated aspect of analyzing outcomes. If you are able to decipher and understand the various incentive structures in place, you can often figure out (with a higher probability) where certain businesses and companies are headed.
- Nomad presents the examples of most retailers. To attract customers, most retailers will offer temporarily reduced prices and hope customers will pay non-discounted items too. This incentivizes customers to be disloyal and just shop around for deals.
- Compare this with Costco, where the customer knows they are only paying 14-15% above costs and they know they are paying less than other places. This incentivizes customers to be loyal, which further allows Costco to grow and pass along even more savings.

From the Partnership Letters: Incentives

DECEMBER 31st, 2008

Incentives. Incentives. Incentives.

In business the question then arises: what do incentives encourage? From the perspective of investors in Nomad, the incentives are helpful if they raise the probability of a favourable destination for our investee firms. Let's take the incentives around high low retailing as compared to scale economics shared retailing. Under the first strategy operating costs are generally high as a result of operating inefficiencies, and prices are high to compensate. To attract customers some products are reduced in price on a temporary basis in the hope that whilst the customer is in the store, they may buy some non-discounted items too (some prices are therefore high and others low, hence the name). The incentives here are awful: customers are trained to buy on deal, be disloyal and shop around, and for the retailer the inefficiencies of pricing and repricing and the volatility of volumes are meaningful. The effect is that, after adjusting for one off reductions in price, sales are lower on a normalised basis than they would be otherwise, which in turn exacerbates operating cost inefficiencies. Yuck.

Scale economics shared operations are quite different. As the firm grows in size, scale savings are given back to the customer in the form of lower prices. The customer then reciprocates by purchasing more goods, which provides greater scale for the retailer who passes on the new savings as well. Yippee. This is why firms such as Costco enjoy sales per foot of retailing space four times greater than run-of-the-mill supermarkets. Scale economics shared incentivises customer reciprocation, and customer reciprocation is a super-factor in business performance.

Scale economics shared works across industries too with the effect that load factors at the low-price Malaysian airline, AirAsia, are superior to high-low flag carrying airlines. And it works online: Amazon have deployed it so well that Amazon's operating costs (per dollar of sales) plus its operating margin are less than some of its high street peers' costs (per dollar of sales). This offers the prospect that, in theory, Amazon's high street peers could price their products at net income breakeven and still not undercut Amazon's prices or profitability. For these high street competitors the game is over. They will leak revenues to more efficient rivals as customers respond to the incentive of consistently low prices and convenience. Over time high street rivals, and less successful online rivals, will need to restructure, change their product, or go out of business. We estimate Amazon's immediate hinterland of high street rivals have combined revenues of U$150bn in the US alone. If these firms go away over the next ten years, as Circuit City, Woolworths, Zavvi and others have recently, and Amazon picks up one dollar in ten of their sales, then this alone would be enough to quadruple Amazon's US revenues over the next decade.

Scale economics works well in bad economic times as well as good. On the busiest day in the run up to Christmas this year, order volumes at Amazon were 16% higher than the previous year and note this compares to industry-wide US retail sales which declined nearly ten percent in December, according to the commerce department! And at AirAsia revenues per seat per kilometer flown rose 33%, whilst costs per seat per kilometer flown excluding fuel declined 10% in the latest quarterly period. Our businesses are surging ahead, even if, in some cases, their share prices are half what they were twelve months ago. In the last few months Amazon has been priced in the market as if it would not grow in the future, despite some of the best growth prospects we can imagine. That is a very rare combination and, combined with other similarly cheap stocks in the partnership, was the basis for Nomad's reopening at the end of last year.

JUNE 30th, 2013

A Different Take on Incentives.
When is six percent, not six percent? Stuck? May we suggest an answer: when it is Nomad's performance fee hurdle? That raised an eyebrow here too, not least because the hurdle is always more than six percent, sometimes a lot more than six percent! Perhaps I should explain.

Zak and I sat down about ten years ago, over a sundown glass of Chardonnay at a bar in a Californian hotel and penciled the Nomad fee arrangements on a spare sheet of paper. It did not take long. We concentrated on the correct philosophical approach to incentives, and so the job was easy: the management fee should not be a profit centre as we do not create value through managing the Partnership per se (hence our break- even cost reimbursement management fee); the performance fee should respect the notion of the opportunity cost of capital (and long bonds had been six percent or so); and if we owned shares for long periods, then performance fees should be at risk for an extended period too. Done, now where did the waiter go?

We did not dwell too long on the heinously complicated practical implications of accounting and administering the arrangement, nor did we foresee the need for a new administrator, a new director associated with the administrator, huge legal fees, and that a six percent hurdle is hardly ever six percent. Oh well, the best laid plans etc.... The reason that six percent is not six percent is two-fold: a linked ten percent loss and a ten percent gain are not mathematically equivalent (duh), and Nomad's performance fee reserve is itself invested in Nomad shares and so is doomed to, in effect, buy high (accrue) and sell low (reimburse). Zak has set himself the task of finding a case when the six percent hurdle might be less than six percent. He may be some time.

If our naivety had been pointed out to us on that sunny evening, we would have recognised the issues but I don't think we would have changed anything. It is not very important to us that a six percent hurdle has been well over ten percent in the recent past, and we would certainly never do anything to lower it. Our slightly unconventional approach to being paid may be worth explaining, and so in this letter I will try to describe our attitude to the financial rewards that can come with running the Partnership.

We have written quite a lot about the power of financial incentives over the years, most recently the extent to which incentives (and rules) can de-moralise behaviour. You could describe the cause of the financial crisis in these terms. And whilst conventional wisdom has, in our view, quite correctly drawn a Pavlovian link between financial incentives and behaviour, money is not the only reason that people behave the way they do. Those tasked with setting compensation arrangements may first wish to ask themselves, why do people climb mountains? After all, it is not for the financial rewards – there is more to life than that.

The author, professor and founder of "The Institute for Advanced Hindsight", Dan Ariely, has studied the power of non-monetary incentives. In a recent talk (TED, Buenos Aires, Argentina, October 2012) he described how early academic experiments looking at motivation attempted to record the effect of taking the meaning out of work. This they did by asking people to build model robots from Lego-like blocks in return for a nominal fee. The fee was lowered for each successive robot built until the builder no longer wished to participate. For one group (the "rewards" group), the finished robots were placed carefully on a shelf for all to see.

For the other group (the "Sisypheans 1") finished robots were broken up in front of the builder and the parts given back with the invitation to build the next robot (again for a lower fee). The researchers found that the Sisypheans built fewer robots and so stopped at a much higher price than the rewards group. This was broadly expected. What they had not anticipated was the magnitude of the difference, as the rewards group produced more than fifty percent more robots and for a much lower price compared to the Sisypheans. The researchers concluded that having their models destroyed took away some of the meaning the Sisypheans saw in their work, and that the lack of meaning was not outweighed by the pay. On the other hand, the rewards group did not see their role as pointless and were happier making models even though the pay was much less.

In the 1940s the food companies began manufacturing a new product, the powdered cake mix, which was marketed as a time saving innovation as the mix required only the addition of water before baking. To the marketer's great surprise - sales were terrible! Something had to be done and so, almost as an experiment, a new product was launched which required the cook to add fresh eggs, milk and sugar and although it took longer to make, paradoxically, sales improved! Anyone who has laboured through assembling Ikea furniture may understand why. To the builder of flat pack furniture or the baker of cakes, the perceived value of the end product is influenced by the input of the consumer's own efforts. In doing some work themselves the builder, or cook, puts a little bit of meaning, perhaps even a little bit of love, into the product.

Ariely was so taken with this observation that he developed a further experiment. One group was tasked with building a complicated origami model and were given instruction on how to do so. When the group had finished the researcher took the model away and asked the builders how much they would be prepared to pay the researcher to keep their model. A second group Ariely tasked with building an origami model, this time without instruction, and when they were finished, he asked them the same question: how much would you pay to keep your model? The findings were interesting: both groups were prepared to pay much more than the market price for origami models built by professionals, even though their own models were inferior. Moreover, those who had laboured without instruction (and built the worst origami!) were prepared to pay the most to have their models returned. In other words, the normal relationship between price and quality had been inverted by the value one placed on one's own work.

In traditional capitalist thinking, Ariely surmised, we tend to have Adam Smith in mind, and the gains from subdividing pin manufacturing into twelve distinct steps. The efficiency embedded in this approach won the day over Karl Marx's concerns about the estrangement felt by workers from becoming an anonymous cog in a larger process. The debate then, and ever since, has been the battle between efficiency and meaning.

The best entrepreneurs we know don't particularly care about the terms of their compensation packages, and some, such as Jeff Bezos (Amazon) and Warren Buffett (Berkshire Hathaway) have substantially and permanently waived their salaries, bonuses, or option packages. We would surmise that the founders of the firms Nomad has invested in are not particularly motivated by the incremental dollar of personal wealth. When we asked Nick Robertson, the founder of Asos, whose paper net worth has increased hugely since we have known him, whether, now he is a rich man, he has thoughts of leaving, his face lights up with the future possibilities of his firm and says he is having more fun now than ever before. In this aspect of his life he has moved on from monetary rewards driving his behaviour, and we are sure the business will be better for it.

The same is probably true for Jim Sinegal before his retirement (Costco), Lord Harris (Carpetright) and some of the other founders of the firms in which Nomad has invested. These people derive meaning from the challenge, identity, creativity, ethos (this list is not exhaustive) of their work, and not from the incentive packages their compensation committees have devised for them. The point is that financial incentives may be necessary, but they may also not be sufficient in themselves to bring out the best in people. In its own little way, this is why Zak and I are quite relaxed about six percent not being six percent. It was an arbitrary number in the first place, and we derive a great deal of value from the meaning of the work we do (challenge, sense of job well done, identity, creativity and so on) not just from the financial rewards (although we will learn to live with those too!). By having an attitude that is somewhat independent of financial rewards, we are sure that Nomad's performance in the long run will be far better too.

Chapter 20

MISTAKES

In this letter we will discuss how we think about mistakes, why the response to the mistake is often more important than the mistake itself, and some of our investment mistakes.

- DECEMBER 31st, 2007

Main Points
- The below segment on mistakes is a fantastic dialogue on Nomad's discussion on mistakes, why the response to the mistake is often more important than the mistake itself and some of Nomad's mistakes.
- We all make mistakes.
- The best way in dealing with mistakes is non-judgmental forgiveness. Once mistakes have been learned, the mistakes are often small compared to the value of what has been learnt.
- In short, mistakes can become net present value positive.
- How we respond is often more important. A mistake is only a mistake if you call it so, otherwise it is a learning opportunity.
- Four mistakes that contribute to more unhappy outcomes than most:
    - Denial: reinvention of reality in the mind because the truth is too painful to bear
    - Anchoring: static, historic vision of a problem

- Drift: how small, incremental changes in thinking build into a big mistake
- Judging (condemning or exalting): stops a lot of rational thought
- Trick to see the world more clearly:
  - Invert! e.g. if one-third of the population wants something, it also means two-thirds don't
  - Focus on what you can control: the biggest risk in investing is the risk of misanalysis → solution is to control risk through the quality of research

From the Partnership Letters: Mistakes

DECEMBER 31st, 2007

How We Think About Mistakes

"If I had to live my life again, I'd make the same mistakes, only sooner".
Tallulah Bankhead (actress).

In our opinion, in dealing with mistakes the best state of mind is non-judgemental forgiveness. Parents will recognise that if their child thinks right, they will make mistakes, work it out for themselves and learn. They do not need to be judged or punished: instead they need support, from themselves and others. If they do learn, then the mistakes are likely to be small compared to the value of what has been learnt. In investment terms, once lessons have been learnt, mistakes can be put on a price earnings ratio of one and the resultant, conditioned, good behaviour on a ratio of more than one. In other words, mistakes become net present value positive.

So why is it that investors are so unforgiving when a company disappoints? If we apply the model above then there is not a problem. If the market was rational and the company an organisation that learns, then the stock price should rise after a mistake. But this is seldom the way the world works. It is as if investors presume that companies do not learn from their mistakes. And that makes some sense, as many organisations struggle with rational behaviour. We wonder if investors' anger is a sub- conscious admission that they invested in a non-learning organisation? An unintended consequence of this is that the financial services industry is structured to allow the embarrassment, frustration and anger to vent through the various asset classes. It is structured to allow investors to be judgemental rather than forgiving. You can just hear people justifying their purchase of a gold fund because that idiot who ran their technology fund made a mistake. And he may have. However, if he learnt from his mistake then the value of the fund, properly calibrated, is likely to be rising just at the time investors are selling. There is not a lot of love going around, in the sense of love for one's fellow man, and because of this there is less learning than there could be.

That is not our model.

We (strapping on the protective armour of the first person plural) have made lots of mistakes. (I will be less cowardly) I have made lots of mistakes. Sometimes we made the mistakes ourselves. Sometimes we learnt from others. Sometimes they were direct investment mistakes. Sometimes they were part of growing up (look out for those private mistakes, they are full of investment lessons). But there they are. Warts and all. This is how life is. We do not justify them, but we do not condemn them either. Indeed, they are best not judged. Our model is to learn from our mistakes and what we learn we hope to give to you, in better performance results (in exchange for a performance fee!).

One way we do this is to practice what we preach, and invest in businesses that have made mistakes. Our current investments in Liberty Global, Games Workshop, Dell, Sony and Ford fit into this category, as do previous investments in firms in bankruptcy such as Telewest (now Virgin Media) and Calpine. For these investments to work over the long haul, what is required is a rational, honest mea culpa and a low share price. The unforgiving nature of the markets often provides the latter. The former is much harder to come by.

Why the response is more important than the original error.

"Life is ten percent what you make it and ninety percent how you take it."
William James (philosopher).

We all make mistakes. What is often more important is how one responds. Take for example the response of two firms to the same mistake. The mistake was to be caught out by the last major property downturn in the early 1990s. The two firms are: MDC a residential property developer, and a sizeable European bank with a large commercial property loan book which, being far better capitalised than SZ and Co, we will refer to as Bank X.

MDC was founded in 1972 by Larry Mizel with U$50,000 in capital. In the 1980s his firm built condominiums and apartments and as the property cycle matured reinvested profits and available borrowings in land for development. This is a classic property cycle error and dooms the purchaser to buying at high prices and leaves little financial flexibility during a downturn. By the early 1990s, revenues had almost halved from the 1988 peak and the firm was left with too much debt and tracts of undeveloped land. The firm averted bankruptcy by selling assets, issuing shares and repurchasing debt at cents on the dollar. The family learnt from its experiences and since then the land bank has been kept to a minimum, debt has been used with great reluctance, and equity capital freed from house sales has been used to equity fund the next venture, pay dividends or, to a greater extent, retained on balance sheet. Whilst management may have learnt their lesson it must have been galling to have pointed out by an investor at a recent presentation "you are going to run out of land"! Plus ca change. The MDC share price has risen ten fold in the last ten years, despite recent industry wide declines in share prices, and today the firm is one of the best capitalised in the industry. It will be interesting to see how they respond to the current industry crisis.

Bank X made similar mistakes in the late 1980s through extending loans to commercial property businesses, although here only a dividend cut was required to repair the capital deficit. According to a company spokesman the lesson learnt from the debacle was that the bank "could not do commercial property". Companies often misclassify their mistakes in terms of outputs rather than inputs, and in so doing allow the original mistake to go unchecked. Psychologists call this denial, and we all do it to some extent. But it was a false lesson. It was not commercial property per se that was the source of the losses, there is no a priori reason why a lending institution cannot make loans to commercial property as this bank continued to in say, residential property, or credit cards. In our opinion, the mistake was in how the company approached commercial lending: it was in how they thought and how senior management were incented to think. However, instead of responding to the mistake by rewiring the corporate cognitive functions the firm condemned the output and diversified internationally and developed investment banking and an investment management operation, as if to dilute the risk. This is a take-three-wives-just-in-case approach and it works in terms of corporate longevity but is rarely equated with share price success: in the trailing ten years the shares of the bank have risen in the order of ten percent, or around one percent per annum. A deposit account at the institution would have returned far more.

There is a second lesson embedded in the contrast between MDC and Bank X, and that is the popular wisdom that diversification lowers risk. This maxim, as homely as apple pie, is fraught with danger. Its ascendancy into the unchallengeable heights of received wisdom comes from the vivid image of seeing one's nest egg disappear because of one mistake. What is not recorded is the cost of the suboptimal outcomes that result from over-diversification which range from lack of investment work, high fees and, most dangerous of all, complacency which allows one to ignore the only real, long term risk, which is the risk of misanalysing a company's destination. Take for example the salami slicing of loans that are embedded in securitisation trusts. Diversification used in this way tries to turn ignorance into an asset. There is something of the zeitgeist in this behaviour: companies routinely subcontract parts of their operation in the name of efficiency, in effect salami slicing their operations into narrow functions. This looks efficient, at least as captured by the profit and loss statements in the early years, but few firms ask: what is lost in this process? Sometimes what is lost is control of subcontracted operations such as Mattel's

Chinese sourced toys, or the BBC's documentary of The Queen. But mostly it is a lack of trust in the institution by the customer and, unfortunately, this sentiment is often reciprocated. If you know a mortgage sold to you by a commissioned pimply youth now resides in one of many hedge funds' balance sheets you will feel differently about it than if your branch manager, who has known your Dad for fifty years, still has it on his books. And the pimply youth feels differently if all he has to do is sell your mortgage. Depersonalisation inevitably leads to customer disloyalty and commoditisation, and that is not good for long term profitability, regardless of what the profits account reads today.

How mistakes can become net present value positive.

> *"It is always a delight to observe other people's mistakes".*
> Anon (Rather, I have not found the source before publishing!)

There is a philosophical argument that a mistake is only a mistake if you call it so, otherwise it is a learning opportunity. That seems like the right spirit to us. Our two biggest analytical mistakes (sorry, learning opportunities) to date were probably Conseco and Stagecoach. We have written about these errors extensively in the past, but in the spirit of the quote above I will précis: Conseco went bankrupt after losses in its manufactured housing loan securitisation trusts impaired capital at its insurance company and A.M. Best, the insurance industry rating agency, declared the business inadequately capitalised. Our analytical mistakes were multifarious, but the most serious was to anchor on analysis at the time of purchase to justify continued holding. The immediate dollar loss was around U$5m for investors in Nomad. However, the opportunity cost loss, the dollar loss adjusted for subsequent Nomad performance (a fairer reflection of real costs) is around U$10m.

Stagecoach was a success in the sense that shares purchased at 14p were sold at a high of around 90p. That is until one looks in the Financial Times to be reminded that the shares currently trade above £2.50. The mistake was to leave £1.60 on the table, and was also caused by anchoring on the original purchase decision analysis (which required a value above 14p), rather than thinking about the destination for the business in years to come. The opportunity cost of the Stagecoach mistake is broadly U$12m today (and counting).

The analytical mistake in both cases was to have a static view of a firm formed at the time of purchase, which failed to evolve as the facts changed. This error was reinforced by misjudgements such as denial (the facts had changed) and ego (we can't be wrong). There was also an over-reliance on price to value ratio type analysis, which can encourage a tighter range of outcomes than occurs in reality. And what did we learn in Investing 101 from Lord Keynes: "better to be generally right than precisely wrong"! At the time we were making these errors we would have held Keynes' quote as true. One has to be so careful; sometimes these mistakes are very insidious. Keynes' dying words were reported to be "I should have had more champagne". No doubt he is right on both accounts.

Destination analysis is consciously central to how we analyse businesses these days. It helps us ask better questions and get to a firm's DNA. What we learnt at Conseco may well have kept us out of the US banks last year, and what we learnt at Stagecoach has helped us continue to own Amazon. These two benefits have been a combined gain in the order of U$60m during 2007 to investors in Nomad. The maths behind this assumption is a little finger-in-the-air and is unadjusted for subscriptions post mistakes, but it is directionally correct and implies that a large proportion of Nomad's performance in 2007 came from the lessons learnt from mistakes in 2003 and 2004. Think of it as a return on prior year losses. And that is just one year's gain. If we have really learnt our lesson, then the gains will continue in future years too. In the meantime we continue to bear down on denial and ego too!

<u>Tips on how to avoid making mistakes.</u>
Understanding how the intellect can become corrupted is probably a life's work, some mystics would argue many lives' work. Noticing the mistakes is a huge advantage and so rarely done. What follows are three mistakes that, in our opinion, contribute to more unhappy outcomes than most. These are: denial, that is the reinvention of reality in the mind because the truth is too painful to bear; anchoring, that is a static, historic vision of a problem; and drift, that is how small, incremental changes in thinking build into a big mistake. Add judging to

the list as well, in the sense of condemning or exalting: that disposition stops a lot of rational thought, and it is almost ubiquitous. One of our favourite Buffett stories came from an interview with Walter Schloss carried in the Outstanding Investor Digest (June 23rd 1989, www.oid.com)

> Walter: *"Warren (Buffett) was playing golf at Pebble Beach with Charlie Munger (Berkshire Hathaway vice-Chairman), Jack Byrne (Fireman's Fund Chairman) and another person. One of them proposed. "Warren, if you shoot a hole-in-one on this 18 hole course, we'll give you U$10,000. If you don't shoot a hole-in-one, you owe us U$10". Warren thought about it and said, "I'm not taking the bet." The others said, "Why don't you? The most you can lose is U$10. You can make U$10,000". Warren replied, "If you are not disciplined in the little things, you won't be disciplined in the big things"."*

I have thought about this story for years, and two things strike me: first, Buffett had to think about the answer, no doubt calculating odds and price. I am always relieved that Buffett's skills had to be learnt and honed, they were not simply innate! Second, Buffett recognised that little lapses in discipline themselves have implications: in other words, he was watching out for drift.

One trick to help see the world more clearly is to invert situations. A newspaper headline claiming that one third of the population wants something, also tells you that two-thirds don't! In our opinion, the best book to hone the skills of inverting was written by Terry Arthur in 1975 and is entitled "95% is Crap – A plain man's guide to British politics". Terry is one of the most modest and thoughtful people Zak and I have had the pleasure of meeting, and he was one of the first investors in Nomad. Enclosed with this letter is a copy of the second edition of Terry's book, updated for modern crap. Once you have read this book, we promise you will not see presented facts the same way again. For those with an interest in such things, we purchased our copies at a discounted price on Amazon. We recommend you buy a copy for everyone you love, on Amazon too, of course.

Mistakes in the Making. Myth: Say-something syndrome lowers risk.

In John Rockefeller's biography, "Titan", Ron Chernow describes how Rockefeller equated silence with strength. In one incident Rockefeller was reported as saying that "weak men had loose tongues and blabbed to reporters, whilst prudent businessmen kept their own counsel". Standard Oil's acquisition led growth could be a problem therefore, as taciturn management could become diluted with a more loquacious, acquired intake. In one acquisition Rockefeller was therefore especially delighted to snare Charles Lockhart, a bearded Scot with a frosty manner who was, in Rockefeller's words "one of the most experienced, self-contained men in business". During negotiations to purchase his firm, Lockhart had listened attentively but hardly breathed a syllable. This elicited Rockefeller's highest praise, "That kind of man I'd like to have go fishing with me".

Taking a leaf from Lockhart's book, the question is, do Zak and I say too much? For example, it is interesting that two of the best performing funds of all time did not disclose their holdings to investors. These were the Buffett Partnership and Walter Schloss Associates, although Buffett wrote extensively about how he thought and approached investing in general. And it was for a good reason that they did not disclose their holdings, they did not wish to be judged, second-guessed or worse (!) as Walter Schloss revealed in the same interview with the Outstanding Investor Digest,

> OID (interviewer): *Is it true that even your clients don't know what you're buying for them?*

> Walter Schloss: *That's correct. And a little story might help explain why we don't tell them what we own. One of our partners said, "Walter, I have a lot of money with you. I'm nervous about what you own." So I made an exception and said, "I'll tell you a few things that we own". I mentioned the bankrupt rail bonds and couple of other things we owned. He said. "I can't stand knowing that you own those kind of stocks. I have to withdraw from the partnership." He died about a year later. That's one of the reasons we don't like to give people specifics."*

> OID: *You should not blame yourself. He might have died anyway.*

(Then again, he might not!) Let's invert for a moment: when we think of our investee companies, the firms which we would quite happily own with no word from them for years are those businesses in which we have the highest confidence of reaching a favourable destination: they are the firms we think we know will work. They are also the largest holdings in Nomad. It is the less certain businesses about which we are more insecure that appear to demand more regular attention. If there is demand for our holdings list, is that what our clients are sub-consciously asking? A bit of handholding please because the trust is lacking? And what does that say of the monthly reporting that passes for industry norm? Thank you for helping us avoid that mistake. Our six monthly writing may be as irrational as monthly reporting, but at what frequency does letter writing become rational? Presumably when one has something meaningful to say. Gosh, that is not very often! A Charles Lockhart disposition would argue for an ad hoc, rather than diarised, schedule to letter writing. Perhaps this is something to pursue in the future.

In previous letters we have discussed the dysfunctionality of disclosing specific investment ideas. The problems are mainly psychological and include the locking in of an idea, the desire to seem consistent, the wish to seem prudent in other people's eyes and so forth. There is then the effect of copy-cat investing, brokers trading against us and, as Walter Schloss found out, dealing with nervous-Nellies and so on. In this letter we have expanded on the topic somewhat.

It is tempting to see the free distribution of our holdings list as an unforced and unnecessary mistake, and so one course of action would be to stop sending them out. However, if we did stop that would also presume that the list was only used for the worst (and I have gone on about being judgemental in this letter already!). We know that some partners have a natural healthy curiosity to see how their money is being invested (if the tables were turned, we would too!) and Zak and I have learnt a great deal from reverse engineering others' holdings, and so we will continue to disclose our holdings, although under separate post.

We ask you to examine your motivation for studying our holdings list. If, for example, you think you are monitoring investment risk in monitoring the share prices of investee firms, then perhaps Nomad is not for you. In our opinion, transient, historic, stock price quotation volatility is not the same as investment risk. Indeed, quite the opposite. If, however, you study our holdings through a joy for the art of investing, our books are open to you (well, with a lag).

Investors will understand that the further distribution of our ideas is contrary to all partners' interests. As ever, our preference is that the holdings list remains private, and we remind you that the contents of these letters are not to be reproduced without permission. We do hope you understand.

We focus on what we control.
The following excerpt is taken from Reverend Norman O'Neal's account of the life of Saint Ignatius Loyola. Prior to conversion, Ignatius had been a soldier in the Spanish army and was injured in a battle with the French.

"During the long weeks of his [Ignatius'] recuperation, he was extremely bored and asked for some romance novels to pass the time. Luckily there were none in the castle of Loyola, but there was a copy of the life of Christ and a book on the saints. Desperate, Ignatius began to read them. The more he read, the more he considered the exploits of the saints worth imitating. However, at the same time, he continued to have daydreams of fame and glory, along with fantasies of winning the love of a certain noble lady of the court. The identity of this lady has never been discovered but she seems to have been of royal blood. He noticed, however, that after reading and thinking of the saints and Christ he was at peace and satisfied. Yet when he finished his long daydreams of his noble lady, he would feel restless and unsatisfied."

Poor Ignatius. One can see how he is credited, by some, with the following prayer:

> *"Give me the strength to accept that which I cannot change,*
> *The courage to change that which I can,*
> *And the wisdom to tell the difference."*

It is a very beautiful statement and is helpful in thinking about the Partnership. In our opinion, the biggest risk in investing is the risk of misanalysis. We seek to control this risk through the quality of our research, especially through applying what we have learnt. The quality of our research-based decisions overwhelmingly determines whether we will do well in the long run. But it has almost no influence over the timing of these results. Zak and I do not control the annual performance figures. It might be nice if we did. But we don't.

We encourage you to focus on what we control too!
To our partners great credit we have never had hand-holding requests and, with the exception of a friend of mine who studies share price charts rather than companies and shall therefore remain nameless, no redemptions. It would be wonderful if this was because our partners have a stoic indifference to short term results. And better still if this was because partners read our letters, know the philosophy and methodology of what we do, and know that this is the engine of future success.

Our aim is have the same relationship with partners during periods of poor performance as we do during the good times. And we aim to do this through encouraging our partners to focus on the things we control. That is quite a goal, and we understand that what we are asking goes against human nature. My father worked as a geologist for the Abu Dhabi Oil Company in the early 1960s, and the unofficial motto amongst the engineers there was "aim high, and grab what you can as you fall". It is in the spirit of aiming high that we ask you to focus on inputs rather than outputs. It is the rational thing to do. If we were all focused on what can be controlled then that would be something special!

A trick to help the rational mind is to put our periods of good performance together with our poor performance. We encourage you to mentally shuffle the surplus from the good years and allocate it to the deficit of the bad years. Especially any future bad years, please! Better still; take away the adjectives used to describe the years. That way one can accept life as it is. After all, regardless of the order in which annual results fall, the destination will be just the same.

Chapter 21

SLACK

"Capitalism does not teach slack, it teaches optimization."
- Nassim Taleb

Main Points
- The crisis [Great Financial Crisis] showed that there was little slack in the system.
    - "Capitalism does not teach slack, it teaches optimization." - Nassim Taleb
    - Assets must be worked, outputs maximized.
    - Itineraries must be filled, students' schedules must be filled with activities, borrowing capacity must be used, holidays must be taken, cash must be put to work.
    - A little slack might have avoided fifty-to-one gearing ratios at the investment banks, burnt out school children, wasted holidays, and nothing-learnt business meetings.
- Charlie Munger told us that slack cash is worth more than cash: "wait for an opportunity and invest the spare million dollars you have lying around."
- Nomad is structured with slack.
    - What does one do with slack? The best activities might be those that refresh the mind, broaden horizons and reinforce good habits.

From the Partnership Letters: Slack

DECEMBER 31st, 2008

Using Up the Safety Net
One of the things this crisis reveals, at least in our opinion, is that there has been little give-in-the-system: that is to say, a lack of slack. Slack in time to think things through, or capital for investment for example. In a recent interview the author Nassim Taleb put it succinctly: "Capitalism does not teach slack, it teaches optimisation". That is capitalism teaches that assets must be worked hard, outputs maximised, returns as high as can be. We all see so much of this line of thinking that it has become part of the landscape so familiar as to not be noticed any more. Itineraries must be filled with meetings, school children's days must be filled with activities (I know my daughters' are), borrowing capacity must be used (or risk an "inefficient capital structure" – we have never really understood what that is), investors answer emails instead of listening to presentations, holidays are to be taken with Blackberries rather than books, or nothing: outputs must be maximised today! And for most of the decade, there has been nothing as sinful in an investor's mind as money idly slouching on deposit, "on the couch" as the investor Seth Klarman put it. Instead, cash must be put to work: its yield maximised. Indeed, and in the parlance of bond investors, "chasing yield" has been one of the maxims of the noughties.

Output maximisation looks efficient at least in the short term, but that is not the same as being long term optimal. The flaw to putting money to work immediately, for instance, is to presume that all relevant opportunity sets are available immediately. By accepting, say, a promoter's promise of eight percent returns (six hundred basis points better than money on deposit), the investor denies himself the right to future opportunity sets which may be far better, like public equity circa 2008 and 2009, we would argue. This is an easy concept to grasp when applied in hindsight, but much harder to see prospectively. A plan sponsor who argued that contrary to the income statement, his cash was not earning two percent but ten percent (a blend of two percent on deposit now and twelve percent from an as yet undefined opportunity set sometime in the future) risks being perceived by his peers as away with the fairies – the lawyers and auditors would not endorse his view - but he was right. That is why, in the hands of Warren Buffett for example, one could rationally argue that cash is worth more than cash. That is not an argument for hoarding cash, as many do today. For the cash to be worth more than cash it must be invested intelligently. It is, however, an argument for a cash buffer, just in case, a little slack in the system. Charlie Munger, Berkshire Hathaway Vice-Chairman, was once asked how to get rich, presumably by someone of youth and modest means. Being of relatively modest means if not youthful ourselves Zak and I were keen to hear the answer: "wait for an opportunity and invest the spare million dollars you have lying around". What Charlie was telling us was that slack cash is worth more than cash. It was not what we wanted to hear. Now all we had to do was come up with a million dollars of slack cash!

A little slack would also have avoided fifty-to-one gearing ratios at the investment banks, burnt out school children, wasted holidays, and nothing-learnt business meetings. "When someone says he is busy, he means that he is incompetent", Nassim Taleb again, "having a stupidly busy schedule isn't a sign of being important. It means that you have become insulated from the world". And we wonder, if you are too "stupidly busy" to think, which part of the brain is making the decisions? Not the rational outer cortex, we suspect. All this busy behaviour looks short term efficient (ten meetings a day!) but, in our opinion, the cost is that things are not being thought through; the end result of a thousand small steps in the current direction not assessed and long-term bad habits creep in. The biggest mistakes are the ones that did not look like mistakes at the beginning, after all bank robbers don't start out robbing banks, they pinch sweets, get away with it, and drift their way up. I suspect many robbers' behaviour later in life would be inconceivable to them when they started. We all drift to some extent. Notice, for example, how company spokesmen use words. To hide reality, the embarrassed use acceptable words to replace accurate words. This is how companies end up talking about "negative growth" rather than declines, and how bank investor relations spokespeople talk of "market turbulence", when what they are referring to, we would suggest, is their own bad lending. If businesspeople are too busy to notice that their use of everyday language has drifted into, let's face it, low level lying, how were they to be honest enough with themselves to recognise the inevitable asymmetry embedded in securitised mortgages? All they were doing was making the next loan and selling it: No assessment of the destination of such behaviour required. The thinking – or non-thinking – was contagious, and if it was good enough for bank X then it must be good enough for bank Y, and both companies reinforced these attitudes through quarterly reporting and annual incentives. The point is that the drift toward poor long-term outcomes is so much harder to spot if your reference periods are short, and one is too busy being busy to notice a lack of real world thinking. Many publicly listed bank executives are certainly subject to these two factors. Is it any wonder these firms are at the epicentre of the financial crisis?

All this is a far cry from the early years of Rolls-Royce Limited, the manufacturer of motor cars, where Frederick "Henry" Royce made the engineers personally sign the parts they were responsible for making. That way, if any component proved faulty, he knew who was responsible and he made them correct the fault in their own, unpaid time – I paid you to make a working part, not a faulty part, he would argue. And that is how he ended up making the best motorcars in the world. That level of personal accountability has been largely lost inside organisations today and has instead been replaced with "efficiency" to the point of Taleb's "busy incompetence" and "real world isolation". Zak and I do not see the ethics behind securitisation trusts, for example, building the reputation of any bank the way that Henry Royce's engineers built the reputation of Rolls-Royce, the manufacturer of the world's finest cars. What passes for industry standard best practice today may look short term efficient but, in any lasting sense of the word, and from the perspective of the long-term business owner, it does not really get the job done.

We do try and run Nomad with some slack in the system. In the June 2007 letter to partners we suggested that one of the benefits of a long holding period was that it allowed time for gentle contemplation, to "retreat and simmer" a little, and we quoted the gardener Charles Jencks: "understanding requires a certain slowing of time. Why else enter a garden?" Notice, "slowing", it is important.

Slack is provided in our company structure: Zak is perfectly capable of running Nomad on his own (someone tell him I do! Zak). This means that straight away we are running at something less than fifty percent capacity utilisation on a normal day, and so we can gear up, in effect, when opportunities arise as they have recently. Capacity utilisation is also kept low by few investments, held for long periods. We have had the blessing of learning some big lessons early in life (there will be more). And we have worked out that, in any real sense, we do not know that much. In our opinion we have the right environment to think things through, think rationally, and come to meaningful long- term insights. Whether our insights are economic or not will be our fault, it will not be due to the environment in which we work. Zak and I don't want to be busy; we want to be right.

Once it has been created, what is to be done with the slack? The best activities might be those that refresh the mind, broaden horizons and reinforce good habits, and it is in this spirit that I have become a governor of a failed school in south east London. What is interesting is not the reasons for the school's failure which seem common enough (unionised teachers employing 1970s teaching techniques, awful facilities and so on). What is interesting is the route out of the soup: incentives. Teachers who previously had no incentive compensation are being given bonuses for attendance (!) and improvements in class results. The children are being rewarded with house points for good work and behaviour, and deductions for poor work. But importantly, there are many more positive house points awarded than negative. This is a desire to be better system, not a punishment and condemnation system. There are other factors involved: new head teacher, new governors, school uniform, five-day teaching week (the previous failed school took Friday afternoons off – unbelievable!), but it is the incentives that reinforce the good behaviour. Other schools have undergone such a reformation with terrific results: for example at one south London school, which is run by the same team as my school, exam results for sixteen year olds have improved from a pass rate of 14% to over 90% in just over a decade. A good incentive scheme is so cheap compared to what is created.

Chapter 22

CONTRARIANISM & GOING AGAINST THE HERD

Following what everyone else is doing may be hard to resist, but it is also unlikely to be associated with good investment results.
— JUNE 30th, 2005

Main Points
- "Following what everyone else is doing may be hard to resist, but it is also unlikely to be associated with good investment results."
- Nomad tries to focus on the price-to-value ratio and ignores performance.

From the Partnership Letters:
Contrarianism & Going Against the Herd

JUNE 30th, 2005

It is a constant feature of the investment landscape that people applaud recent gains when they should be thinking more about the future. We all do this to some extent. We all like rewards and like to be associated with success. And it is hard not to be drawn toward the crowd. One of our favourite cartoons, carried by

Punch in the 1970s (and reproduced in the book "*Influence: the Psychology of Persuasion*" by Robert Cialdini some years later) makes the point.

Following what everyone else is doing may be hard to resist, but it is also unlikely to be associated with good investment results. Zak and I concentrate on the price to value ratio of the Partnership and ignore its performance as much as is practical, and we would encourage you to do the same. In our opinion you should be more pleased with the improvement in the price to value ratio of the Partnership than the gain in the price of the Partnership this year. That's easy to say when results have been reasonable. But it would feel quite different if the Partnership had declined in price instead. Unfortunately nature does not always help us to think rationally. Psychologists (McClure, Laibson, Loewenstein and Cohen 2004) have found that the brain perceives immediate rewards differently to deferred rewards because two different parts of the brain are involved. Immediate gains are perceived positively compared to larger deferred gains as the limbic (survival) system has the ability to over-ride the fronto-parietal (analytical) system. Interestingly, stress induces this over- ride, and of course, money induces stress. So, the more stressed we are, the more we value short-term outcomes! This is not without reason, for if starving is a real possibility, a meal today is more important than a feast in a week's time, and the brain's wiring reflects that survival bias. Such notions are embedded in popular phrases such as "a bird in the hand is worth two in the bush". But at Nomad we try to be more analytical: it is the two birds in the bush we are concerned with and how they compare to the bird in the hand. In our opinion, today, the birds in the bush are around 47% (68c/100c) bigger than the bird in the hand. This compares with only around 37% (73c/100c) bigger at the end of last year. The Partnership is up this year, but you can see that it also does not mean very much compared to the deferred gains. It is price to value that's important.

DECEMBER 31st, 2008

<u>Happier Times</u>

Let me finish with a story told by the radio presenter and car collector Chris Evans that has parallels to the stock market bargains of today and helps demonstrate the merits of doing some proprietary work, sniffing out a great investment, and holding forever. First a little background. In the late 1950s Ferrari motor cars successfully competed and won almost all the major GTO class races of the time, but by the early 1960s they had started to lose ground to new slippery shaped Aston Martins and the AC Cobra, amongst others. The solution was Ferrari's first wind tunnel designed car: the 250 GTO, which was launched in 1962. It was an instant success, and beautiful to boot. 250 GTO owner Paul Vesty recalls childhood memories of seeing five GTOs line up on the start of the Goodwood TT in Sussex, England "immediately all the other cars looked ancient – instantly we all wanted one". The car won almost everything going and became an immediate classic. It was also very rare: one hundred cars should have been built to qualify the vehicle for GT class racing but, in the end, only thirty- six were actually produced. The effect today is that fifty and sixty year olds, looking to buy their boyhood dream car, may have to pay world record prices, think U$10 to U$15m, the next time one sells at auction. After some successful seasons the GTO was replaced with faster models and during the mid 1960s Ferrari sold off its racing vehicles to enthusiasts. At about this time the third James Bond film, Goldfinger, was launched which featured the now iconic Aston Martin DB5. Back to Evan's story:

[In the mid 1960's] *"a very famous collector, who has one of the finest noses for sniffing out a deal, hears a whisper that the first James Bond Aston Martin DB5 may be for sale...The word is that for the right money, the original James Bond car can be bought directly from the movie studio. So he makes a few calls, he tracks down the production guy...*

"It's gonna have to be 15 for the pair"

"You mean there are two?"

"Hey man this is show business, there is always two... at least"

"But 15 for the pair" says our man. *"I wasn't counting on spending that much and I don't really want two – I just want one"*
"When that is the deal. Take it or leave it."

..."*Fifteen thousand pounds – a lot of money now, a load of money then. Our hero hesitates for a moment, but his nose knows better. It tells him to deal. He buys the car. The cash is to be paid on delivery of both vehicles. The day arrives, the trailer pulls up, the cars roll off. The invoice reads: FIFTEEN HUNDRED POUNDS. Yes, friends both original Bond cars for £1500, but it does not end there. Be prepared to run for the hills screaming. Our man then swaps one of the Bond cars for a GTO. That's a GTO for £750. That's the cheapest GTO ever and...he still has it today."*

Of such stuff are dreams made. Now, let me rephrase this story from the perspective of an equity investor. The collector thought outside the box, rolled up his sleeves, did some proprietary analytical work, and found a contrarian investment opportunity with great growth potential that few of his peers recognised at the time, lucked into a low price, owned it forever and, in the end, it did not matter what price he paid particularly, as the growth in underlying value made his purchase one of the best investments of all time. Zak and I aspire to such a road map.

JUNE 30th, 2009

"This Abstract, which I now publish, must necessarily be imperfect. I cannot here give references and authorities for my several statements; and I must trust to the reader reposing some confidence in my accuracy. No doubt errors will have crept in, though I hope I have always been cautious in trusting to good authorities alone. I can here give only the general conclusions at which I have arrived, with a few facts in illustration, but which, I hope, in most cases will suffice. No one can feel more sensible than I do of the necessity of hereafter publishing in detail all the facts, with references, on which my conclusions have been grounded; and I hope in a future work to do this. For I am well aware that scarcely a single point is discussed in this volume on which facts cannot be adduced, often apparently leading to conclusions directly opposite to those at which I have arrived. A fair result can be obtained only by fully stating and balancing the facts and arguments on both sides of each question; and this cannot possibly be here done."

So begins paragraph three of "On the Origin of Species by Means of Natural Selection" by Charles Darwin, the bicentenary of whose birth falls this year. The book took Darwin twenty years to write and may have done more than any, with the exception of the Bible, to shape man's self-perception. But just look, if you will, at the language of the introduction:

"This Abstract must necessarily be imperfect...no doubt errors have crept in... I can here only give the general conclusions...I am well aware that scarcely a single point is discussed on which facts cannot be adduced, often apparently leading to conclusions directly opposite to those at which I have arrived...A fair result can only be obtained by fully stating and balancing the facts on both sides".

One can hardly accuse the man of promotion! Darwin knew he was right but his findings troubled him personally. He was a Christian, in a Christian society, indeed he had considered studying theology before setting sail on HMS Beagle, and his new ideas challenged the church, his countrymen and his conscience. At major turning points in society, such as he was suggesting, how many of us, we wonder, would be modest about what we had discovered? Darwin's humility is an attractive human quality, perhaps because such understatement recognizes that the ideas were bigger than the man. Which, of course, they were. It is an interesting subconscious psychological tendency that truths are often spoken with a whispered voice whilst shaky suppositions are shouted for all to hear. It is not so much us that the shouters are convincing, as the need to convince themselves. We all shout to some extent, with agents usually shouting louder than principals: and that should tell us something. In the Nomad ecosystem we do try to keep the volume down somewhat. Like Darwin, perhaps, but on a very different scale, we recognize a few simple truths and we are conscious that our views, in the eyes of our peers, may not be very popular.

DECEMBER 31st, 2009

The Locker Room Culture

The attitude of the builders and sellers of these new things may be akin to what Charlie Munger called the "locker room culture". This is an attitude whereby the players just have to win, and they are not too squeamish about the means. And if winning, for some, meant securing a bigger bonus than others, then, in the case of the mortgage market, any way to get people to buy expensive paper was just fine, and to hell with the consequences. This is a proud, manipulative, points-scoring orientation that manifests itself in all walks of life, but may be especially evident on Wall Street, although some salesmen, sportsmen, chief executives, politicians, warlords and hedge fund types are notably not exempt. It is perhaps the dominant, get-ahead mindset of our times and it is inherently focused on vivid, short term outputs. Sales targets and profit margins achieved through cutting corners may be inherently worthless in the end, but they can dazzle for a while, and that is their value to the locker room set.

If we are honest, we have all been tricked by the unscrupulous salesman and his short-term promises. It is, perhaps, part of growing up. Zak and I have certainly responded, with order sheet and pen at the ready, to firms that have explicitly promised revenue and margins targets, without really considering how those targets were to be earned or whether they were sustainable. Oh dear! One-nil to the locker room set. In the end though, the sin and folly of the locker room culture, with its win at any costs attitude, does huge damage to us all.

A great deal has been penned on why the locker room mindset exists in listed businesses. However, it is interesting that the commentary has, to date, been almost deferential towards shareholders, who are cast more as victims of scandals rather than sowers of their own misfortune. We would argue a contrary view: if the shareholder base of a listed firm is dominated by, say, mutual funds that, in turn, are seeking short term performance, then that too will be what they will seek in their investments. An odd pact may, therefore, develop between the immediate business imperatives of the salesforce-controlled mutual fund and, say, the consumer goods company with earnings to hit. Both parties will care for short term outputs and will take from the long-term to meet their needs. All parties will invariably be in denial that this is the case, at least to their clients but, we ask, how are the incentives aligned? We would argue that not only do companies get the investors they deserve, but investors also get the companies they deserve.

Schlock begets schlock, as it were.

Operating inside the bubble, it is hard for many participants to see this. The author Upton Sinclair, commenting on the attitude of businessmen and almost one hundred years to the day before the current credit crisis, had it about right, "it is difficult to get a man to understand something when his salary (or bonus) depends on his not understanding it". So, the mindset is prevalent because it pays in the short term. But this does not make it the right thing to do, nor does it make it profitable over the long-term.

Doing what is right rather than what plays well

Zak and I far prefer a different approach. We would argue that locker room behaviour is more likely to be spotted by patient, generalist investors deploying common sense, as it helps to be outside the bubble to see the bubble. It may also aid one's thinking if the investor is prepared to make a meaningful, long term investment as this breaks the in-out, get-rich-quick spell of the salesman (and, let's face it, the salesman in one's own head!). Our anti-locker room disposition was echoed by the founder of one of Nomad's investee firms, who, in a private meeting, put it as follows: "if you want to be successful, and we do, then you have to be willing to be misunderstood, and do things that do not seem sensible to most people". For example, "if you (employees) come into the office in the morning thinking how you are going to beat number one, two or three in the industry" - how many times have we heard companies articulate that view? - "then, our firm is the wrong place for you. We start with the customer and work backwards." Oh, sweet nectar! He continued that rather than set your standards by what others do, the firm benefited from a "divine discontent" with the status quo, which kept colleagues on their toes and the firm improving, irrespective of what the competition were doing. In other words, his company had an internal compass with true north pointing to what was right for the customer.

This orientation strikes us as the antithesis of the locker room set.

Chapter 23

INDEX THINKING

> We are walking down the road less traveled when we argue that the index is not risk free, it is one, of many, opportunity sets.
> — DECEMBER 31st, 2006

Main Points
- Nomad does not focus on the index or beating the index.
- Most common mistake investors make is to view the index as a risk-free "home". Not risk-free.
- Other mistakes include:
    - Requirement to have an opinion on everything inside the index
    - Unwillingness to invest in other better opportunities
    - Over-diversification
- Don't be envious of index returns.
- Goal is a track record to be proud of and aim to earn returns on par with great investors they admire (Ruane, Tweedy, Klarman, Whitman, Hawkins, Miller, Schloss, Berkowitz).

From the Partnership Letters: Index Thinking

JUNE 30th, 2004

Nomad's year to date performance is sufficiently close to the index (at the time of writing the differential is just 2%) to raise an eyebrow given the disdain with which we hold closet index managers. These are a sub-specie of professional fund managers that charge high active management fees whilst delivering index-like (i.e., non-active) performance. We can promise you that any resemblance Nomad may have to the closet index trackers is entirely coincidental. Our portfolio is nothing like the index. Indeed, it is not quite like anyone else's. And note, unlike the closet index trackers, at Nomad, no performance means no fees. That is the way it should be. (A notion to be slipped into your mutual fund manager's suggestion box!).

DECEMBER 31st, 2006

So there is no confusion: the index is not our benchmark. Zak and I spend no time at all thinking about the index (indeed we were unaware of the index return until I set about writing this letter) and its inclusion at the top of this letter reflects our genesis in an index-relative investment firm more than our orientation. If we started Nomad again today, I'm not sure we would present results this way but, be that as it may, we will leave the index at the top of this letter for now, as for some Partners it may be helpful in placing our results in context.

Zak and I have witnessed many investors make terrible investment decisions from thinking via the index. The most common mistake is to view the index (indeed any index?) as a risk-free "home". That this disposition still exists after the irrational index bubbles that preceded the Asian crisis and technology collapse may be testament to the strength of the marketing skills of the financial establishment. Once the index is seen as risk free the mistakes that follow cascade and include: requirement to have an opinion on everything inside the index regardless of one's circle of competence, an unwillingness to invest in other better opportunities, and over diversification. These three mistakes destroy a lot of capital. We came across one country manager's report claiming that although his country had done poorly it had proved valuable as a "portfolio diversifier" in a global fund: Many a furrowed brow these last few weeks figuring out what that means! Even so, index relative funds are the industry norm because they sell. And they sell because the client does not trust their manager with the keys to the Ferrari. It is a ghastly Faustian pact.

We are walking down the road less traveled when we argue that the index is not risk free, it is one, of many, opportunity sets. This year that opportunity set beat us. It may do so again next year too. And the year after that. We should all be prepared for that possibility and stoic at its occurrence. A rational mind understands that it is the destination that is important, and if we have some skill in picking stocks (please, no answers on a post card!) then, whilst annual returns may bounce around, our destination will be some way ahead of the index. Zak and I are not envious of index returns and we encourage you not to be either. We see our goal as far more personal than that. Our goal is a track record to be proud of, we wish to accomplish something meaningful, and to do that we aim to earn returns, over time, on par with those investors we greatly admire (Ruane, Tweedy, Klarman, Whitman, Hawkins, Miller, Schloss, Berkowitz). In no way do we guarantee returns, but if we can approach their results then, over time, we will beat the index too.

Chapter 24

INTERDISCIPLINARY THINKING & SCALING LAWS

What we are saying is that because so many fund managers are constrained by their mandates excess returns ought to exist for the unconstrained.
- DECEMBER 31st, 2006

Main Points
- Santa Fe Institute (SFI): a group of scientists who strived for an interdisciplinary, collaborate approach to problem solving. Describes themselves as studying the Science of Complexity.
- Need to borrow from idea from across disciplines to better understand reality.
- What can investors learn from Scaling Laws? The question that needs to be answered is: why is it predictable that a business will grow from a mouse to an elephant?
- A business ought to be able to self-fund its own growth, and if the opportunity set is large, then the return on capital needs to be suitably high.
- Barriers to entry should increase with size; that way a company's moat is widened as the firm grows. To do this, the basic building block of the business, its skeletal structure, is probably best kept very simple.

From the Partnership Letters:
Interdisciplinary Thinking and Scaling Laws

JUNE 30th, 2007

An Introduction to the Santa Fe Institute

One way not to fool oneself is to spend time with one's intellectual superiors and it is in this spirit that Zak and I became members of the Santa Fe Institute (SFI) some years ago. The SFI was founded by Murray Gell-Mann and seven, principally Los Alamos, scientists who were frustrated with the gaps between contemporary academic disciplines. To this group, traditional academia discouraged broader interests (physicists study physics, not biology) and this left many problems unsolved because they fell across disciplines. Their solution was an interdisciplinary, collaborative approach to problem solving.

Witness the SFI's description of the economy. Traditional economists argue that people are rational beings who seek, what economists call, utility maximization, that is, the maximum output for any one input. This old guard are hostile to assertions of non-rational behavior, perhaps because the idea that we are all rational is just so elegant. Scientist and External SFI Professor W. Brian Arthur argues that this static, equilibrium based model of the world does not sit easily with the biologist's view that individuals act in self-interest, make mistakes, learn and evolve. Or the psychologists' view of the world that there are systematic biases to individual decisions – that is, we have these little wobbles in our decision-making processes. Brian Arthur's approach is to borrow what he needs from all the academic disciplines to describe a reality that is a little wayward compared to that the traditional economists would expect. As Gell-Mann puts it, the real world "is not just a look up table". Instead, Arthur describes the economy as a Complex Adaptive System that evolves as agents (people) learn.

The SFI describes itself as studying the Science of Complexity and, in our opinion, that seems like a better model to explain reality. After all, how can economics not be behavioral – who is making the decisions after all? In our opinion, Brian Arthur's Complex Adaptive System and the behavioral finance work pursued by the likes of Professor Richard Zeckhauser at Harvard are the new economics in waiting. As the saying goes, one scientist would rather borrow another's toothbrush than his ideas, and it is with this attitude that, and with apologies to MBA students, the new economics of Complexity Science is unlikely to be taught to any great degree in academia until the utility maximizing old guard, that dominate academic institutions, die off.

After a recent speech Gell-Mann was asked, "So, how do you have creative thinking?" His answer was: 1. Start thinking about something, gather data to the point of saturation, recognise anomalies and recognise that you are now stuck; 2. Retreat and simmer, mull it over and a period of incubation ensues with the unconscious mind deployed; 3. Whilst doing something else a solution to the problem surfaces (Archimedes' eureka revelation); 4. Go and verify the new solution. To Gell-Mann, taking time is important in creative thinking. The landscape architect Charles Jencks, who designed the "Garden of Cosmic Speculation", echoes this sentiment. Jencks's garden is an attempt to put the new Science of Complexity into garden design and symbolism. (If in Dumfries, Scotland in June we thoroughly recommend a visit, and take us with you! – but note it is only open to the public for one day a year). To Jencks "understanding requires a certain slowing of time. Why else enter a garden?" There is a lot to be said for gentle contemplation. And of course, a long investment holding period allows one time between decisions to "retreat and simmer" a little.

An Introduction to Scaling Laws

It is perhaps only in a supportive, interdisciplinary institute such as the SFI that Geoff West could embark on a study of scaling laws. Two questions concerned West: why do small animals live for less time than bigger animals, and why do humans live for around one hundred years rather than say, one thousand years, or one year? The simplest of scaling laws concerns body-mass and skeletal strength. As an organism increases in size its body-mass grows with volume (to the cubed) whilst the shear strength of the skeleton only increases with the width of the bones (to the squared, or a power law of 3/2). Without a bigger bone structure, mass soon overwhelms strength, and the organism collapses under its own weight! (A few companies we know have followed a similar pattern). Metabolic rates (as measured by oxygen used) also rise with body mass, but at a declining rate (a power law of 3/4). This implies there is an economy of scale to mass in animals, further evidence of which might be that heartbeats per minute also decline with mass. This is Kleiber's Law and it states that literally a kilo of mouse costs more energy to live than a kilo of say, whale. West put the two power laws together and realized that if longevity increases with mass, and the heart rate decreases with mass, then it follows that all life shares a common number of heartbeats (indeed, around one billion). A mouse uses up its billion heartbeats in about four years (at a rate of five hundred beats per minute) whilst an elephant uses up its billion heartbeats in seventy years (at a rate of twenty-five beats per minute). It seems that evolution has not changed this basic constraint: a billion heartbeats it is, careful how you use them!

Chart1: A billion heartbeats it is: careful how you use them!

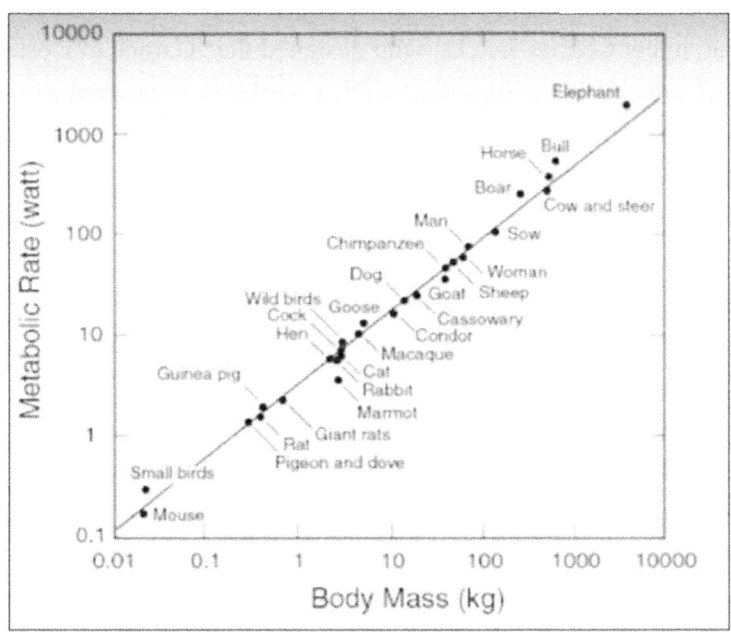

Source: Santa Fe Institute

But even so, why does the mouse heart beat so quickly? In all animals the aggregate cross sectional area of the blood vessels increases with distance from the heart. The purpose of this is to overcome the viscous drag created by blood coming into contact with vessel walls. Smaller animals do not have the space in their body to allow for much cross sectional widening, and so the mouse heart works harder to overcome the blood's resistance to flow. In larger animals the distance between the heart and the body's cells is much greater and so the cross sectional area can be increased much more.

In other words there is a very basic function to longevity with skeletal strength allowing for size, size allowing for circulatory efficiency, and efficiency allowing for longevity. The answer to West's question is that man lives for around a hundred years as this is all his heart can cope with, given body-mass and skeletal strength.

What can Investors learn from Scaling Laws?
This might be the right way to think about scaling in organisms, but does it tell us anything about companies, and especially firms as they grow? The question that needs to be answered is: why is it predictable that a business will grow from a mouse to an elephant? This is a little like asking the meaning of life, and we will try hard not to give an answer as intractable as Douglas Adams' suggestion in The Hitch-Hiker's Guide to the Galaxy (where the answer to life, the universe and everything was "42"!). Several tenets are important.

- A business ought to be able to self-fund its own growth, and if the opportunity set is large, then the return on capital needs to be suitably high.
- Second, barriers to entry should increase with size; that way a company's moat is widened as the firm grows. To do this, the basic building block of the business, its skeletal structure, is probably best kept very simple.

In short, we want a skeletal structure that can support growth from mouse to elephant without too much skeletal re-engineering.

Let's consider traditional high street retailing. Goods are sent from the supplier to the retailers' central warehouse, where they are stored until demanded by the shops. Goods are then sent to the high street stores. These are expensive pieces of real estate, and have high operating costs. Price aside for a moment, the quality of service the consumer perceives is largely a function of staff levels, staff helpfulness, product range, shop furnishings and so on. So there are lots of constantly variable elements to service quality at the most expensive end of the distribution system. It seems to us that the skeletal structure is highly complex, and many things can go wrong.

Contrast this to the internet model. Goods are sent from the supplier to a central warehouse, but often only after the order has been taken. The goods are then sent direct to the customer with the expensive high street real estate missed out. The quality of service perceived by the customer is the speed of delivery, the feel of the web site, functionality of the web site (such as recommendations), breadth of product range and so on and these factors are inherently more controllable. They are fixed in terms of expense and also customer experience (a web site viewed in New York looks the same as the same website viewed in London or Hong Kong). So whilst quality is inherently patchy at most high street retailers, it is fixed at Amazon. This is important as it is complexity that is one of the main reasons firms fail as they try to grow.

It seems to us that the basic building block of internet retailing, its skeletal structure, is far more robust, scalable and cheaper than the high street equivalent. In other words its power law is very high, and implies that businesses with the simplicity of operation as say, Amazon.com, have a shot at being far bigger, quicker and more profitable than their high street equivalents. Nomad has an investment in Amazon for more reasons than the firm's simplicity of operations. But when this basic building block is combined with the scale efficiencies shared model (which increases the moat as the firm grows), customer centric orientation of the firm's founder, as well as his healthy disdain for Wall Street, this combination makes us think that we may have a mouse that can turn into an elephant. To those who argue Amazon is large already we ask two questions: what do you think e-commerce will be as a proportion of US retailing in ten years time, and what do you think it was last year? Write both numbers down and turn to the end of this letter*** for the answer to the second question.

After the doubling in the share price and the weighty resultant position in the Partnership it would be easy for Zak and me to claim victory, high five, and sell our shares in Amazon. However, the high weighting makes sense given our understanding of the destination of the businesses and the probability of reaching that destination. In previous Nomad letters we have argued that the biggest error an investor can make is the sale of a Wal-Mart or a Microsoft in the early stages of the company's growth. Mathematically this error is far greater than the equivalent sum invested in a firm that goes bankrupt. The industry tends to gloss over this fact, perhaps because opportunity costs go unrecorded in performance records. For example, our greatest error was the sale of Stagecoach (which has risen ever since sold), not the purchase of Conseco! We wonder, would selling Amazon today would be the equivalent mistake of selling Wal- Mart in 1980 (a similar time period after both companies' IPOs)?

DECEMBER 31st, 2006

<u>Why do Problems go Unsolved? Because they Fall Across Disciplines</u>
Whilst Zak and I are delighted at the doubling of the value of Nomad shares between 2001 and 2004, this would be for nothing if returns had been given back in the last two years. As it is, we have been able to reinvest the portfolio in new opportunities and the fund has continued its rise. There are several funds that, over the last few years, have created a similar track record to ours by investing in specific countries (Russia, India, Egypt etc.) or sectors (gold, oil, basic materials). Investors with holdings in the fields listed above should be aware that more narrowly focused funds will find it hard to maintain their performance if the bull market in their fields starts to fail.

What we are saying is that because so many fund managers are constrained by their mandates excess returns ought to exist for the unconstrained. The turn-of-the- millennia technology fund manager could not invest in Stagecoach (a bus operator) even if he had wanted to. For this reason, it seems to us that there is more to the private equity boom than just low interest rates.

In a world where traditional fund management is compartmentalised by attributes such as geography, sectors, investment styles (value, growth, garp, momentum), tracking errors, beta, listed or unlisted status, (stay awake at the back) equity or debt, bankruptcy or solvency then those with broader powers, such as private equity, and indeed Nomad, should have an advantage over constrained incumbents. Woody Allen once quipped that being bi- sexual doubled the chances of a date on Saturday night, curiously that principle also applies to investing.

Rules based systems always contribute to societal non-thinking, but it's not the mandates so much that are the source of risk to investors in constrained funds. It's the attitude of the non- thinkers running the funds that is so destructive. The following excerpt taken from the December 2003 Nomad Letter to Shareholders summarizes our views:

"The Weetabix offer is only one of many privatisations of cheap, small and mid capitalisation businesses in the UK. Institutional shareholders have abandoned these firms in favor of mega-caps, and the shareholder base is left dominated by one or two inside interests and a tail of small holders. Our view is that the discount that the shares trade at in the market is an asset to be harvested for the benefit of all shareholders through share repurchase. But human nature being as it is, insiders will be incented by the low valuation to buy the shares for themselves. A Scheme of Arrangement is the most ruthless method of asserting one party's will over a fragmented and non-professional shareholder base and coupled with irrevocable acceptances allows takeover offers to be presented as a fait accompli to shareholders. Please note: bad practice spreads. Despite this, and the almost daily occurrence of privatization proposals in the UK, there has been almost no criticism by shareholders, the authorities or in the media. In no other sphere of capitalism can your property be seized in exchange for cents on the dollar (except compulsory purchase on the grounds of national interest). But fund managers, who in their private capacity would be insulted if someone offered less than their house was worth, happily sell shares in their professional capacity at discounted prices to smart buyers. And no one cries foul."

The fund managers understand what is going on. These are intelligent, highly paid individuals who could defend their clients' interests much more vigorously. They could, for example, own much more of the target company and block the bid. Or, if mandate constrained to only invest in listed equity, why not explain the situation to their clients and seek to change the rules of their funds to allow ownership of, say, unlisted equity? But not a squeak. Many fund managers would rather sell your shares for a small takeover premium now (and market their short-term performance to new investors) whilst turning a blind eye to the doubling in the value of the sold business over the next few years. It's a scandal.

The December 2003 letter again,

"Whilst we have a profit on our investment in Weetabix, shareholders should be careful what they wish for. Before congratulations are in order, Partners need to weigh in their minds short-term profits against value forgone in the discounted offer price and the incentive provided by the success of seizure for potentially more of the same in the future."

Just look at what is happening in the markets now: 2006 was a record year for private equity funds. As the bids often come from the private equity fund operating in joint venture with management then, in our opinion, they are best understood as insider trading with the takeover rules being used as a bulk purchasing facility. In the UK (and some former colonies) there is some protection against corporate wallet lifting as dissenters (those wishing not to sell) cannot be compulsory acquired if they own more than 10% of a company. The situation is far worse in many other countries – for example in the United States there is no universal protection against compulsory purchase! Back to the December '03 letter:

"So, what is to be done? The best defense is to own enough of the company to influence the outcome. In most cases [in the UK] in excess of 10% of the shares outstanding would suffice. Those that advocate market liquidity of their investments over other considerations might like to bear in mind an investor's inability to influence outcomes whilst owning a de- minimus proportion of a

company. Should Nomad continue to grow in size, we intend not to make this mistake."

To this end Nomad is now the largest shareholder in Games Workshop Plc., a significant shareholder in Jarvis Plc., and part of the dissenting group at Whitehead Mann Plc.

Whitehead Mann has a reasonably entrenched position as the largest headhunter to FTSE 100 CEOs and used this cyclical revenue stream to fund the acquisition of several competitors (often with insiders cashing out!). As revenues declined the interest burden overwhelmed failing cash flow and the share price declined from a peak of £4 to around 50p when we first went to meet management two years ago. At the time the firm was seeking more capital in the form of a bankruptcy avoiding rights issue and placing. It seemed odd to us that the insiders were not buying shares in the firm along with their shareholders and so we declined to participate, "we'll be bullish when you are bullish" we told the MD. Even so, capital was raised at 40p per share from other investors and we sat and watched from the sidelines. Then last year the company announced that management, along with a private equity fund, were offering 42p to buy the whole company and had secured irrevocable undertakings from shareholders to purchase around seventy percent of the shares outstanding. In other words, having saved the company investors were being offered a return of 2p (five percent) for their trouble! And insiders, who had chosen not to invest in the bankruptcy-avoiding placing, now wished to buy as much as they could (via the bulk purchasing facility) and so we also made an investment. Today we are part of a dissenting shareholder group that own around 19% of the shares, enough not to be compulsory acquired. As we will continue to own our unlisted shares we propose, in the absence of more information, that the shares be valued in Nomad at the takeover price (42p) plus (or minus) retained earnings. We look forward to seeing what management can do for us, now they have (leveraged) skin in the game.

Chapter 25

SHORT TERM VOLATILITY

The volatility does not bother Zak and me one jot.
- JUNE 30th, 2007

Main Points
- Common for portfolio construction to be a result of stock weightings starting from one or two percent and up to a target holding.
- You can also invert and start at a hundred percent weighting and work down.
- The volatility of holdings does not bother Nomad.

From the Partnership Letters: Short Term Volatility

JUNE 30th, 2007

Short-term volatility and stock weighting
It is common-place for overall portfolio construction to be as a result of stock weightings built up from one to two to three percent of a portfolio and so on up to a target holding. This means that weightings are anchored at a small number

with only outliers reaching double digits. There is another way to construct a portfolio, which is to invert and start at a hundred percent weighting and work down! If fund managers did this, I am sure they would end up with completely different portfolios. Now we are not advocating all the fund in Amazon (well, not just yet at least), but in allowing past habits to anchor portfolio construction we have probably made the mistake of a starting holding that was almost certainly too low. Be that as it may, one effect of having one sixth of the Partnership invested in a volatile stock, such as Amazon, is that our results will also be more variable over the short term. Please bear that in mind in future performance. The volatility does not bother Zak and me one jot.

Our results since inception have been large, out-sized multi-year gains during periods of market distress (2001 to 2004) and reasonable, index matching/bettering multi-year results during stock market boom periods (2005 to 2007). This follows the predicted path outlined in the June 2002 Nomad letter when we quoted a Buffett Partnership letter from 1960:

"I have pointed out that any superior record which we might accomplish should not be expected to be evidenced by a relatively constant advantage in performance compared to the Average. Rather it is likely that if such an advantage is achieved, it will be through better-than-average performance in stable or declining markets and average, or perhaps even poorer-than-average performance in rising markets."

And we certainly do not have a relatively constant advantage compared to the index!

Chapter 26

HARD & FAST RULES

Any year that you don't destroy one of your best loved ideas is probably a wasted year.
— Charles T. Munger

Main Points
- Don't adhere to hard and fast rules. Revisit and question them.
- If you remove the rules from a system and instead ask people to think for themselves, the system works better.
- Don't adhere to hard and fast rules.
- Some rules that Nomad had to reviewed:
    - Low share price is better than a high share price, all else being equal. This proved unwise as the low market capitalization undermined the shareholders' bargaining position in the recapitalization.
    - High ownership is a good thing. In the case of Northwest Airlines, a high insider ownership actually hindered the process that would have lead to a more viable airline, as the unions reasoned that management would not have let the company go into bankruptcy (high ownership) and held out for the last dollar.

From the Partnership Letters: Hard and Fast Rules

JUNE 30th, 2005

"Any year that you don't destroy one of your best loved ideas is probably a wasted year", Charles T. Munger.

In January this year, the market town of Carlisle (located between the English Lake District and the border with Scotland and incidentally home to your manager's family-in-law) was flooded when the River Eden broke its banks. Parts of the city centre were under many feet of water and residents were shown on national TV being evacuated from roof tops by helicopter. As the water receded the city slowly returned to normal, although the damage remained extensive, and included the traffic light system at Hardwicke Circus, a junction of seven roads controlled by a series of traffic lights dotted throughout approaching roads and a central roundabout. Although the lights remained out of use, the authorities opened the roads and trusted the residents to drive with care. Soon afterwards, drivers began to suspect that the traffic flowed better through the complex junction without the traffic lights than before, and in March this year the City Council began a trial in which the lights were covered up, and drivers left to get on with it. What they found confirmed public suspicions, the speed of traffic through the intersection had indeed risen, and better still, it appeared that the number of accidents may actually have fallen as well. What they found was entirely contrary to accepted wisdom in council planning, that the roundabout was faster and may also be safer without the traffic lights! Ayn Rand would recognise what was happening, as may members of the Santa Fe Institute (which recently published a study entitled "How Individuals Learn to Take Turns: Emergence of Alternating Cooperation in a Congestion Game and the Prisoner's Dilemma"). The point is that, often, if one removes the rules, and instead ask people to think for themselves, the system works better.

We criticise hedge funds for their fee scales and short investment time frames, but they have a point when it comes to investment rules and certain regulations. Traditional investment management can become heavily burdened by bureaucracy, compliance and corrupted by marketing expediency. These business forces can work at the expense of the investment process, and the trick for any growing investment firm is not to sap the life out of the investment team through stapling them to the bureaucratic equivalent of the US Department of Agriculture. We think of ourselves as reasonably entrepreneurial, but even we suffer to some extent from this culture drift. The solution is not hard to come by. What is required is for people to behave in such a way that, in the words of Charlie Munger, one builds "a seamless web of deserved trust". The operative word is "deserved". The problem is that rules do not require people to think, and how are people to deserve trust if first they don't think? Degenerative spirals of behaviour do not build good results (or fast roundabouts), but that is where the industry is going, and it is a destination we will all do well to avoid.

We try not to be too hard and fast about rules. In previous letters we have quoted H.O. Hirt, founder of Erie Indemnity, and it would be a shame not to do so again. Hirt posted the following notice to staff:

> "***RULES***
> *Are for **INFANTS**, **INCOMPETENTS**,*
> ***INCARCERATED CRIMINALS** and **IMBECILES***
> *- **NONE** of **WHOM** should have any place in*
> *the **ERIE FAMILY**."*

Even so a few rules end up slipping in over time and need to be viewed with great suspicion. One was that a low share price was better than a high share price, all other things being equal, which proved unwise when the low market capitalisation undermined shareholders' bargaining position in the recapitalisation of Conseco a few years ago. This year we shall have to discard another strongly held bias which is that high inside ownership is a good thing. This too is not always helpful, as shareholders in Northwest Airlines are finding out. In this instance the unions appear to reason that management (who are the largest group of shareholders) will not risk placing the company in bankruptcy and are holding out for the last dollar in negotiations. Oddly here, high inside ownership is hindering the process that would lead to a more viable airline. Who would have thought that a low share price and high inside ownership could be bearish? But they can. I wonder what other "best loved ideas" we will need to rethink in the coming years.

Chapter 27

THE PRINCIPAL/AGENT PROBLEM

What I am describing is one aspect of the principal agent conflict, that is, the interests of you, the principals, are different from ours, your manager, the agent.
- DECEMBER 31st, 2005

Main Points
- The principal/agent problem is a conflict in priorities between a group and the representative that is authorized to act on that group's behalf.
- In investing and fund managing, the principal (the investors) and the agent (the managers) have different priorities.
    - The Principal (the investors): maximize returns
    - The Agent (the managers): maximize the *fund's* returns by gathering large amounts of assets and charge a management fee; larger amounts of assets also lead to decreased returns
- Nomad's Solution: focus on maximizing returns, not assets

From the Partnership Letters: Principal/Agent Problem

DECEMBER 31st, 2005

What I am describing is one aspect of the principal agent conflict, that is, the interests of you, the principals, are different from ours, your manager, the agent. There are two ways to approach this situation:
1. Maximise the conflict for the sake of maximising short-term agent revenues (standard industry practice), or
2. Set about minimising the difference through behaving and thinking like principals.

Zak and I have followed the second path. I know we are agents by virtue of the Nomad performance fee and perhaps that is the lot of young men with mortgages and families. But I do not think it is our natural disposition. There comes a point when turbo charging is counter- productive and there will come a day when we will be able to waive the performance fee. Before you start rubbing your hands, it's not around the corner, no really, it isn't! But we mention this in writing now so that hopefully you will remind us of it in years to come, and hold us to account! Our motivation is to do a good job. If we do that then the mortgages will take care of themselves.

Which brings me to the subject of the existing performance fee. Eagle-eyed investors will not have failed but notice the near 200 basis point difference between gross and net performance this year, reflecting the performance fee earned. We are in this position because performance for all investors is in excess of 6% per annum compounded. But given historic performance, that may be the case for a very long time. Indeed we are so far ahead of the hurdle that if the Partnership now earned pass book rates of return, say 5% per annum, we would continue to "earn" 20% performance fees (1% of assets) for thirty years, that is, until the hurdle caught up with actual results. During those thirty years, which would see me through to retirement, we would have added no value over the money market rates you can earn yourself but we would still have been paid a "performance fee". We are only in this position because we have done so well, and one could argue that contractually we have earned the right by dint of performance, but just look at the conflicts!

Given the incentives, we should buy treasuries, and to keep us on our toes, you should rightly withdraw your investment and immediately reinvest to reset the base line. That's not the relationship we want. Now, we are not going to buy treasuries (at least not for that reason), or equities that look like treasuries for that matter (check your other managers for those!) and to your great credit, no one has tried to game the system through withdrawing and reinvesting, and we would be mortified if you did. And given the way both investors and your manager appear to think and behave, I may be guilty of fixing a problem that does not exist. But even so, and at the risk of a belt and braces approach, I would like to propose that from this year the performance fee be amended so that the high water mark also compounds at 6% per annum, and I will write to you shortly to ask approval for that amendment to the prospectus. That way each new year has a hurdle of 6%, and the hypothetical pass book return goes unrewarded. No one has criticised the status quo. We are under no pressure to change anything. But I simply do not want to earn a "performance fee" if future returns are below 6% each year, that is not what we are about, and I want to be able to shave in peace in the morning!

Chapter 28

PER SHARE DISCIPLINE & DILUTION RISK

Per share discipline is much misunderstood by investors.
- JUNE 30th, 2003

Main Points
- Per share discipline is something that's rarely discussed. Management who don't own much shares in the company don't care much for issuing shares, thereby diluting existing shareholders. The problem is compounded if the shares are issued below the firm's intrinsic value.
- Nomad suggests that there are two ways to benefit from share issuance:
    1. Be a beneficiary of share issuance by purchasing investment liabilities (bonds, redeemable preferreds).
    2. Invest in a company capable of compounding value from a static share base.

From the Partnership Letters:
Per Share Discipline and Dilution Risk

JUNE 30th, 2003

Per share discipline is much misunderstood by investors. The long-term rate of share issuance in the US is over three percent per annum, comparable to the trend growth in the economy and far exceeding population growth. And whilst it can be argued that something is normally being bought with the shares issued, it is also true that some items, such as incentive compensation, have a shorter shelf life than newly issued shares that may remain outstanding forever. Buying transitory outcomes (e.g., a manager with a one-year employment contract) with permanent capital is a duration mismatch a bond investor might understand, but short-term equity investors care little about, and so the dripping tap of share issuance is rarely turned off.

There are two ways to tackle this phenomenon: first is to be a beneficiary of share issuance, usually through other investment liabilities such as bonds or redeemable preferred stock, witness Nomad's investment in Lucent 8% Preferreds (more later). Second is to be an owner of a business capable of compounding value from a static share base, such as Weetabix. What is required is an understanding and mandate to invest across the capital structure (bonds and equities).

The modern investment management industry generally lacks this ability. The system has become rules-based and managers straight-jacketed into geography, sector, style, market capitalisation or security type specific mandates (this list is not exhaustive). These managers are unable to purchase investments outside these narrow constraints, regardless of the case for doing so. H.O. Hirt, the founder of Erie Indemnity, posted the following notice to staff:

*"**RULES***
*Are for INFANTS, **INCOMPETENTS**,*
INCARCERATED CRIMINALS** and **IMBECILES

> *- NONE of WHOM should have any place in the ERIE FAMILY."*

Source: "In His Own Words" by H.O. Hirt, original emphasis.

We would not go quite as far as H.O., but when it comes to the modern fund management industry he is on the right lines.

JUNE 30th, 2008

Dilution risk occurs when companies issue equity at less than the firm is worth. This risk is always with us but is most pernicious at stock market troughs. Let's take a, not wholly, theoretical example: a firm is worth, under normal market conditions, say U$2bn, divided by 60m shares or U$33 per share. A value-oriented buyer may start to buy shares at around U$15, thinking he has bought dollar bills for less than 50c. But what if the firm issues say, 30m new shares at U$10 to fund U$300m of cyclical losses. Under this scenario intrinsic value per share, adjusting for the U$300m in loses, falls from U$28 to U$22. Purchases made at U$15, thought to be at 47c on the dollar of value, turn out to have been made at 68c on the dollar. Worse still, dilution risk accelerates as the share price declines: if the firm raises the same amount of new capital (U$300m) at U$5 per share, then intrinsic value after the capital raising falls to U$16 per share; and if capital is raised at a price of U$1 per share then intrinsic value afterwards falls to U$5.50. In the final example, original purchases made at U$15, at what was thought to be less than half value, end up proving to have been made at three times intrinsic value! Investors can protect themselves from this risk by putting in their proportional share in any new capital raising. The problem comes when investors start to question the size of the capital raising. Perhaps the firm needs more than U$300m? Is the business really worth U$2bn? How can we know for sure? The doubt manifests itself in further share price declines and increases the dilution from not participating in a capital raising. Dilution risk comes from doubt about one's original analysis.

Short sellers know this and whilst it is tempting to criticize their widely circulated 150 page marketing documents (it is interesting that, in contrast, the longs tend to keep their best ideas to themselves), the shorts' regulated anonymity, their desire to keep the doubt going and create an outcome (i.e. share placing) what the shorts are really testing is the shareholders' conviction, and on this level, in our opinion, institutional holders also have much to answer. For example, dilution risk virtually disappears if large institutional shareholders backstop capital raising at reasonable prices. This would require a firmly held view of what a company is worth, shareholders and management that do not game the system (rarer than hen's teeth) and is best done, in our opinion, by way of rights (with rights not taken up underwritten by large holders). Take for example the arrangement between Assured Guaranty and Wilbur Ross. It appears that Ross has agreed to provide up to U$750m to the company as, when and if the company requires. Management are free to raise capital elsewhere if they choose. In effect, Ross has gone a long way to under-writing the equity value (although not entirely) and for the time being the shares trade around book value. None of the other bond insurance companies, including MBIA, have this arrangement and all trade well below book.

The shorts know the institutions are weak minded. And the institutions themselves know they are weak. They are weak because, although equity is permanent capital, the owners of the equity are short term oriented. Institutional money managers appear to reason: why take a stand today when the shares could be half this price if I wait, and why buy shares today when I might get some shares in a placing at an even lower price? It is as if they suddenly do not know what a firm is worth. In taking such a timid view they sell their investments, themselves and their fellow shareholders down the river. Worse still, the preference in the United States for placings over right issues (gosh, the investment banks are good at marketing) means that current shareholders can be cut out of the capital-raising loop entirely. Under this model of stock market participant behaviour the early contrarian buyer, who by himself is too small to influence the outcome by providing the capital required, is severely punished. So, however cheap MBIA may appear, the prospect of a future capital raising means that one cannot place a valuation on the business per share without knowing the number of shares outstanding, and we cannot know that until we know the size of the losses and the price of any future capital raising. In this Alice in Wonderland world, the stock's biggest attraction, its apparent cheapness, becomes the investor's Achilles heel, and it was for this reason that we sold our MBIA shares. And it is also for this reason that recent purchases by Nomad, which are not enough to recap businesses in their own right, and where there is meaningful dilution risk, have been modest in size.

So where have all the long-term investors that could be backstopping businesses gone? In our opinion, what we are witnessing is the effect of a generation or two of the ascendancy of the marketing people and risk managers in the investment management function. The business model at many firms is not to make investments, to research and provide permanent capital; instead, the business model is to gather and retain assets. Fund managers at such organizations may have a strong financial incentive not to stick their neck out, and instead wrap themselves in a grey cocoon of rented stock portfolios. In other words, the marketing guys have won. When I described this conclusion to one fund manager he replied "but, dear boy, they always do".

Chapter 29

INVESTMENT HOLDING PERIODS

Lord Keynes predicted that this trend would intensify as even 'expert professionals, possessing judgment and knowledge beyond that of the average private investor, would be concerned, not with making superior long-term forecasts of the probable yield on an investment over its entire life, but with forecasting changes in the conventional valuation a short time ahead of the general public.'

- JUNE 30th, 2008

Main Points
- Investment holding periods by institutional investors have declined from an average of 7 years in the 1950s to less than a year by 2006 (according to the Bogle Institute).
- The average holding period of US stocks held in Nomad (excluding Berkshire Hathaway) is 51 days (one twenty-fifth the time Nomad expects to hold an investment).
- The current "investors" are renters and cannot have an idea on the long term value of the company. Therein lies the opportunity.

From the Partnership Letters: Investment Holding Periods

JUNE 30th, 2008

Duration

Tom Stoppard, the playwright, is credited with saying "*If an idea is worth having once, it's worth having twice*" and it is in this spirit that we will quote Jack Bogle's work again. Investment holding periods by institutional investors have declined from an average of seven years in the 1950s to less than a year by 2006, according to the Bogle Institute. Well, I am sure Jack and his colleagues are right, but we can't see it in our investments. The average holding period for the US stocks held in Nomad (excluding Berkshire Hathaway) is fifty-one days! That is approximately one twenty- fifth of the time that we expect to hold an investment. Those that set the current prices for our investments (the renters) cannot have an eye on long term value, and that, in a nutshell, is the investment case for Nomad.

And that raises an important point: the costs of short-termism, such as dilution risk, are borne by investors when management mark the share price to market and issue equity. In other words, it is borne early in Nomad's expected holding cycle. The gains from short-termism, such as our ability to purchase shares for meaningfully less than they are worth, will take far longer to materialize. In the example above, the buyer of 10% of the company at U$15 a share and 10% of the capital raising at U$1 per share would in the end see an overall profit of U$80m on his U$120m invested, even though his book loss at the time of the capital raising would be 93.4%! It is pain today and gain tomorrow. Our misanalysis of dilution risk at MBIA for example has cost Nomad investors about 1.5% of NAV this year, but the gains from our continued investment in AirAsia will, we expect, earn Nomad investors 20% of NAV in years to come.

Jack Bogle refers to his senior thesis at Princeton University regularly, even though it was written in 1951, and did so again in the following excerpt from a speech given to the Haas School of Business at the University of California in October 2006:

"Then, prophetically, Lord Keynes predicted that this trend would intensify as even 'expert professionals, possessing judgment and knowledge beyond that of the average private investor, would be concerned, not with making superior long-term forecasts of the probable yield on an investment over its entire life, but with forecasting changes in the conventional valuation a short time ahead of the general public.' As a result, Keynes warned, the stock market would become 'a battle of wits to anticipate the basis of conventional valuation a few months hence rather than the prospective yield of an investment over a long term of years.'

"Simply put, what went wrong was a pathological mutation in capitalism—from traditional owners' capitalism, where the rewards of investing went primarily to those who put up the capital and took the risks—to a new and virulent managers' capitalism, where an excessive share of the rewards of capital investment went to corporate managers and financial intermediaries."

Be that as it may, and although we are financial intermediaries ourselves, we don't like it. One reason we don't like it is we cannot for the life of us figure out why society at large is served by having company owners swap seats every few months? We all know it is pursued in the name of the efficient allocation of capital and liquidity, but it fails at the former and the latter is prized by the insecure. Has this reached an extreme? We do not know, but we did enjoy the following exchange between an analyst and the CEO of one of our investee firms recently:

Analyst: *"Was the exit [in terms of business performance] from March stronger or weaker than the entrance?*

CEO: *"Sorry this is getting ridiculous, next question, please?"*

It is not our system. The point of equity is that it is the only permanent capital in the balance sheet. It is there to weather storms, such as the current economic backdrop, and provide a stable base, and of course to earn the rewards of enterprise. This basic building block of society is broken when those with their hands on the permanent capital change their minds with their underwear. It is no coincidence perhaps that pass-the-parcel and musical chairs are children's games.

Charlie Munger described an alternative model at this year's Wesco Financial annual general meeting. According to Munger the English establishment was so outraged by the speculation of the South Sea bubble and subsequent share price collapses, that in the early eighteenth century Parliament passed the Bubble Act, which outlawed the issuance of shares! That ban remained in place for over a century (1720 to 1825) and, it could be argued, during that century Britain set the stage for the Industrial Revolution, the greatest step forward in modern society. It is not clear we need to trade shares to be successful.

But trade shares we do. According to Empirical Research Partners, an independent investment research firm, the current period is the greatest momentum market since the dot com era, which was one of the greatest momentum markets on record. (A momentum market is one where the best performing stocks this month were those that did best last month and so on. It is unusual because rationally one would expect shares to become less attractive as prices rise. However, currently investors chase stocks in order to own today what they should have owned yesterday. In effect prices rise just because they have already risen. Economics students will recognise this as a "Giffen good").

It is unusual for investors to repeat the last mistake (dot com behavior) so soon. Psychologists argue that the last mistake is so vivid that, if anything, we tend to over- correct, as anyone with a whisky-hangover will tell you. The insanity of bubble-like valuations was well captured by Scott McNealy in a 2002 interview in Business Week when he was still CEO of Sun Microsystems (source: James Montier, Société Générale, Cross Asset Research Group),

> *"But two years ago we were selling at ten times revenues when we were at U$64. At ten times revenues, to give you a ten-year payback, I have to pay you 100% of revenues for ten straight years in dividends. That assumes I can get that by my shareholders. That assumes I have zero cost of goods sold, which is very hard for a computer company. That assumes zero expenses, which is really hard*

with 39,000 employees. That assumes I pay no taxes, which is very hard. And that assumes you pay no taxes on your dividends, which is kind of illegal. And that assumes that, with zero R&D for the next ten years, I can maintain the current revenue run rate. Now, having done that, would any of you like to buy my stock at U$64? Do you realize how ridiculous those basic assumptions are? You don't need transparency. You don't need footnotes. What were you thinking?"

More to the point, what do they continue to think? Why has, say, Potash Corporation of Saskatchewan, a miner of potash and manufacturer of fertilizer (share price up ten-fold in three years, to twelve times sales) taken over from Sun Microsystems, a manufacturer of servers (share price up ten-fold in the two years to 2000, peak valuation around ten times sales)? The answer, along with an unshakable belief in the sustainability and longevity of Chinese urbanization, emerging market demand, resource booms, search for inflation hedges and so on, may have something to do with the decline in investor time horizons – the average holding period for shares of Potash has declined from nearly two years to six weeks as the share price has risen, and if you own the shares for just six weeks, then what do you care if, in two years' time, current prices turn out have been a bubble? Lord Keynes was spot on.

Chapter 30

MOMENTUM INVESTING

We can all do momentum investing, but it is emotional investing and I just don't think it is that intelligent, or profitable.

- JUNE 30th, 2008

Main Points
- Nomad views momentum investing as emotional investing; something that anyone can do, but it's not intelligent or profitable.
- Nick Sleep's mistakes in bidding for a Savoy Hotel item (chrome wall protector in the shape of an 'S') being auctioned off to the public
    - Vanity ('S' for Sleep)
    - Soft spot for the hotel
    - No idea what the intrinsic value for the item was
    - Bidding for the item

From the Partnership Letters: Momentum Investing

JUNE 30th, 2008

Momentum Investing Revisited

In December last year the contents of the Savoy Hotel in London were auctioned to the public. There were several interesting lots: silver trays, pepper and salt pots stamped with the hotel's insignia and so on, although one that caught my eye was a chrome wall protector in the shape of an 'S'. 'S' for Savoy, 'S' for Sleep (such vanity – first mistake), and well, I have always had a soft spot for the hotel (second mistake) and whilst I had no idea what the intrinsic value of such an item might be (third mistake), I placed a bid (fourth mistake). There were a dozen 'S's for sale with lots available over three days. On the first day the prices rose from £350 to £500. On the second day they started down a little at £400 but rose to £800. And on the final day they started at £600 and rose to £850. Notice that the lowest price of each day was the first price and how prices rose steadily throughout the three days. Why? The answer, it seems to us, is first, scarcity, as the auction continued the stock of available 'S's declined. Second, social proof, once one person had set a high price it was seen by others to endorse the value of the item and they too could pay a higher price knowing they were not alone. And what price did your author pay? Well, let's just say I bought on the last day...and I justified it by telling myself that it was a one off, the Savoy is special, I won't get this chance again, 'S' for Savoy, 'S' for Sleep, and so on. And I just know I overpaid (Mrs. Sleep's withering what-have-you-done-now-look said it all). We can all do momentum investing, but it is emotional investing and I just don't think it is that intelligent, or profitable.

Chapter 31

THE QUIET APPROACH

"Advertising is the price you pay for having an unremarkable product or service".

- Jeff Bezos

Main Points
- The quiet approach: most of the companies Nomad was invested in shun commonplace promotional activity and are no less successful.
    - Amazon / Costco do not advertise.
    - Berkshire Hathaway and Games Workshop don't provide earnings guidance.
    - Amazon, Costco, AirAsia, Carpetright, and parts of Berkshire give back margin to the customer.
- These companies are run by people who behaved as if they ran private firms.
    - Amazon (Jeff Bezos quote): ""Advertising is the price you pay for having an unremarkable product or service".

From the Partnership Letters: The Quiet Approach

JUNE 30th, 2009

Empty Vessels and a Quieter Approach
Upon reflection, it is curious that this quiet attitude extends, in its own way, to the companies in which we have entrusted your dollars: Amazon and Costco do not advertise (no shouting here); Berkshire Hathaway and Games Workshop do not provide earnings guidance (popular with baying fund managers and stockbrokers); Amazon, Costco, AirAsia, Carpetright, and parts of Berkshire give back margin to the customer, we would argue that is a pretty humble strategy too. In other words, around two thirds of the portfolio is invested in firms that in some major way shun commonplace promotional activity and they are no less successful as a result. If one steps outside of stock market listed companies to instead observe private firms run by proprietors and founders, it is the quiet approach that is far closer to the norm. Let's invert: why are publicly listed companies so promotional about their affairs? Are these companies shouting to inform shareholders and customers or convince themselves?

Nomad's investments may be in publicly listed firms but these firms are also overwhelmingly run by proprietors who think and behave as if they ran private firms. Amazon for example struggles with institutional investor relations so much so that the good people that man the IR department do so knowing that the firm's founder, Jeff Bezos, thinks their role is all but a waste of time! Poor souls. Bezos was also quite forthright on the subject of product promotion and advertising at this year's annual general meeting:

> "Advertising is the price you pay for having an unremarkable product or service".

It is interesting to note that the other end of the promotional scale is exemplified by the pop star razzle of General Motors which had the largest advertising budget of any company whose annual report we read this year (actually that title went to GM last year, and the year before, and the year before...). The advertising spend was U$5.3bn in 2008, or U$630 per car delivered. It is fun to muse that had the company made cars that required little advertising support, then the firm's last five-years' advertising spend may have been sufficient to retire half of the company's debt, at par, instead! But, it seems, it was easier to call Madison Avenue than build cars that sold themselves. In our opinion, GM is very much the empty vessel making the most noise, in this regard. Our portfolio takes a different path. The whispered voice of price givebacks is economically fruitful but only if the customer reciprocates in the form of more spending, even in the face of more promotional approaches by competitors. For evidence that this is the case with our whisperers look no further than the average revenue growth rate of the largest investments in Nomad (including some of the companies mentioned above, err, not GM!) which, in the most recent reporting period, was in excess of ten percent!

Why? In a word, price. It is in times like these that the hyper-efficient low-cost providers, who share the benefits with their customers, often take permanent market share. This fact rather reminded us of a quip by Wal-Mart founder, Sam Walton, who, when asked about the recession of the early 1990s, stated:

"I've thought about it and decided not to participate".

Amazon, for example, is choosing "not to participate" in as much as trailing twelve- month revenues have risen by over sixty percent since the onset of the credit crisis, say mid 2007. Not that the steady growth in revenues has always been apparent in its stock price, as the chart below describes. As a youthful analyst I used to have a notice on my desk that read, "share prices are more volatile than corporate cash flow, which is more volatile than asset replacement cost". It was reminder to concentrate on non-transitory items. Today I would update such a notice to read, "share prices are more volatile than business values", but the gist is the same: a reminder to focus on lasting value, not transitory prices. More on this subject later in this letter.

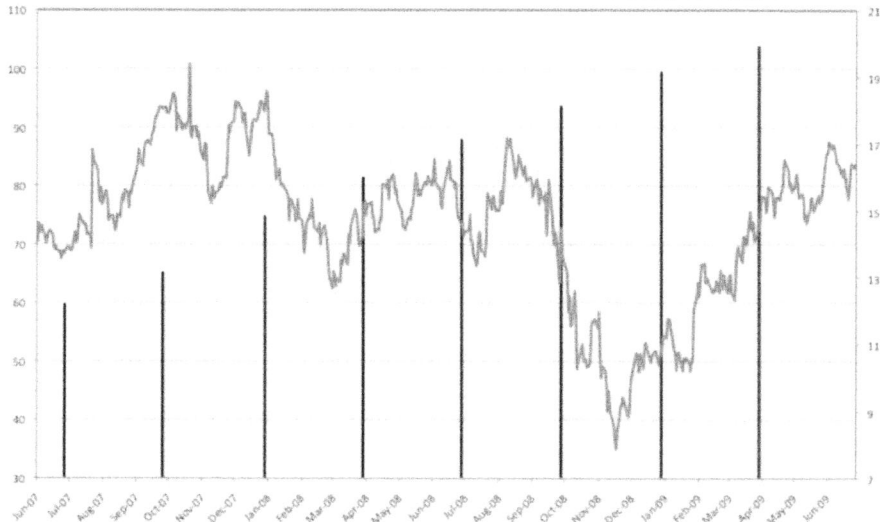

Chart 1: Make up your mind, U$100 or U$40? Amazon.com trailing twelve month revenues (in billions of dollars, rhs) and share price (lhs).

Source: Company accounts, Bloomberg, Sleep, Zakaria and Company, Ltd.

Chapter 32

FUND SIZE & GOVERNANCE

When we find a pool of good ideas of reasonable size, we will be in touch. However, we will not open just because Nomad will be independent or due to some dreadful manifestation of the principal agent conflict.

- JUNE 30th, 2006

Main Points
- Nomad was very disciplined and shareholder-friendly in the way they ran their fund.
- They weren't focused on asset gathering and were instead focused on generating returns.
- They closed the fund to additional capital when they didn't have any ideas.
- They refused capital from those they found unsuitable or irritating. They made it clear to their investors that Nomad was not suitable for those with less than a 5-year horizon.
- They charged a tiny annual management fee that just covered their costs (instead of the annual 1 or 2 percent of fees).
- They received 20 percent of the fund's investment profits, but only after 6 percent annual return.

transitory prices. More on this subject later in this letter.

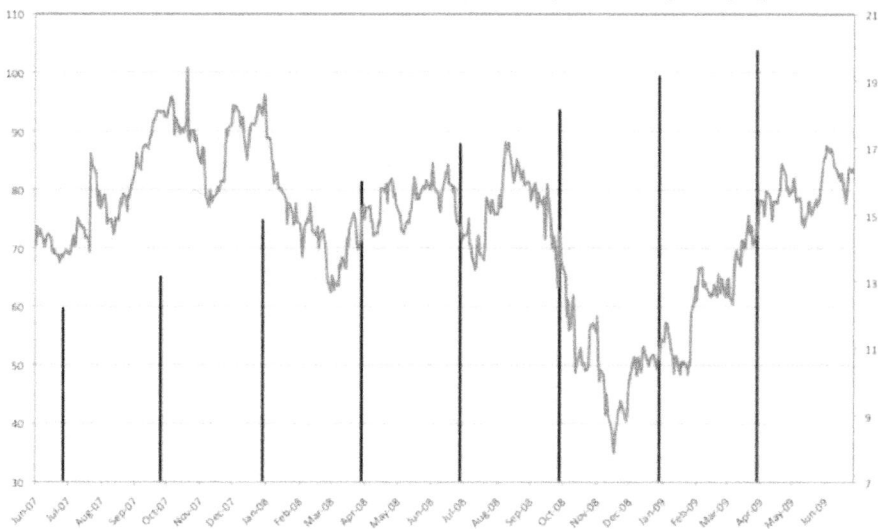

Chart 1: Make up your mind, U$100 or U$40? Amazon.com trailing twelve month revenues (in billions of dollars, rhs) and share price (lhs).

Source: Company accounts, Bloomberg, Sleep, Zakaria and Company, Ltd.

Chapter 32

FUND SIZE & GOVERNANCE

When we find a pool of good ideas of reasonable size, we will be in touch. However, we will not open just because Nomad will be independent or due to some dreadful manifestation of the principal agent conflict.

- JUNE 30th, 2006

Main Points
- Nomad was very disciplined and shareholder-friendly in the way they ran their fund.
- They weren't focused on asset gathering and were instead focused on generating returns.
- They closed the fund to additional capital when they didn't have any ideas.
- They refused capital from those they found unsuitable or irritating. They made it clear to their investors that Nomad was not suitable for those with less than a 5-year horizon.
- They charged a tiny annual management fee that just covered their costs (instead of the annual 1 or 2 percent of fees).
- They received 20 percent of the fund's investment profits, but only after 6 percent annual return.

- Later on, they decided to make it even harder by placing their performance fees in a holding bucket; if Nomad fell short of its 6 percent hurdle, they would refund a portion of the previously earned fees.
- In short, Nomad was structured to be a vehicle for maximizing returns, not assets.

From the Partnership Letters: Fund Size & Governance

JUNE 30th, 2003

Our results to date place Nomad at or very near the top of any investment fund league table over the same time period, regardless of whether the opposition employed leverage, options, shorting or such like – again, we employ none of these techniques. The effect is that, in all likelihood, Nomad's funds could be grown quite rapidly if we allowed the floodgates to open and take all comers. This we will not do. We have only one chance to grow Nomad to a reasonable size before it is closed, and the quality of investors when the doors are shut is of great importance to us. To date, we have declined almost as many investment dollars as we have let in, a ratio that the industry does not track and a habit that the industry is not good at keeping. But even so, whilst we hope that the fund will grow over time, we are in no hurry to do so, and will endeavor to maintain the quality of the Partners with whom we will share results, bad and good.

DECEMBER 31st, 2003

Partnership Growth

At the time of writing the Partnership is nearly five times bigger than at inception, with the smallest contribution having come from investment performance! The balance is due to subscriptions made by new and existing investors. These contributions have been welcome, from the viewpoint of making Nomad a viable commercial activity, but it has only been appropriate to accept subscriptions as we have been able to put incremental capital to good use.

It is only fair to report that due to a quirk in your manager's character, growth in assets from this source drives him mad. The reason is the dilutive effect it has on overall performance. Take, for example, our investment in Resorts World, a Malaysian casino. At the time of purchase the holding was 5% of assets and yet despite the shares doubling in the last two years the holding today is smaller as a proportion of the Partnership than two years ago. Likewise, Kersaf and Television Broadcast, whilst Stagecoach would have peaked at around 25% of fund assets but peaked at 15% due to dilution. So, what is to be done?

There are three alternatives:
1. Accept subscriptions as they come and place cash on deposit until suitable investments can be found. The problem here is that money can easily arrive faster than good investments, almost inevitably so, with dilutive consequences for existing investors, and suboptimal outcomes for new investors.
2. Accept subscriptions as they come and buy a little of everything to replicate the existing portfolio. This sounds attractive as, dealing costs and liquidity constraints aside, prospective returns from the Partnership as a whole are broadly maintained. But it does have one major, subtle drawback. There are very few absolutes in investing, but one thing about which we can be certain is that as prices rise prospective returns go down. If a business is worth U$40, the purchase of shares at U$30 has to be inferior to their purchase at U$20. We expend a great deal of mental effort preserving the integrity of our purchase decisions and would rather not have the thinking muddied by purchases made at ever-higher prices due to subscriptions. In our opinion, this alternative risks devolving the initial investment decision back to the subscribing party, who are likely-as-not unaware of their additional role as stock picker.
3. Match subscriptions to new ideas with a right to draw down or defer subscriptions as necessary. In our opinion this is the superior strategy as incremental funding is invested in new fifty cent dollars, thereby lowering the price to value ratio of the fund and with the effect that new investors bring something to the party. We have guestimated that we may be able to find incremental investments at the rate of one per month.

This is a best guess on our part and if pushed we will concede that it looks high; ideas may be far less frequent than that. New holdings average 5% of Partnership assets at purchase, a fact that dictates incremental funding is limited to around 5% of assets per month.

Route 3 is the most equitable way to run the Partnership in our opinion but does require patience on the part of new investors whose subscriptions may need to be staggered over several quarters. Even so we have been surprised by the support this eccentric regime has received. The largest non-Marathon investor in the Partnership noted that one of the reasons they chose to invest was precisely because of the emphasis placed on performance over asset gathering. This investor then offered to pro-rata their subscription should we request, in effect extending their subscription period to make way for other co-investors. Such courtesy is exceptional in this industry but captures the spirit in which we are trying to run the Partnership. Bravo! We have no interest in diluting the quality of our Partners from what we believe to be a very high level.

Partnership Closure
Our preferred state of affairs is to close and for growth in assets to be investment-led. We will close when any of the following conditions are reached: it is no longer possible to invest a unit size; time spent marketing rises above a very low level, say 1% of the working year; or when we feel the quality of the client base is being diluted. In all likelihood this means closure when the Partnership is still small by industry standards and we are very comfortable with that.

JUNE 30th, 2004

Partnership Governance
In May, the balance of the funds waiting to be invested in Nomad were drawn down at a time when stock prices allowed us to lower the price to value ratio of the Partnership, and when insider buying, and share repurchase picked up at investee companies. The bulk of this incremental capital was invested and leaves a cash balance of around 16% of assets. This too will be invested as and when

prices allow. The Partnership has grown considerably in the last eighteen months to just over U$100m and should now be considered closed. This is our natural state of affairs, and one that will be punctuated with open periods in response to price opportunities.

Job one, two and three for your manager is investment performance, not asset gathering. Few practice this approach. We work under the assumption that if performance is reasonable then the level of interest in what we are doing will increase and, if appropriate, the Partnership will grow in time. Common sense and simple maths dictate that it will be opportune if growth can be channeled to coincide with depressed prices, and not market tops. We must aim for this standard, even though it is contrary to common practice in the industry. Had we adopted the industry standard open-house approach the Partnership would be approximately three times its current size, but the results worse, and the quality of Partners meaningfully impaired. It is important to us that we all understand the investment process (a reminder is contained in the appendix, in the form of an interview published in the Outstanding Investor Digest), try hard to keep a healthy indifference to results achieved (certainly no extrapolation of annual results please) and maintain a patient temperament. Investment dollars work best when they occupy a different psychic space to almost any other form of savings you may have.

The size of any future reopening will be proportionate to the opportunity set: a melt-down in large capitalization shares (please), a debt market swoon like the one recently experienced in the US, or an emerging market crisis as occurred a few years earlier, would allow the Partnership to be many times its current size and improve its potential returns. Today, the opportunities are mainly small and mid-capitalization companies, especially in Asia, and mainly turnarounds in nature (which bring with them reinvestment risk once the stock is sold). And so, for the time being the Partnership will retain its modest size. Over time this may change, but the timing of that change is outside our control.

When we do reopen, we will write to those that have expressed an interest in investing more. This is likely to occur during periods of market stress and we will have to trust that indications made during rosier times turn into contrarian subscriptions. Very few organizations practice this common-sense approach because they understand how human nature works. They suspect (or know!) the average investor will be bearish at the bottom. There is no point taking that particular horse to water. At Nomad, we believe our Partners to be exceptional. Take the drawn down of the queue in May. Within forty-eight hours of indicating our preference, all those in the queue had consented to subscribe their full amount, at little notice, and with several offers for more if we wished. Wonderful. And thank you. You have quietly let us get on with the job of investing without the prodding and poking that is commonplace throughout the industry. In turn, we have felt trusted and free to invest in ways we think is appropriate to the benefit of all our results. We are aware that the industry's record in raising capital at market lows is not good. But we are happy to trust you to be contrarian at the next market swoon.

DECEMBER 31st, 2004

How big is Nomad?

There is no getting around it, Nomad is stapled to a fund management organisation three hundred times its size. This was important for Nomad's genesis, and I wonder if it would have survived this long if truly independent. But it is a problem also. Particularly when picking stocks. This is because your manager wears two hats, that of analyst to the main Marathon funds, and that of Portfolio Manager to Nomad. The problem comes when an order for Nomad is aggregated with those of the main funds. Then Nomad, whose own size is small, in effect behaves as if it was a U$30bn fund (Marathon's total assets under management). This is not ideal, but it is hard to devise a system which does not amount to a worse outcome for one party or the other. We struggle with a satisfactory system, but you should be under no illusion that Nomad's returns, such as they are, are a product of its size alone. We look like a mouse but move like an elephant. It is not a good combination, but it is what it is.

DECEMBER 31st, 2005

In May 2004, we drew down part of the queue that was waiting to invest in Nomad, and since then the Partnership has gained around 35%, compared to a gain of around 25% for most stocks. When we look back at the investments we made, there was, in practice, a very high limit to the amount of money we could have invested and still maintained performance. Several hundred million dollars could have been invested in each of Costco (US), New World Developments (Hong Kong), Amazon.com (US), Telewest (UK) and Liberty Media (Europe and Japan). But as each idea came one at a time, with a lag in between, we were reluctant to open the Partnership for the sake of one new idea. We erred on the side of investment performance rather than maximising fund size. I know this is not how the industry thinks and behaves, but at Nomad we see our job as running an investment partnership first and commercial enterprise second. Which raises an interesting wrinkle: if we had opened Nomad, drawn down the whole queue, and invested the capital well, then in five years-time Nomad would be billions of dollars in size. Say we then found that the opportunity set was small: could we give the money back?

There is a difference between investment returns measured as a percentage gain, and results when measured in dollars. Doubling a hundred dollars through stock picking is not economically equivalent to a ten percent gain on a thousand dollars, although the dollar profits are the same. It is for this reason that investment results are rightly presented in percentage terms, however, in some respects this is only half the equation, as doubling a billion dollars is clearly a better outcome than doubling a hundred dollars. The key ingredient for evaluating the case for taking on more funds must be that the incremental, new dollars do not inhibit performance in percentage terms for the first dollars. That way the bus is always running at full speed with the number of passenger optimised to maintain maximum speed. The industry skirts around this point and talks about relative performance instead, as commercial pressures encourage lesser performance on vastly increased pools than better performance on smaller pools. It is as if the industry aspires to run the equivalent of the Calcutta commuter bus, so burdened with paying passengers piled on the roof that all it can manage is to trundle, unsafely, in the slow lane!

But let's turn the proposition on its head: the intrinsically low-cost structure of the investment business, so often used to earn super normal profits for business owners, would instead allow a shrinking of the investment pool for the purpose of protecting investment returns. I don't think many managers have thought about it this way, most in the industry have taken to heart Winston Churchill's instruction to "keep buggering on". They hope that declining returns go unnoticed, and besides, they argue, who knows how fast the bus would be going if they let some passengers off. But what we are asking is, in practice, how would you feel about us returning capital to you on investment grounds? At Nomad we hope that it would never come to that, but it may. And it is important that we all understand a road map that allows for a shrinkage before we first grow the Partnership. And to add another layer of complexity, how would you feel about us changing our mind some time thereafter if the opportunity set improved markedly and we could take more money? This raises the interesting notion that if we returned capital to you would Zak and I have some moral responsibility for the dividended funds? I think we might. In other words, as investment results are maximised by Nomad expanding and contracting with the opportunity set, how can we reflect this reality in the structure of our Partnership? It's amazing to us that most investment companies are silent on such an obvious, common sense issue, but such is industry obfuscation of uncomfortable facts these issues go undiscussed. Even so, our ability to expand and shrink will be an important tool sometime in the next twenty years. I guarantee it. And it seems silly to set off without it. I would value your thoughts on this greatly.

DECEMBER 31st, 2006 (Appendix II)

The Nomad Investment Partnership currently charges a management fee of 10 basis points per annum, a levy which leans somewhat on the in-place infrastructure at Marathon and which is insufficient to sustain a stand-alone operation. We would therefore like to propose a new management fee that will reimburse the operating company (Sleep, Zakaria and Company, Limited) for its costs incurred in running the operation (salary, rent, accounting, research, legal etc.). We guestimate this will be between 0.7% and 1% of the Partnership per annum at its current size, and we will cap the reimbursement at 1% of NAV and fund any deficit out of pocket if need be. Philosophically our position is that the management fee should not be a profits centre (although a small surplus float is prudent). This is not a blank cheque: Zak and I will take a salary cut to run Nomad, and a total remuneration cut that questions our sanity, but as I have said, this is not a traditional business. As the Partnership grows in size the management fee will decline as a percentage of assets and, that way, all investors share in the natural scale economics of the operation.

The performance fee also needs addressing, as there is an inconsistency between multi-year investments, multi-year orientation by investors and an annual payout for the manager! The performance fee should be appropriately calculated for the job, be at risk for subsequent poor performance and reflect the cost of capital. We will therefore propose that the existing six percent cost of capital hurdle remain (approximating five-year bond rates) and that the performance fee be deferred and subject to repayment in the event of subsequent underperformance. There are several ways this could be achieved, the easiest of which may be to bank the performance fees, and for the bank to drip fees to us if performance remains reasonable, or drip reimbursements back to you to the extent we fail to maintain our advantage. One way our advantage may be compromised is if size becomes a meaningful drag on performance, as I said in the last letter to investors "our ability to expand and shrink will be an important tool sometime in the next twenty years. I guarantee it...". Our intention is that "the bus is always running at full speed with the number of passengers optimised to maintain maximum speed", and so we will also take powers to return cash to you should we find the opportunity set is small. I don't expect that we will return cash to you that much, and I would be delighted if we did not at all, but it seems silly to set off without the ability to do so. Again, the prospectus will elaborate.

The investment philosophy and methodology will be unchanged. All that changes is that Zak and I will be dedicating one hundred percent of our time to

Nomad, rather than something less than one hundred percent, and that one hundred percent of our personal investments will be in Nomad, rather than something less than one hundred percent. Otherwise, it is business as usual and there will be no change in our fund administrator (Daiwa Securities Trust and Banking in Ireland) or auditor (Ernst and Young).

JUNE 30th, 2006

We do not mean to be so evasive, so let me explain the conditions under which we may reopen. The golden rule is that we will only reopen if incremental dollars bring something to the party, through lowering the price to value ratio of the Partnership as a whole. This aside, any increase in size is also accretive to performance as the management fee in dollars is, within certain parameters, fixed and will decline as a percentage of assets as the Partnership grows. That way growth also offers a saving to all investors. Capital raising will first take place by a rights issue to existing investors with rights not taken up returned to us and then offered to those that have indicated an interest in investing and satisfactorily completed a due diligence questionnaire. The queue is ordered with principals ranked above agents, and agents ranked according to various criteria. However, it is not ranked according to the size of the investor's pot. It is far more important to us, and our existing partners, that we all see Nomad in the same light – we simply do not have the will or inclination to offer bespoke services, cater to a different crowd or to be particularly large. When it comes to the Partnership opening, we are happy to adopt the motto of the Brooklands Motor Racing Circuit whose pre-war posters showed cars speeding around its famous banked corner whilst well-dressed spectators ate picnics on leafy verges, with the slogan "the right crowd, and no crowding". We are very respectful of the trust existing partners have placed in our ability to compound their savings and have no appetite to pack in all and sundry, regardless of the incentives.

I am sure we would make poorer investments if we did and be unhappier to boot!

When we find a pool of good ideas of reasonable size, we will be in touch. However, we will not open just because Nomad will be independent or due to some dreadful manifestation of the principal agent conflict. The cost-reimbursement management fee means we do not need to open to put bread on the table. To date, we have turned U$1 into around U$2.70. Our aim is to turn this onto U$10 within a decade (approximately fifteen percent compound per annum) and we are somewhat indifferent as to how much money we carry with us during the process: For Zak and I, it is all about the destination.

JUNE 30th, 2007

<u>The Terms of Future Capital Raising.</u>
Before there is any sucking of teeth, we do not have any plans to raise capital. Really. But we do wish to set out our stall now for the next investment crisis, and that crisis could come quickly. As we have always said in the past, capital should only be raised in response to investment opportunity sets (to be slipped into the suggestion box of marketing-oriented fund management operations). Rightly or wrongly (and there is a perfectly rational case that we are wrong) we have an over-riding bias to keep our operation small. However, we are also conscious that a repeat of the Asian crisis or the junk bond crisis would allow us to invest multiples the current size of Nomad with better results for all concerned. So, for illustration, let's say Nomad is a U$1bn Partnership and there is a new crisis and we raise a further U$1bn with the result that after the crisis has abated, Nomad is say, U$4bn in value. U$4bn is not a small amount of capital, especially in a concentrated portfolio. The rational thing may be to return the crisis capital to investors and right size back to the original capital. So, our suggestion is that a future capital raising would, in effect, be a rights issue of redeemable shares, which would give Zak and me the option of shrinking. We are flagging this now, and we welcome your thoughts on the subject. Speak up or forever hold your peace!

JUNE 30th, 2012

Our Management Fee

Nomad's cost-reimbursement management fee (Zak and I meet the costs of running the operation each month and are reimbursed at the beginning of the following month) will have an annual run rate of fewer than ten basis points in the near future. We may not quite get there this year, but we are going in that direction. Our management fee was a philosophical decision for us. We thought that in managing the Partnership we had not added value per se, and so the management fee should meet the Partnership's costs, but not be a source of profit. A by-product of this is that as the Partnership grows in size the management fee declines as a percentage of assets, and so the incremental dollar brings something to the party, as it were. In the last six years the management fee has fallen from circa fifty basis points to close to ten, and with little scrimping of costs: Zak's and my salaries have normalised after several years of being in family-holdback-start-up mode, we travel all we need, we purchase the research resources we value, and the rent has just gone up. The saving to our partners, who are mainly charities and endowments for charitable causes, is not trivial: approximately U$15m per annum compared to the industry standard one percent management fee, or over U$30m per annum compared to the hedge fund standard. We mention this to pop the illusion that investment management is a Giffen good (one where, paradoxically, demand rises with price). Indeed, Zak and I would take it a step further and say that incentives (and rules) can de-moralise behaviour, and what the industry needs more than anything, perhaps, is a sense of right and wrong. It can be hard to separate right from wrong when there is so much money sloshing around. It is a contentious thought but, if one could lower management fees across our peer group, one may end up improving aggregate industry behaviour in the process!

Chapter 33

INFORMATION AS FOOD

Information, like food, has a sell by date, after all, next quarter's earnings are worthless after next quarter. And it is for this reason that the information that Zak and I weigh most heavily in thinking about a firm is that which has the longest shelf life, with the highest weighting going to information that is almost axiomatic: it is, in our opinion, the most valuable information.

- JUNE 30th, 2012

Main Points
- All food has an expiration date. Similarly, information also has an expiration date.
- Nomad viewed information as something that should be consumed only if it has a long shelf life. Once you view information through this lens, you realize that most pieces of "information" are no longer useful after a few days or weeks.
- The most valuable information are those that are still relevant years or decades (even centuries) later; these are the pieces of information that should be weighted the most heavily.

From the Partnership Letters: Information as Food

JUNE 30th, 2012

Information as Food

The castaway for the seventieth anniversary edition of BBC Radio 4's Desert Island Discs was the naturalist, David Attenborough. Kirsty Young, the host, introduced David Attenborough as follows:

> Kirsty Young: *"He has seen more of the world than any person who has ever lived. The depth of his knowledge and breadth of his enthusiasm have had a fundamental effect on how we view our planet. From sitting hugger-mugger with the mountain gorillas of Rwanda, to describing the fragilities of the flightless Kakapo: the wonders of the natural world are his stock-in-trade. His passion can be traced right back to the days as a lad when he cycled his bike through the Leicestershire countryside trawling for fossils. He says he knows of no deeper pleasure than the contemplation of the natural world. David Attenborough, you visited the North and South Poles, you witnessed all of life in-between from the canopies of the tropical rainforest to giant earthworms in Australia, it must be true, must it not, and it is a quite staggering thought, that you have seen more of the world than anybody else who has ever lived?"*

> David Attenborough: *"Well...I suppose so...but then on the other hand it is fairly salutary to remember that perhaps the greatest naturalist that ever lived and had more effect on our thinking than anybody, Charles Darwin, only spent four years travelling and the rest of the time thinking."*

Oh!

David Attenborough's modesty is delightful but notice also, if you will, the model of behaviour he observed in Charles Darwin: study intensely, go away, and really think. It is Darwin, he argues, who has contributed more. In other words, Attenborough is saying that the human mind trumps endless data collection. We could be more specific: the frontal cortex of the brain, which is charged with rational thought and information processing, can make more sense of the world, given enough time to think it through, than the senses themselves can make sense of the world.

In today's information-soaked world there may be stock market professionals who would argue that constant data collection is the job. Indeed, it could be tempting to conclude that today there is so much data to collect and so much change to observe that we hardly have time to think at all. Some market practitioners may even concur with John Kearon, CEO of Brainjuicer (a market research firm), who makes the serious point, "we think far less than we think we think" - so don't fool yourself!

Whilst Zak and I applaud John Kearnon, we try to take Charles Darwin's approach: de-emphasise the data collection and think. When we study truly great businesses, we find that very often it has been simple human attributes that have led to their success: you feel differently drinking a Coke than a no brand cola or, you may feel differently towards a business that consistently undercuts the competition in price or, a delivery service that literally goes the extra mile and picks up returned items – and the reason you have these feelings, and the stimuli that produce them, have hardly changed in millennia. When we try to understand the factors that made great businesses great, in our opinion, there is lots of time to think.

For example, it is interesting to note that the business model that built the Ford empire a hundred years ago and is illustrated in the chart below (dated 1927), is the same that built Sam Walton's (Wal-Mart) in the 1970s, Herb Kelleher's (Southwest Airlines) in the 1990s or Jeff Bezos's (Amazon.com) today. And it will build empires in the future too. The longevity of the model is not difficult to understand as Jeff Bezos pointed out "I can't imagine that in ten years from now customers are going to say: I really love Amazon, but I wish their prices were a little higher" or Amazon was less convenient, or they had less selection.

Chart 1: Production Volumes and Cost (to the consumer) of Ford Cars 1908 to 1924.

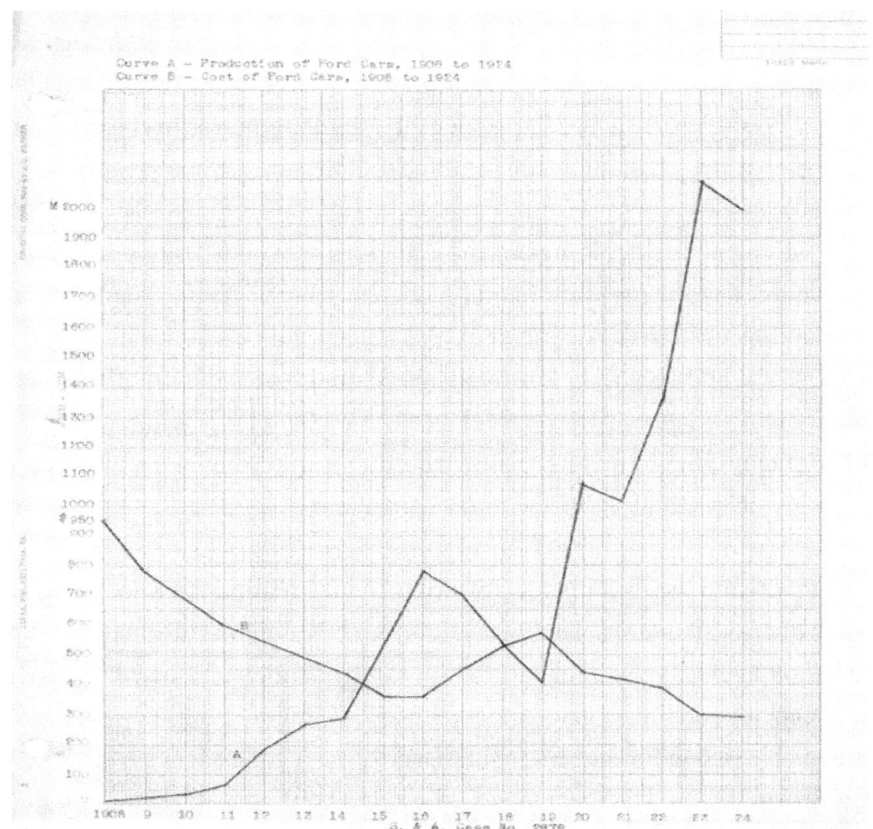

Source: The original 1927 report of the Franklin Institute of the State of Pennsylvania for the Promotion of the Mechanical Arts, recommending "Mr. Henry Ford, of Detroit, Michigan" for the Institute's Elliott Cresson Medal. Line A illustrates the volumes of cars produced, in this case from zero to just over two million per annum. Line B describes the decline in cost (probably to the consumer) of the Model T Ford from U$950 to around U$300. The x-axis refers to the calendar years 1908 to 1924.

Whilst the basic business models that lead to success don't change that much and there aren't that many of them, there is still all that data to deal with. So, how should we think about information?

The journalist and technologist, JP Rangaswami, argues that the most helpful way to think about information is the same way we think about food. His analogy may even have some scientific grounding. In the "Expensive Tissue Hypothesis" anthropologists Leslie Aiello and Peter Wheeler state that for a given body size a primate's metabolic rate is relatively static, what differs from primate to primate is the balance of tissues, most notably the tissues that are expensive to operate, principally the nervous system (including the brain) and the digestive system. In man we have small stomachs and large brains, in pigs the opposite is true. If you want a larger brain you have to live with a smaller gut, and of course the large brain provides the thinking power to organise the world in such a way that one is not required to constantly graze.

Leaving the science aside, Rangaswami's analogy is wonderfully provocative: in the cultivation of food there are hunter gatherers who are free to roam, or farmers who put up fences to define ownership; the same is true in information, is this not what patent and copyright law is all about? In the preparation of food we can either choose distilled nutrition (a beef steak, for example) or a smorgasbord that allows for the mixing of raw nutrients; the same is true when we are served with a conclusion or instead ask for the underlying data.

And then there are the differences, for instance information does not always have food-like quality standards. There is little-to-no labelling of information presented on television, so fact and fiction can be deliberately fused and have given rise to "docudramas" and "mocumentaries". In literature the same phenomenon exits and has been popularised following the success of books such as Dan Brown's "The Da Vinci Code". To avoid confusion, one solution may be to label information for its fact content, in the same way we label food for its fat content.

And what of the implications of over-consuming? Clay Shirky, the writer and internet consultant, claimed that "there is no such animal as information overload, only filter failure" which, using Rangaswami's analogy, implies we need to think about data diets and information exercise to prevent the buildup of toxins and disease. "When I saw [Morgan Spurlock's documentary film] 'Super-Size Me'" joked Rangaswami in a recent speech "I started thinking, now what would happen if an individual had thirty- one days nonstop Fox News?" What, indeed?

Information, like food, has a sell by date, after all, next quarter's earnings are worthless after next quarter. And it is for this reason that the information that Zak and I weigh most heavily in thinking about a firm is that which has the longest shelf life, with the highest weighting going to information that is almost axiomatic: it is, in our opinion, the most valuable information. No doubt Charles Darwin would agree.

Chapter 34

THINKING IN DECISION TREES

When investors value a business they have in their minds, consciously or not, a decision tree with the various branches leading to all possible futures and probabilities attached to those branches. The share price can be thought of as an aggregate of the probability weighted value of these branches.

- JUNE 30th, 2010

Main Points
- Below is a fascinating way Nomad used decision trees to map out the value of a business.
- When investors go about valuing a business, they inadvertently create a decision tree with various branches leading to all the possible futures with probabilities attached to those branches.
- The share price can then be thought of as the aggregate of the probability weighted value of these branches.

In this example below, they used AirAsia.

From the Partnership Letters: Thinking in Decision Trees

JUNE 30th, 2010

The Subtle Implication for Long-Term Investors

The opportunity for Nomad's investors comes from realising to whom these firms are more valuable. Certainly not the short-term investor, who will be indifferent as to whether Amazon, Asos or AirAsia will be the most valuable retailer/fashion e-tailer/airline in the world in ten years' time. The institutional fund manager may be similarly indifferent. This collective professional myopia presents the true long-term investor with the spoils, but the mechanism for this wealth transfer from short-term holder to long-term investor is subtle.

When investors value a business they have in their minds, consciously or not, a decision tree with the various branches leading to all possible futures and probabilities attached to those branches. The share price can be thought of as an aggregate of the probability weighted value of these branches. The problem, as Santa-Fe Institute scientist Ole Peters most recently pointed out (SFI Bulletin 2009, volume 24), is that this is not an accurate representation of what the future will be! The next step for the company will not be to visit all of those branches simultaneously. In reality the firm in question will only visit one of those branches before proceeding to the next and so on. Short-term investors spend their time trying to handicap the odds of each branch.

Guessing which-branch-next can be a crowded trade, but it's fine, as far as it goes. However, it rather misses the big picture, in our opinion. We would propose that some businesses, once they have progressed down the first favourable branch, stand a much greater chance of progressing down the second favourable branch, and then the third, as a virtuous feedback loop builds. The process takes time, but a favourable result at any one stage increases the chances of success further down the line, as it were. Think of it as a business' culture.

Take AirAsia: The firm was born with a no frills, cost culture with the result that, we estimate, it is the lowest cost airline in the world: this is favourable branch one. Favourable branch two: the employees take pride in the firm, suggest their own savings and the savings are implemented. Branch three: the savings exceed the peer group and are given back to customers in the form of lower prices. Branch four: the customer reciprocates and revenues rise. Branch five: further scale advantages lead to more savings per seat flown. Branch six: further customer reciprocation. Branch seven: the network builds and crowds out other, less efficient airlines. Branch eight: competitors go out of business?

The point is that the odds associated with any of these branches are not static but, in a hugely important way, they improve as one travels from branch to branch. Imagine the payoff in a game with these attributes? If investors recognise the inevitability of these improving odds they are also usually indifferent to them, perhaps viewing the eventual greatness of a business as simply outside their time horizon. Nevertheless, the effect of this indifference on share prices is to leave long-term success undiscounted (note, share prices are an aggregate of all possible future worlds, not the actual future) and the rewards from that observation may be enormous for the patient few. We certainly expect so.

Chapter 35

SUPER HIGH-QUALITY THINKERS

In the office we keep a list of companies assembled under the title "super high-quality thinkers". This is not an easy club to join.

- JUNE 30th, 2004

Main Points
- Nomad kept a list of companies that fall under the category of "super high-quality thinkers". How does one make the list?
- Companies that do the right thing when their backs are against the wall, have the ability to out-think their competition, or allocate capital over many years with discipline to reinforce the firm's competitive advantage
- This list of companies is something Nomad called "the terminal portfolio". In short, this was the portfolio that Nomad wanted to strive for.
- Yet why wasn't Nomad's portfolio mirror this list? Price. They didn't want to overpay and would only pay 50 cents for these companies.
- From their perspective, the odds that a high-quality company would fall to 50c on the dollar in the next few years are pretty good and when they did, Nomad would be ready to scoop up the shares.

From the Partnership Letters:
Super High-Quality Thinkers

JUNE 30th, 2004

The Likely Evolution of Partnership Investments

In the office we keep a list of companies assembled under the title "super high-quality thinkers". This is not an easy club to join, and the list currently runs to fifteen businesses. Entry is reserved for the intellectually honest and economically rational, but that alone is not enough. There are many companies that do the right thing when their backs are against the wall, and this list excludes those temporarily attending church. The anointed few are there because they have chosen to out-think their competition and allocate capital over many years with discipline to reinforce their firm's competitive advantage. Good capital allocation takes many forms and does not necessarily require a firm to grow. The Partnership's successful investment in Stagecoach has been due to the firm's shrink strategy, not its growth, although that may come in time. At National Indemnity (an insurance subsidiary of Berkshire Hathaway), the firm's ability to write insurance only when pricing is good and stand back when pricing is poor, even if revenues decline by 80% and remain depressed for many years, is a wonderful example of capital discipline and good capital allocation. After all, why grow if returns are going to be poor? However, surprisingly few companies have the strength to just sit it out, or shrink, as the pressure to grow is often overwhelming. The clamor comes from within the company (reinforced by poorly constructed incentive compensation), Wall Street promoters and short-term shareholders. When faced with this barrage, the voice of the long-term shareholder often goes unheard. We ask companies with poor economics why they want to grow. And senior management, with their hands on our purse strings, look back at us incredulous at our line of questioning. It is just not that easy to resist the urge to grow, even if economic results look so so. The "super high quality thinkers" are our best guess of those firms whose shareholders could abdicate their right to trade stock (allocate capital themselves) sure in the knowledge that their capital will be well allocated for years to come within the businesses. This list is a group of wonderful, honestly run compounding machines. We call this the "terminal portfolio". This is where we want to go. The question is, why is this list not the same as the current Nomad portfolio?

This is not an easy question to answer. But let us return to the church analogy for a moment. When we think about companies, the over-riding analytical consideration is the quality of the business and quality of management's capital allocation decisions. <u>The longer investors own shares the more their outcome is linked to these two metrics.</u> What separates a corporate hero from a loon is an intellectually honest appraisal of business prospects, and armed with that knowledge an appropriate allocation of discretionary resources. There are only two reasons companies behave well. Because they want to, and because they have to. Our preference is to invest in those that want to. If we can find enough of these heavenly opportunities they will in effect put us out of a job, and you should be pleased with this happy outcome (even we will be pleased, if a little bored). The problem of course is price. In paying up for excellent businesses today, investors are already paying for many years growth to come, in the hope that, as the saying goes, "time is the friend of a good business".

We can all observe that stock prices, set in an auction market, are more volatile than business values. Several studies and casual observation reveal that individual prices oscillate widely around a central price year in year out, and for no apparent reason. Certainly, business values don't do this. Over time, this offers the prospect that any business, indeed all businesses, will be meaningfully mispriced. Even the mighty Berkshire Hathaway with its stalwart long-term shareholder base was demonstrably half priced in early 2000. And Marathon bought shares (unfortunately pre-Nomad inception). It is just a matter of time. Those that chase high prices today, leave less gunpowder for the future. In effect, they value future opportunities close to nil. So opportunity cost is partly behind our decision as well. Today, we have made two investments in wonderful compounding machines, and only one of those is meaningfully represented in the portfolio (Costco Wholesale). What is the probability that say, over the next ten years, a good portion of these "super high quality thinkers" will be priced at 50c? Our betting is that the odds are reasonable. Even though prices are generally high, the trick is to do the work today, so that we are ready.

Chapter 36

THE EQUITY YIELD CURVE

Our peers are trading shares at the short end of the equity yield curve where the competition is the greatest, and we are investing at the long end where competition is the least. We respond to completely different stimuli.
                                    - DECEMBER 31st, 2006

Main Points
- The equity yield curve is the concept that patience has a value and returns increase with time in the equity market as they do on a normal bond market yield curve.
- Nomad believes that business outcomes can be more predictable several years out than they are in the near term.

From the Partnership Letters: Equity Yield Curve

DECEMBER 31st, 2006

An Overview of the Partnership
Good investing is a minority sport, which means that in order to earn returns better than everyone else we need to be doing things different to the crowd. And

one of the things the crowd is not, is patient. Readers of our letters (there must be some) may be familiar with the notion of the equity yield curve, and our thoughts were covered in an interview for the Outstanding Investor Digest (reprints available upon request, do ask Amanda) a few years ago. (<u>In brief, the equity yield curve is a concept that argues that patience has a value, and that returns increase with time in the equity market as they do on a normal bond market yield curve).</u> In the bond market the higher yield is there to compensate for the increase in risk that the principal will not be repaid, or that the principal may be devalued by inflation. That is not how it works in the equity market: in our opinion business outcomes can be more predictable several years out than they are in the near term. For example, we have no idea where the market will end this year but given corporate strategies, capital allocation and starting valuations, I think we have some idea of how our companies will evolve over the next few years. In other words (at this point economics students may wish to cover their ears) the return from investing in shares can be both increased and de-risked by time.

There may be a blind spot in academia as the overwhelming methodology for research in Economics has been to take observations over short time periods, as if cause and effect sit on top of each other. Habits can take years to form. What, we wonder, would academics have to say of Coke's century long advertising program and the eventual establishment of the World's most valuable brand?

It is interesting to us that Nomad's performance by vintage bears evidence of the equity yield curve. Take the current portfolio: stocks held for over four years have superior annualized returns compared to those held for between three and four years, which have higher annualized returns compared to those held for two to three years and so on down to stocks purchased last year, which are a pretty mixed affair and contain several losses! The numbers are skewed by survivorship bias (no Conseco) but exclude stocks sold that have continued to do well (notably Stagecoach, which has risen ever since we sold it!). There is opportunity set bias in these numbers too ('02 may be a better year for making new investments than '06) but even so, the steepness of the curve (over 1000 basis points per annum) is cause for optimism, as it implies patience is rewarded.

It is with some interest that, on average and weighted by size of holding, the investments in the Partnership today are just over one year old. In other words, Nomad is a young portfolio, perhaps one fifth of the way through its normal life expectancy. The competition is so great that we have little advantage at the short end of the equity yield curve – after all the average holding period of US mutual funds is less than one year – and so one might expect current returns to be so-so. However, if the past is our guide and as the portfolio matures, its best years may yet lie ahead.

Our peers are trading shares at the short end of the equity yield curve where the competition is the greatest, and we are investing at the long end where competition is the least. We respond to completely different stimuli.

Chapter 37

INSTITUTIONAL DYSFUNCTIONALITY

Time will tell whether these investment institutions were right to sell but, if they turn out to be, it will be for the wrong reason: they did not make an investment decision, they sold because it was commercially expedient, and that may be to our great advantage.

- DECEMBER 31st, 2005

From the Partnership Letters: Institutional Dysfunctionality

DECEMBER 31st, 2005

A worked example of Current Institutional Dysfunctionality

Our returns over the next twenty years will, in part, be derived as a consequence of the failings of the institutions that dominate the markets. The good news is these companies are stuffed with internal rules and contradictions necessary for them to perform as businesses, but which foster the psychological mistakes mentioned above that compromise investment returns. Take an institutional favourite, liquidity (the number of shares of a company that trade on the stock market, crucially this is usually measured over a short time period). The institutional desire is to have high liquidity, it appears, so to lower the probability of being caught in a poorly performing share, and dare we say, having to explain that to clients and their agents (another strike for the principal agent conflict)! Being in the wrong stock strikes me as an analytical mistake, not a liquidity mistake (if there is such a thing) and hiding analytical mistakes through selling shares in my opinion borders on fraud. But even so, the point is that companies with poor liquidity can be sold by institutions because they have poor liquidity and regardless of price, and that creates opportunities for those less constrained. Take for example one of our holdings, Matichon Pcl, a Thai newspaper which we described in the first Nomad letter to Partners as follows :

> *"We do not read Thai and take it on trust from Thai friends that the editorial content is pro- reform, and it is certainly tabloid in style which sets it aside from Thailand's largest newspaper (Thai Rat) which is more "old Thailand". Matichon is probably not the Washington Post, but it's healthily questioning, nonetheless".*

Perhaps a little too *"healthily questioning"* as, in September last year, the firm was subject to a takeover attempt backed by, it is reported, the Thai Prime Minister, who had been regularly criticised in Matichon's pages! The offer was debt financed and orchestrated through another local media business which was making the bid. In the weeks before the attempted takeover we were approached by several other sizeable shareholders and asked if we wished to sell our shares in a block with theirs to the bidding party. We were a little surprised at the role reversal, as one might expect the bidding party to make the pitch, not one's fellow shareholders, and besides the price seemed low!

What could these other institutions be thinking? There had been no analytical mistake, we had all done quite well with our Matichon holdings, and yet as the stock had become increasingly illiquid (in part because we all owned so much of the company) one of our fellow shareholders confessed to us that there was a business pressure to sell, and it was for this reason they had called us. Just look at the psychological mistakes these institutions may be making, their thinking would appear to be as follows: the stock has risen in price so it is OK to sell (vivid evidence), our peers want to sell (social proof), therefore it must be OK for us to sell too (group psychology), there is a business reason to sell (principal agent conflict), the shares are illiquid (vivid evidence), we do not want to get stuck in an illiquid holding (impatience, more principal agent conflict and poor probability based thinking – highly priced shares are rarely illiquid!).

To our way of thinking in-market insiders buying on leverage are unlikely to provide the highest offer for our shares, and we declined on the grounds that the economics of buying looked good to us! But everyone else sold, except it seems Nomad, the company founder, allegedly the Thai Prime Minister and his associates, and other members of management. Following the institutional exit, the firm has begun a sizeable share repurchase program, not good for liquidity perhaps, but the repurchase program does imply a healthy compounding of value per share for the remaining owners. Time will tell whether these investment institutions were right to sell but, if they turn out to be, it will be for the wrong reason: they did not make an investment decision, they sold because it was commercially expedient, and that may be to our great advantage.

Chapter 38

NON-TRANSITIVE DICE & INVESTING

The prices the market sets reveals information about a company's prospects which may or may not provide an opportunity, it is up to investors to either take the market up on its offer, or wait for another price, another day.

- JUNE 30th, 2006

From the Partnership Letters

JUNE 30th, 2006

If a > b and b > c, then it would normally follow that a is also > c. This is a transitive sequence and is embedded deeply in our mental problem solving apparatus. It all seems quite logical. Non-transitive, or "magic", dice challenge this assumption. A set of magic dice contains four dice whose faces are labelled as follows:

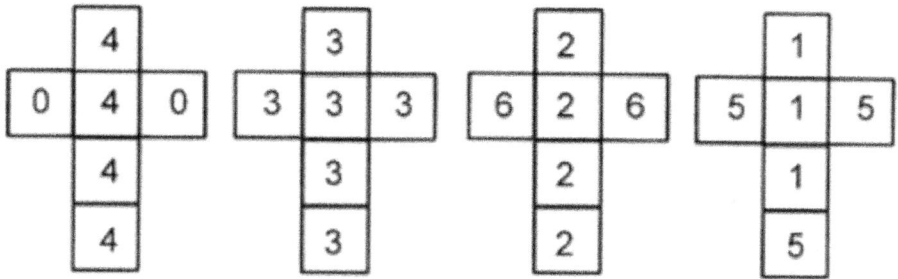

To play magic dice a host invites an opponent to choose one dice, which the opponent will roll against the host, the one with the highest number wins. The process is repeated and it's best out of ten. Some players might chose the dice with the numbers five or six, without observing the number's frequency. Others may reject the dice with zeros (surely that can't win a round?) without observing that the dice's four fours beat the number three dice two-thirds of the time. As displayed in the diagram above, the dice on the left beats the one on its right, and so on across the diagram, but the dice on the far right also beats the one of the far left! It would appear that if a > b and b > c that c is also > a!

Of course there is nothing magic about it, but at first the circularity appears counter- intuitive. A winning dice thrower must correctly assess the probability or frequency with which a dice will produce a superior number, after all a winning dice may not win on the first throw. And the dice thrower can only answer that question if first he knows what dice he is up against. The trick is to allow your opponent to unwittingly reveal some more information, and get him to pick a dice first!

Non-transitive dice offer two handy investment models: first, just as any dice can win for a while, so any superiority an investment process may have will only emerge with time, so patience is important. Second, the stock market posts prices every day, this is the equivalent of making your opponent chose his dice first. The prices the market sets reveals information about a company's prospects which may or may not provide an opportunity, it is up to investors to either take the market up on its offer, or wait for another price, another day.

Chapter 39

"SO, HOW DOES ZECKHAUSER PLAY BRIDGE?"

The right way to think is the way Zeckhauser plays bridge, it's just that simple.

- Charlie Munger

From the Partnership Letters

DECEMBER 31st, 2005

Speech given to the board of The Investment Fund for Foundations at the invitation of Mike Costa and David Salem, September 26th 2005, New York City.

In his brief for this talk, Mike asked me to talk about emerging markets. This may have something to do with my firms' track record of investing in emerging markets, principally south east Asia, but also serendipitously in places like South Africa and Mexico. When I sat down and started writing, I found that I had a lot to say. I tried to cut it down a little, but it lost something. Now if I was a great orator, like Bill Clinton, perhaps I could deliver my talk off the cuff and look cool and nonchalant? But the truth is I pick stocks for a vocation, and that puts me at the geek end of the spectrum: so if you will forgive me, for the most part I will read what I have to say. Some of this stuff is important and I want you to understand it.

In main established markets of the world our output, that is to say our track record, has been to beat the indices in almost all geographies, over almost all time frames by 4 to 500 basis points per annum. But if one burrows down to look at our experience in emerging markets it is much, much better than that. And that is a very interesting phenomenon. I mean how is it that three guys (Jeremy, Zak and myself) in a room in London, doing broadly what we do elsewhere in the world do much better in one territory than in the other? And how is it that we have done better than our peers with armies of analysts stationed in capitol cities throughout the region? I mean, how can this be? And how sustainable is it? And as you have money invested with us, I am sure you will want to know how sustainable it is too!

At this point I should probably explain something about my background. I studied Geography at Edinburgh University, Scotland. Geography is a subject that hardly exists in north America. A Harvard Professor once told me that they had a Geography course at Harvard but it had a reputation for homosexual lecturers and was closed down. I am not sure what to make of that particularly, I suspect it is not cause and effect, but at any rate Geography is a subject with an identity crisis – it is the confluence of geology, physics, chemistry, oceanography, climatology, biology and that is just physical geography. Human geography deals with sociology, psychology, statistics, economics – so it is the ultimate polymath course. Geography just reached in to other subjects and grabbed what it thought it had to have. Indeed the reason I studied Geography at all was because of this polymathic quality although I got there through an odd route…

I went to Edinburgh to study Geology, because that's where the best Geology course was, and in my first year I developed an interest in Architecture and IT but I was discouraged from studying these off subject courses by the Geology department who thought I ought to be doing the hard sciences, and so I transferred to Geography and began a dissertation of architecture and business parks! But because Geography is so broad, it claims little territory of its own, that's why Harvard closed it down, and at various times in its history the subject goes through identity crises. Because Geography is seen as an academic gate-crasher practitioners have had to ask themselves questions that other more homogenous subjects such as physics or chemistry have not.

And so at Edinburgh we spent a whole year on the philosophy and methodology of what we were doing, and that year opened my eyes. I just loved it.. I mean it really changed my thinking. And I was reading "Zen and the Art of Motorcycle Maintenance" by Robert Pirsig at the time, and the two just combined to change how I viewed the world. So I have this tendency to return to the basic questions. And what I am going to do here is talk about the philosophy and methodology of what we do as investors, and assess why performance is better in Asia as a logical subset of a much more important question, which is "what is your competitive advantage in investing?"

Bill Miller was asked that question recently and gave the following answer: there are broadly three advantages one may have: informational, analytical and psychological:

An informational advantage would be that I know a piece of information that the market does not, and that information has value. Nathaniel Rothschild built one of Europe's great banking fortunes that way. He had faster couriers and carrier pigeons than everyone else, and everyone knew that, and so he was first to market with the knowledge of the war won (or lost). And because everyone knew that he knew, it was hard for him to fail. That advantage is pretty much dissipated today. It is either illegal following insider trading and Reg FD like regulations, or the information is instantaneous and omnipresent. I have tried not to look, but I guess some of you will have checked your blackberries since I started talking?

The second is analytical, that is one can cut up the information everyone else has in a different way to arrive at different conclusions. Lets see what Wittgenstein had to say on the subject. **Slide 2.** Wittgenstein's point is the description you use, will frame how you think? So is it a coat hanger or a door wedge? If someone described it to you as a piece of cheese, you would think about it differently than if they had told it was a mountain, or a pyramid that's fallen over. The point is that perceptions change as descriptions change – and they change independent of the facts. My favourite example here is the way advertising and marketing budgets are treated in public accounts. That is they are expensed as a debit to earnings. Because the accountants have this sound overriding bias to draw up accounts with reference to conservative values, and don't know how to capitalise it, its valued at nil. Estee Lauder has a huge advertising and marketing budget which dominates its profits statements. So much so that the residual cash flow that drops down to the profits of the business is almost a rounding error on the larger amount. But its that little residual that the markets use to value the company.

Slide 2:

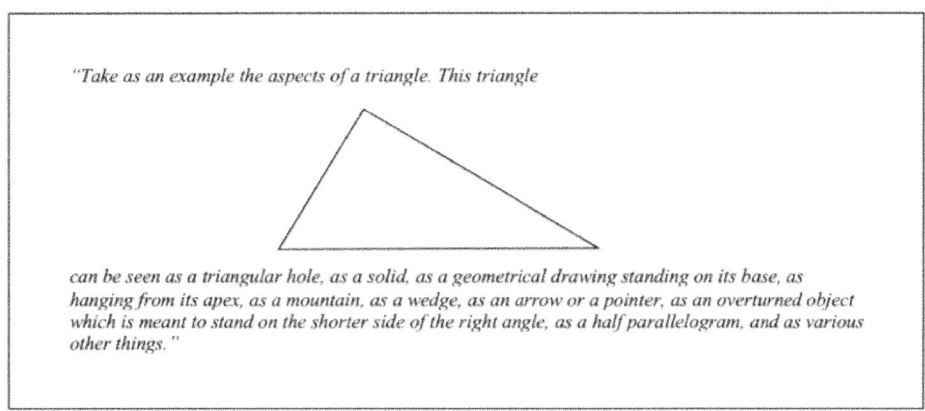

Source: Ludwig Wittgenstein, Philosophical Investigations

In the case of the Estee Lauder Company the share price fell! when they announced a rise in the ad spend. In other words the market viewed "all costs as bad costs" – well they had to have been buying something with the money! And so the question is: what have Estee Lauder bought with that advertising budget? Ditto Nike, Coke or one of our investments, Scotts Miracle Grow. And this factor goes on again and again. And it can be applied to other expensed investment spending such as R&D. So we do a fair amount of turning numbers around, looking at things no one else looks at, such as share of voice versus share of market, which is a way of assessing advertising spend, we assess customer loyalty, we covering up the name of the company and analyse the business and so on.

You have to array the information in such a way as to be able to properly weigh its value, and that is not always the same way the accountants use. And I think we have some analytical advantage in that compared to the crowd. But I like it most when it is combined with the final source of competitive advantage and those are…

Behavioural and psychological. At this stage my talk could turn into a variant of Charlie Munger's "Psychology of Human Misjudgement" speech given at the Harvard Law School in the mid 1990s and which is the finest investment speech ever given. Not that he talked directly about investments. And that tells you something. But the most enduring advantages are psychological. And the trick here is to first understand them. And then train yourself out of them!

Well the list here is just so many: over-confidence, incentives, commitment and consistency tendency, deprival super-reaction, anchoring, jealousy/envy, I could go on and on, and Charlie had 24! But what I will do here is focus on four that I think lead to more misjudgements than most, especially when they combine with each other.

First, Social Proof/Group psychology. Well we all know something about the dysfunctionality of group based decision making, you've got one guy leading the debate, he's the authority figure, he suggests a course of action, everyone anchors off that suggestion, maybe bonus time is looming so no one wants to object. You are all aware that a competitor across the road has just taken the same course of action. And nobody objected. Social Proof. And of course it's a perfect disaster. We all know that social decisions can be suboptimal, but even so, that is how most decisions are made… At least on the boards of public companies and investment firms I know.

Slide 3. This is a chance to bring in one of my favourite cartoons which was carried in the book "Influence: The Psychology of Persuasion" by Bob Cialdini. I can't look at this cartoon without seeing that angel as a metaphor for the investment management industry. We sit at the top of the capitalist pyramid, collecting our rent from the layers below, and we should be thinking differently from the crowd. We should behave with some integrity. But what is the angel doing? ...I was at a Santa Fe Institute meeting the other day, and Jim Surowiecki the author of "the Wisdom of Crowds" told me that Stanley Milgram actually performed this as an experiment. And what he found was, as the size of the crowd increased, so the proportion of passers-by that stopped and looked up, at nothing, increased too. I have not seen the study but I bet the relationship wasn't linear. That it had these step functions to it. No one stops if there's just one guy standing there, but perhaps a group of three would get some passers by looking up...and by the time it's a big group almost everyone is stopping...anyhow, that's the way it works in the markets...

Slide 3: The Punch Cartoon

In Cialdini's book he talks about the unhappy case of Kitty Genovese who was slowly murdered whilst people just stood by watching each other? And because no one was running to her aid no one else did?

And how many people bought tech stocks in 1999 because everyone else was?

How else do you explain how you get these waves of massive overinvestment such as occurred in the Thai cement industry in the mid 1990s. In my opinion what happens is once one company starts building they all do through fear of missing out. Once Siam Cement had built all the capacity Thailand could need there was no need for Siam City Cement to join in. Let alone TPI Polene. But they all went mad. Combine social proof with envy jealousy, and financial incentives and boom, there you go.

My second source of misjudgement is availability, or the tendency to overweight the vivid evidence or the evidence easily obtained. Here my favourite example is given by Dick Thaler, who runs an investment company and teaches behavioural finance at the Chicago School of Business. And Dick uses a short video clip of 20 seconds or so, which shows three people dressed in white and three people dressed in back. And each team passes a ball between them whilst moving around the floor. And Dick asks, count the number of passes made by the white team. At the end he asks the audience how many passes they observed. 18? A few hands. 19? More hands. 20 and so on. It is interesting that we cant all agree on that! That tells you something. Then he asks did anybody see anything else? Now I have seen this done a few times now and in only one class did someone spot what actually happened. Dick asks, did anyone see a man dressed in a gorilla suit walk into the middle of the screen beat his chest and walk off?! Almost no one sees this.

Well we all do this to some extent. We tend to look hard at the task in hand and miss the bigger picture. Looking around you is the most important skill, and is largely innate, although Prof. John Stilgoe who is also at Harvard is trying to teach it and wrote an interesting book recently entitled "Outside Lies Magic". And in the markets investors tend to latch on to what can be measured, aided by the accountants as we discussed just now and to some extent by their own laziness.

The adage that "if its in the headlines its in the price" is very largely correct. I mean who would want to put up with this. **Slide 4**. There are over 640,000 headlines under Xerox and bankruptcy on Google! I know investors that screen for that by the way, but there are not too many people that want to own the most despised company in the market, which any Joe on the street that reads a newspaper knows is in some kind of trouble, as anyone who has owned Asia at the pit, or Xerox, Lucent and Primedia these last few years will know.

Slide 4

My third misjudgement is from an inability to perform probability based thinking. In one of Charlie Munger's talks he makes the statement "the right way to think is the way Zeckhauser plays bridge, its just that simple". Well, to a young man in London that is a very infuriating statement. I mean, who is Zeckhauser, and how does he play bridge? Well it took me about a year to track down Richard Zeckhauser and answer that question.

He was world bridge champion in '66 and runs a brilliant Behavioural Finance course at the Kennedy School of Government at Harvard. And the reason that his course is at the Kennedy School at all is very interesting. I mean what is a Behavioural Finance course doing at a "School of Government" in the first place? Well, the reason is that his course was rejected by the deans of the economics department who claimed it was not economics. Instead he took the course to the Kennedy School where it has been held ever since.

Zeckhauser's split with the economists' view of the world is their reliance on a rational utility-maximising framework. The old guard are hostile to assertions of non-rational behaviour, I mean the idea that we are all rational is just so beautiful, as I'm sure Ayn Rand would agree. Well this does not sit easily with the psychologists' view of the world that there are systematic biases to individual decisions – that is we have these little wobbles in our decision making processes. Or a biologist's view of the world that individuals act in self-interest, make mistakes, learn and evolve. Well Brian Arthur at the Santa Fe Institute refers to the economy as a complex adaptive system that learns as agents learn. And that seems like a way better model to me...

So, Behavioural Finance takes a pragmatic, multidisciplinary approach (a little like Geography!) and puts the rational economists' view of the world together with that of the psychologist and biologist. After all how can economics not be behavioural – who is making the decisions after all?

It is my personal opinion that the thinking presented by Zeckhauser, and at the Santa Fe Institute should be thought of as the new economics in waiting, but it will likely only become mainstream consensus once the old guard has died off. The fact that these courses are still considered Moonie conventions and are rejected by the Harvard economics department shows how far away establishment, consensus thinking is. I am aware of only one large fund management organisation that has internalised these ideas and when Zak and I joined the Santa Fe Institute last year we represented only the second European investment company to do so.

And even we have trouble getting these ideas adopted – there is a tendency for people to say "thanks Nick, that behavioural finance stuff was really great", but then they go back to their desks and carry on as they did before. Articulating this stuff is easy, internalising it is not. That's the hard work. Einstein's theory that space and time were relative had already been thought of by Lorenz. But what Einstein did was put it central to everything – whilst everyone else kept the concept peripheral. And it changed the word. That's how behaviour finance should be used. But it probably wont...Murray Gell-Mann at the Santa Fe Institute is fond of saying "one scientist would rather use another's toothbrush than his nomenclature". But those that can adopt these ideas will be streaks ahead of the competition in my opinion. But I'll come to that later.

So, anyhow, how does Zeckhauser play bridge? Well he thinks via decision trees and attaches probabilities to the various branches. And as the facts change, change the probabilities. Now I've been droning on a bit, so let me say it again, because its key...Zeckhauser thinks via decision trees and attaches probabilities to the various branches. And when you are dealing with probabilities you can be indifferent to gain or loss outcomes, but that's normally a trained response. And when you are dealing with probabilities, and the vast expanse of opportunities such as the global stock and bond markets, you don't have to be too conservative with your bets.

But people don't think well with probabilities. This was famously demonstrated in the Monty Hall problem, named after the host of a 1970s game show "Lets make a deal". The contestant chooses one of three doors. One contains the keys to a car and the other two a picture of a goat. The choice made, Monty opens one of the two other doors, and the rules of the game require him to show you a goat. The question is should the guest switch to the remaining closed door? And why? When this problem was posed in the New York Times they received 10,000 letters insisting that the wrong answer was right! I mean the mind is not naturally arranged in a way to answer probability based questions. It is not instinctive.

I'll give you another example. One person in a 1000 suffers from a particular disease. Your friend tests positive for the disease with a 99% probability that the test is accurate. What is the chance that your friend has the disease? The answer is one in eleven, but according to surveys that's not what most doctors think!

They think your friend is toast! – well the chances are he isn't! It takes just a little thinking through. And this is why they test for dreadful diseases like HIV twice, because the tests aren't that accurate and doctors aren't good at maths! So an inability to think like Zeckhauser and arrange outcomes in probabilities is a considerable error causing bias in investors decision making processes. It is interesting that this was essentially the central message in Rob Rubin's autobiography and Buffett's Chairman's statement this year.

So for example the biggest mistake an investor can make is to sell a stock that goes on to rise ten fold! Its not from owning something into bankruptcy. But that's what everyone thinks, at least judging by the questions we get from clients. Only last week we got questions about our holding in Northwest Airlines rather than the sale of Apple earlier this year. But selling Apple has cost us more. People look at actual costs, not opportunity costs, and what did we say about over-weighing the vivid evidence? And if you understand that, and you understand probabilities, then you'll know Northwest wasn't worth calling us about.

My last psychological hurdle is patience, or the lack thereof. At the beginning of the AGM of the Berkshire Hathaway Company they show this little video and each year Buffett is asked what's the main difference between himself and the average investor, and he answers patience. And there is so little of it about these days. Has anyone heard of getting rich slowly?

What is it Jack Bogle tells us? That the holding period for stocks is down to 10 months and the average mutual fund is held for 2 years? What's that all about? In my opinion quarterly reporting borders on an obsessive compulsive disorder. And how did we get to this state of affairs?

Well I think that the problem is you get two agents – the fund manager, and his immediate client – and they try to eek out some value added in the mind of their clients and it creates these counter productive consequences. You would never get this level of reporting nonsense if it was on a principal to principal basis! And who is to blame? Well I side against the investment institutions. These are largely rich organisations and should behave with integrity, not bow to dysfunctional requests. Behaving like Molly Malone and flashing your knickers at the boys on a Dublin Friday night is not the right way to build a lasting reputation, but that's how these institutions behave.

And it is so unnecessary: we own the only permanent capital in a company's capital structure – everything else in the company, management, assets, board, employees can change but our equity can still be there! Institutional investors have never really reconciled their ability to trade daily with the permanence of equity. I mean are they long term or short term? Zak told me a joke I really enjoyed: two hedge fund managers meet at a cocktail party and one asks "how are you?" – and the other replies "yeah, I'm up 3% this month". Good investment process is not apparent in one quarter's worth of transient stock price quotations, or one year for that matter!

In a small investment partnership that I run we make people sign a form saying they understand that the fund is not suitable for those with time frames less than five years. No one else does that. We make them do it by the way, to try and put the investment in a different psychic space than other savings they may have. And to avoid the pressures of social proof and jealousy/envy I mentioned earlier. Incidentally we have average holding periods well over five years as judged by recent results.

So, patience, social proof, vividness and probability based thinking are the four psychological hurdles I have chosen to highlight and I think we understand these perhaps a little better than the average investor out there...and, I'm not always sure about that. I certainly blew Argentina three years ago, mainly due to over-weighing the vivid evidence - especially the temporary vivid evidence - and that has cost us. I mean, you think you understand this stuff, but you have to keep at it...

But if so, so what? What does all this have to do with our emerging market performance.

Well lets go through some of these psychological misjudgements from an Asian perspective: Well, the Asian emerging markets are Chinese, even in Thailand, Indonesia, the Philippines and Malaysia, which have large indigenous populations, the business elite is Chinese. And the Chinese like to gamble – one of our largest investments is in an old Malaysian casino and its chocked with Malaysian Chinese from KL on a week day, and you should see it at the weekend! - well that does not sound like "patient money" to me. And what have we just learned, that patience matters.

There is very high social cohesion to Asian societies. That is people think alike, and they think literally. This is true in the west, but I think it is probably more true in the east as eastern societies tend not to celebrate the individual to the extent we do in the west. So social proof and herd mentality may be more acute. That is, contrarian thinking seems to be more rare. And at the trough things are very, very cheap.

There may also be a foreign angle to the cheapness too. Most of our competition comes from regional specialists – these people suffer from the same restrictions that tech fund managers suffered in 1999 – they have no where else to go. When they are given funds to manage the covert instruction is to buy growth, not value. The vivid evidence is that Asia is growing – just look at China!

And they have a principal/agent conflict. That's Zeckhauser's other pet subject, the principal agent conflict. They have set up offices in every capitol city as if in a marketing exercise to assert local expertise – well its all there on the Bloomberg, at the end of a phone line and in annual accounts. You don't need local correspondents as well. And you certainly don't need the drift into group decision making that implies.

So the foreigners in the region typically think like bullish agents, but that is not how the main shareholders think! the families that control Asian companies view is not the institutional agent capitalism we grow up with in the west (and the self promotion that goes with that) – its dynastic, confusion capitalism - that is they think like principals. So in Asia there is this huge dispersion in orientation, between the Chinese gambling mentality of the masses and the tycoons dynastic orientation. The way to bet is not to align yourself with the market patsy, but to think like the tycoons – and our long holding period helps in that regard – back to patience.

In my opinion there is a "false asset class" element to demand for investment product in the region, and this has bred "fake specialisation" in my peers. I mean they know the shape of the economy, but they don't know what a company is worth. Westerners do not invest in Asia to be contrarian! The point is that specialising by geography is not the same thing as specialising in investing.

And we try to specialise in investing. So we don't sell dedicated funds, and we don't go marketing Asian specialisation and when things are unattractive we go looking elsewhere on the planet, and I think that helps. We don't have to be there. Our generalisation by geography and specialisation by discipline is a huge help.

We are trying to be people of good judgement and do intelligent things with money. And so we go to Asia looking for businesses that fit our experience of being in situations that will work, at prices we like. But few people start with that bias. Our peers seem not to be looking at what we are looking at. Like Siam Cement or Jardine Matheson for example, these are huge businesses (JM is the largest private employer in the region, and SCC represented 4% of the Thai economy at one point) and they were priced at sizeable discounts to replacement cost, with better than replacement cost normalised economics, and they have been ten baggers for us. You could not look at Asia and not see these companies. They dominate.

But the point is our performance is better because there is less competition for our shares. Period. And that's because there are less people with our approach. We have found that when we are buying shares our competition is the trade buyer who cannot negotiate 100% of the company at the price at which we can buy a fraction on the stock market. Take a look at Siam City Cement. The day Holderbank bought control of the company, from the family, for Tb170 per share, which equated to replacement cost of the assets – the stock that day close up one baht to Tb48 – less than one third of what the trade buyers were paying. That stock has risen ten fold since.

Well, is this sustainable? Perhaps not, what is it Brian Arthur at the Santa Fe Institute tells us: that people learn and the economy is adaptive. It seems reasonable to expect that over time that advantage will may diminish. As Buffett joked at one AGM – "the secret to a successful marriage is not looks or money...its low expectations". And I think that is a healthy starting point when thinking about our emerging market performance.

However, it is true to say that some of the behavioural traits I have mentioned here are as old as the stars and were as valid when Graham wrote the first edition of Security Analysis in 1934 as it is today. Even so, and whilst I recognise that fact, I think it is healthy to think in evolutionary terms and to plan to stay ahead, and we have some clues to where the leading edge in investment thought is going. Let me read you what Mike Mauboussin at Legg Mason, who is streets ahead, had to say on the subject of decision making:

Slide 5

"Individuals who achieve the most satisfactory long-term results across various probabilistic fields (gambling, cards, horses, investing in common stocks, investing in a new plant) have more in common with one another than they do with participants in their own field."

Slide 5

> - *"Individuals who achieve the most satisfactory long-term results across various probabilistic fields have more in common with one another than they do with participants in their own field."*
> - *"Distinguishing features of probabilistic players include a focus on process versus outcome, a constant search for favourable odds and an understanding of the role of time."*
> - *"Success in a probabilistic field requires weighing probabilities and outcomes – that is an expected value mindset."*
> - *"One key to success is a high degree of awareness of the factors that distort judgement."*

Source: Michael Mauboussin, Legg Mason Funds Management

Well that just has to be true. Amarillo Slim was the world poker champion in 1972, and his autobiography was published last year into the new poker boom, and is entitled "Amarillo Slim, in a world of fat people" – and if you understand Michael's point, you can see why Slim called his book that. Puggy Pearson was also a world card champion, and he argued that to win you needed to understand the 60/40 end of the bet (when the odds are on your side), know money management (how much to bet), and know yourself. Well that sounds awfully like good investment decision making to me.

Mauboussin again...

> *"Distinguishing features of probabilistic players include a focus on process versus outcome (I hope I have done some of that today), a constant search for favourable odds and an understanding of the role of time."*

That is Patience.

It is still amazing to me that everyone assesses a fund manager on his output, not his process. They don't admit that of course. But that's what happens.

> *"Success in a probabilistic field requires weighing probabilities and outcomes – that is an expected value mindset."*

Well...think like Zeckhauser.

I'll let Mauboussin have the last word...

"One key to success is a high degree of awareness of the factors that distort judgement". Well, amen to that.

And now I will take any questions you may have…

Slide 1: Speech Title "So how does Zeckhauser play bridge?"
Slide 6: Final slide, "The right way to think is the way Zeckhauser plays bridge, it's just that simple" Charlie Munger.

Chapter 40

DESTINATION ANALYSIS

Destination analysis is consciously central to how we analyse businesses these days. It helps us ask better questions and get to a firm's DNA.
- DECEMBER 31st, 2007

Main Points
- Destination Analysis: how Nomad analyzed businesses with a focus on where a company was headed, as this helped them ask better questions to understand the firm's DNA
- Questions include:
    - What is the intended destination for this business in 10 or 20 years?
    - What should management be doing today to raise the probability of arriving at that destination?
    - What could prevent the company from reaching its favorable destination?
- Focus on questions provided insights with a long shelf life.

From the Partnership Letters: Destination Analysis

DECEMBER 31st, 2007

Destination analysis is consciously central to how we analyse businesses these days. It helps us ask better questions and get to a firm's DNA. What we learnt at Conseco may well have kept us out of the US banks last year, and what we learnt at Stagecoach has helped us continue to own Amazon. These two benefits have been a combined gain in the order of U$60m during 2007 to investors in Nomad. The maths behind this assumption is a little finger-in-the-air and is unadjusted for subscriptions post mistakes, but it is directionally correct and implies that a large proportion of Nomad's performance in 2007 came from the lessons learnt from mistakes in 2003 and 2004. Think of it as a return on prior year losses. And that is just one year's gain. If we have really learnt our lesson, then the gains will continue in future years too. In the meantime, we continue to bear down on denial and ego too!

Let's invert for a moment: when we think of our investee companies, the firms which we would quite happily own with no word from them for years are those businesses in which we have the highest confidence of reaching a favourable destination: they are the firms we think we know will work. They are also the largest holdings in Nomad. It is the less certain businesses about which we are more insecure that appear to demand more regular attention.

DECEMBER 31st, 2011

The simple deep reality for many of our firms is the virtuous spiral established when companies keep costs down, margins low and in doing so share their growing scale with their customers. In the long run this will be more important in determining the destination for our firms than the distractions of the day.

Part II

Case Study #1

International Speedway (2002)

From the Partnership Letters

JANUARY 18th, 2002

International Speedway (approx 3.7% of the portfolio at year end) owns and operates 12 motor racing circuits in the US including Daytona, Watkin's Glen and Talladega, and plays host to 20 of the 39 Nascar races. The National Association for Stock Car Auto Racing (Nascar) was founded in 1948 by Bill France who had organised motor races at Daytona Beach in the period before the war. During the war the beach circuit fell into disrepair and so on his return France set about renting local circuits to host races, but he felt that the sport really required a sanctioning body to set common standards for competitors and track safety (a relative rarity at the time) to lift its image from its moonshine legacy. After the American Automobile Association refused to endorse his idea France established Nascar himself, and was announced its first president in 1948. From the beginning France intended Nascar to be exciting and publically accessible, as well as sponsor friendly, and the formula evolved toward big fields of very fast cars (200mph+) on banked circuits surrounded by large atmospheric stadia.

Until quite recently motor racing has been a very fragmented sport: sanctioning bodies have tended to splinter into rival factions which form their own leagues, and the race tracks have developed on an ad hoc basis (some were originally perimeter roads to local airstrips) and remained under family ownership. Formula One with its dominant sanctioning body and almost totalitarian leadership under Bernie Ecclestone is both the exception, and due to its huge commercial success, the benchmark. International Speedway has grown through building and buying circuits throughout the south east and more recently elsewhere in the US. But the real prize from consolidation is that the firm has substantially improved its bargaining position with the broadcasting companies. Instead of their being more tracks and sanctioning bodies than media buyers, the tables have now been reversed. The attraction to advertisers is that Nascar runs races most weekends (good for filling programming schedules), is US only (unlike Formula One) and attracts middle America in droves. When the industry recently negotiated an exclusive seven year media rights contract the rate doubled in year one, and for the period to 2007 are contracted to rise by a further 17% per annum. Whilst this is promising in itself such events are quickly discounted by the markets, and the shares rose to a peak at US$70 two years ago.

Our interest is in how the windfall is being distributed: the France family (which owns Nascar) will take 10%, note this sum compares with much closer to 100% for Mr. Ecclestone's take of Formula One revenues, 65% is divided between the tracks (of which ISCA earns the lion's share), and 25% goes in prize money to the drivers and teams. This final point may be important because as prize money increases it may establish a virtuous cycle of new entrants attracted by the increased "pot", which in turn may raise viewing audiences and media attention. It is encouraging that the Chrysler racing team have recently announced their return to Nascar after a multiyear absence. In other words the firm may be deferring part of the windfall to fund future growth, which will be incremental to the escalating media income.

The price of ISCA shares at the time of Nomad's investment (around half their peak level) was a small premium to replacement cost of the circuits and a valuation which discounted only low single digit growth in profits. Cash flow growth will likely be cyclically subdued in the near term and investors with a short term time horizon, which appears to us to be the majority of professional investors, will have little to excite them. This is fine by us, because the outlook for the next five to ten years is very positive. Finally, how do CBS and Fox feel about their new Nascar contracts? They claim they are very encouraged, they now have to negotiate with one party to fill 40 weekend programming schedules and viewing audiences have exceeded their budgeted projections. Fox has recently bought a dedicated motorsport cable channel to host their Nascar coverage. Roll on contract negotiation in 2006! In discounting growth of just 3% to 4% the market valued the business as if it was just an average firm, when in our opinion International Speedway is a rock solid franchise with improving economics and could be a multiyear winner for investors that are patient enough to wait.

Case Study #2

Matichon (2002)

From the Partnership Letters

JANUARY 18th, 2002

Matichon (3.2% of fund at year end) is Thailand's second Thai language newspaper and is a company we have known for many years and in which Marathon is also the third largest shareholder. We do not read Thai and take it on trust from Thai friends that the editorial content is pro-reform and it is certainly tabloid in style which sets it aside from Thailand's largest newspaper (Thai Rat) which is more "old Thailand". Matichon is probably not the Washington Post, but it's healthily questioning nonetheless. The paper appeals to the new generation of Thais that have grown up with a much higher living standards and more western values than their parents and it is interesting that circulation has grown at an accelerated rate since the Asian crisis. The firm is family run and has avoided the pitfalls of straying into new media or gambling on new titles. Instead the firm has focused on raising longer term readership and margins. In an effort to promote circulation the cover price has been kept low but this has the effect that the majority of revenues comes from advertising which is far more cyclical and means that revenues declined by a third peak to trough. The cost cutting effort however has been amazing, with the effect that cash flow in 2000 is 40% higher than 1996, on sales one third less! 2000 is the first year of a cyclical recovery in advertising, and rates are now 20% above their trough but around 50% below the previous cyclical peak. In other words there may be a long way to go.

So, what is Matichon worth? The shares peaked at Tb300 (U$12) in 1994 and have now declined to Tb50 (U$1, adjusting for the decline in the currency). The share price decline is all the more amazing as the firm is without debt. Our company is presently valued at 0.75x revenues or four times our estimate of normalised free cash flow. This is approx one third of our estimate of its worth, and may be as low as one quarter of the valuation of its western peers. The family owns 25% of the shares and has taken the gains from cost cutting to raise the dividend three fold since the trough, and so investors now have a 9% dividend yield whilst they wait for the cycle to improve. And improve slowly it is, rates are expected to rise gently this year and next, so patience is likely to be rewarded here too.

Case Study #3

Xerox (2002)

From the Partnership Letters

JUNE 30th, 2002

In this edition I thought we might discuss an investment you are likely to have read about in the press, Xerox Corporation, and an error in analysis, Monsanto Company, which we sold. That way you will be under no illusion about the fallibility of your manager.

Xerox will be familiar to many as the manufacturer of presses, copiers and printers. The firm has annual revenues of U$17bn and a niche in high end (U$100,000+) printers where the firm has around 70% market share. It is a reasonably profitable but modest growth operation. The firm enjoyed several good years in the early and mid 1990s following the introduction of a new generation of machines but by the late 1990s growth had declined markedly. Perhaps aware that Wall Street rewarded earnings growth above all other metrics, management asserted that earnings per share would rise by 15% per annum and the shares began to rise to discount the near certainty they would. However 15% growth in earnings is tricky to achieve for any length of time especially from a 5% revenue growth business and management began, and indeed was egged on by Wall Street, to find growth from an alternative source.

In a cartoon carried in the Wall Street Journal two accountants sit opposite each other in a prison cell. You know, one says to the other, in accounting it is best to think inside the box! Xerox management would have done well to read this cartoon in 1996 or 1997 as it was about that time that management began to push too hard to grow earnings. One of the ways this was achieved was through booking profits from long term lease contracts upfront. It is quite possible, indeed likely, that one could have a happy and successful life without knowing about lease and sale accounting, so if the topic bores you, skip the next paragraph.

For everyone else, welcome to the Statement of Financial Accounting Standards No. 13 "Accounting for Leases". We will try to be brief. There are two types of leases, operating and sale-type. Under an operating lease a lessee rents an item for a short period and the total rent payments are usually a fraction of the value of the rented item. Car rental contracts are usually of this type. The difference between an operating lease and a sale-type lease is a matter of scale. A sale-type lease is usually for a much longer period and in effect transfers a much larger portion of the economic value of the asset to the lessee, a contract for the use of an airplane for the rest of its economic life would be a sale-type lease. The former is rental contract, the latter more of a sale. Now for the accounting. The accountants differentiate between the two using SFAS 13 which states that that contracts which transfer 75% or more of the economic life of the leased asset, or where minimum lease payments are 90% or greater than the fair value of the asset, be treated as a sale-type lease, with lesser values treated as an operating lease. The crucial difference is how they are recorded in the accounts. Sale-type leases require the leased asset to be booked as if sold outright, in effect bringing forward revenues and profits. In contrast, payments under an operating lease are booked incrementally over the lease term. It is important to note that whether a transaction is deemed an operating lease or a sale-type lease, cash flow is unaffected. The customer still pays the rental as required, it is only the accounting that implies something else has happened.

When Xerox leases an expensive printer it is often in the form of a five year contract which bundles equipment, a service contract and financing. However, in a bundled contract there is some discretion as to how much is attributable to the value of the equipment and how much should be deferred to later years in recognition of financing, maintenance and service. One can therefore understand how management, plump with stock options and growth in earnings per share related bonuses, were strongly incented to recognise earnings up front and SFAS 13 allowed them to do this. The value of the equipment was incorrectly raised relative to service, financing and maintenance which allowed the firm to treat the transaction as a sale-type lease and required that the inflated equipment value be booked as if sold. A double whammy of inflated revenues and profits recognised early. This does not appear to be illegal, although it is hardly conservative. It may even have mattered less if Xerox had not relied upon the commercial paper market to fund its receivables business. When the company announced that earnings would be below Wall Street expectations, the SEC announced an investigation into the firm's accounting and the auditors were replaced, the result was that the credit markets all but closed to the firm, and the shares declined to 7% of their peak price.

It is important to put this in perspective. In the five years to 2001, cumulative revenues at Xerox approached U$90bn, of which U$6.4bn was incorrectly booked. Cash flow and free cash flow, the basis of our valuation of the firm, is completely unaffected. Customers continued to pay their bills monthly as arranged. Operating blunders associated with product extensions, again designed to raise the growth rate, have been reversed and investment in research and development maintained at around U$1bn per annum regardless of the turmoil all around. Earlier this year the firm completed negotiations with its banks to repay the debts over the next few years in easily digested increments that should be funded from internally generated cash flow and U$1.8bn of cash on hand. The operating turnaround is now well under way, and a new product cycle, in some lines the first new products for ten years, will see products launched at twice the rate of the late 1990s. Even after new auditors have been appointed the debate about the accounting continues. It is with some irony that the replaced accountants protest that Xerox's profit is now understated. Xerox might be alone in corporate America in this regard. And, as if to prove that truth is stranger than fiction, the new accounting methodology will result in higher revenues and profits over the next few years than under the previous discredited policy. This matters not a jot to us, note again: cash flow is unchanged.

So what is the business worth? The firm has around US$1bn in free cash flow per annum after interest, taxes and maintenance levels of investment spending (capex, marketing and R&D) which should permit the net debt of around US$2bn (US$17bn of total debts are offset against US$15bn of trade and long term receivables and cash) to be repaid over the next few years. Indeed, if the apple cart is to be upset, it is likely to come from a dilutive share issuance, something we are lobbying management to resist, hopefully more effectively than the bankers who are egging them on. The current market valuation of US$4.5bn is just four and a half years free cash flow or four and a half years research and development spending. We estimate the capitalised value of the R&D asset may be around US$7bn or approximately 50% more than the current market capitalisation. As a cash cow the firm may be worth around US$14 per share in our opinion, although the increase in new product launches from two per annum to four per annum during the next three years may result in modest growth as well. Presently the firm is valued at US$6 per share, less than half our appraisal of its real worth. Trading volume of Xerox stock implies investors own the shares for under four months on average, a time horizon which implies few investors are focused on the long term value of the business but rather are betting on the next quarter's outcome. Rich pickings, we suspect, for the patient.

Case Study #4

Monsanto (2002)

From the Partnership Letters

JUNE 30th, 2002

Now for our analytical error. Monsanto manufactures and markets genetically modified seeds and fertilizers and is a business with good economics, good growth potential, good management and a low share price. It is right up Nomad's street. However, it is also a business with a past. In the mid 1990s Monsanto consisted of the seed business, a commodity chemical business (Solutia) and the G.D. Searle drug operations. In 1997 Solutia was spun off to shareholders in Monsanto and early in 2000 Pharmacia Corp bought the remaining Monsanto operations, before spinning out the seed business in order to retain the Searle drug business. The wrinkle however comes in the form of potential environmental clean up costs and punitive damages relating to Solutia's PCB plant in Alabama. Solutia's own balance sheet is encumbered with healthcare liabilities and debt and any award which cannot be met by Solutia passes on to the parent company, in this case Pharmacia. However, and here is the catch, Monsanto has indemnified Pharmacia for any environmental or punitive damages incurred as a result of Solutia's operations. We do not know if any, or indeed the size of any damages that may be awarded, and legal council cannot ascertain where an award would rank in the list of creditors in the event of Solutia's bankruptcy. This means we do not know how much, if any, of the liabilities would revert to Monsanto. What we are aware of is that value for us, the Monsanto shareholder, may be decided by a judge in an Alabama court, and on that basis we are nervous. In our original analysis we missed the indemnification and it was only on reading recent company filings with the SEC that the indemnification buried in the notes to the accounts came to our attention. The effect is that we are no longer confident of valuing Monsanto with any certainty and the prudent thing to do was to sell our shares for approximately the price we had paid. We have indeed been fortunate as the shares have since declined to half our sale price.

Case Study #5

Stagecoach (2002)

From the Partnership Letters

DECEMBER 31st, 2002

In previous letters and Global Investment Reviews we have discussed the investment case for Saks, International Speedway, Matichon, Xerox, Hong Kong and Shanghai Hotels, Conseco (augh!), Kersaf, and one of our sales Monsanto. That's approximately 30% of the portfolio covered. This time I would like to discuss our investment in Stagecoach (8.6% of Partnership assets) and Costco Wholesale (3.1% of Partnership assets).

Stagecoach is the largest bus operating company in the UK, operates the commuter train services from London's Waterloo station, and bus services in Scandinavia, Hong Kong, New Zealand and the US. The firm was listed in London when shares were sold to the public at 20p in 1993. In the early 1990s and after years of national ownership, the UK bus system was deregulated with the right to operate services, depots and buses sold in auction to private companies such as Stagecoach. The system was ripe for an overhaul, buses were poorly time-tabled and run for the convenience of the driver and conductor rather than the passengers and fares irregularly collected. Brian Souter, Stagecoach's entrepreneurial and straight-talking CEO, started his career as a bus conductor and was good at doing the simple things right, such as
collecting fares, putting on more buses during the rush hour, handing out mugs and flags to passengers on new services, painting buses bright colours and most

of all undercutting the remaining state owned competition. Bus deregulation proved to be a huge success in the UK as passenger numbers grew, and was copied abroad with the result that Stagecoach had a natural advantage exporting its brand of deregulated bus services. By 1996 as the firm developed businesses in Scandinavia, Hong Kong and parts of Africa, and within ten years of listing revenues and profits grew ten-fold and the share price reached a peak of £2.85 in 1998. One City research note struggled with the price of the shares at the time but concluded a "Souter premium" might be appropriate! Souter went into semi-retirement in the late 1990s as one of the richest men in Britain and handed day to day operations to the next generation of management, apparently leaving them with instruction to maintain the dividend.

It was about the same time that the problems started. It was no secret that running buses could be a reasonable business and as deregulation spread bus companies from around the world wanted to be running bus operations elsewhere and the price of franchises rose. A similar pattern has followed the deregulation of US utilities and telephone services in the late 1990s. Stagecoach began looking for growth elsewhere, and purchased a minority stake in a Chinese toll road operator, and control of a train leasing business which it sold shortly afterwards. However, the big mistake came with the hubristic top-of-the-cycle purchase of Coach USA, itself a debt funded roll-up of several disparate bus, taxi and charter coach operations which had been assembled by investment bankers and a leveraged buy out (LBO) fund. The price paid was too high, the operations had little economic merit on their own, let alone bundled together, and the acquisition had been debt funded. In short the company had geared up to buy a company worth a fraction of the purchase price. It then got worse. Improving the operations of Coach USA required a heavy investment program (thank you, LBO fund) at the same time as the firm had committed to renew the UK bus fleet. The US operations were quite unlike the simple time-tabled commuter bus operations the firm had operated in the UK, and required more management time, to the detriment of the UK business, which was ignored and began to flag. It is not hard to run a profitable bus company "but you do need to keep the plates spinning [do the simple things right]" claimed Souter, and management had stopped spinning plates. The shares which peaked at £2.85 in 1998 reached 10p in late 2002, or half their IPO price ten years earlier. When the final dividend was cut in July 2002, management were sacked and Souter returned from semi-retirement.

Souter began cutting away the weak businesses, a process Charlie Munger, vice Chairman of Berkshire Hathaway refers to as the "cancer surgery approach". This often works because there is normally a jewel at the heart of most companies that has often been used to fund new ventures or is taken for granted by impatient management. As the jewel becomes diluted by less successful projects aggregate performance declines and valuations atrophy or even fall. The star in this regard and in which Mr. Munger invested, is Coca-Cola, which in the mid 1980s had become a poorly defined conglomerate including a shrimp farm, winery, film studio and shudder to think, even owned its own bottling plants! As the poorer businesses were cut away, to reveal the jewel that is the syrup manufacturing and marketing operation, the shares of Coca-Cola rose over ten fold in the succeeding decade.

At Stagecoach the fix is relatively simple: cease investment in poor US operations, sell the worst businesses for asset value, repay the debt and in doing so return the business to its jewel, the UK bus operation. When Marathon met Souter in early December he referred to the UK operations as being under the shadow of more recent acquisitions (a "Cinderella Business") but that "they [management and employees of UK Bus] were the only people happy to see me back": Souter is looking forward to spinning plates again. The firm has the relative luxury of a modern bus fleet and so the firm's high levels of free cash flow can be used to repay debt. The banks have been supportive, even to the extent of allowing the company to repurchase its public debt (at sizeable discounts to face value) even though the public debt is due after the bank's own debt facilities expire. All creditors are unsecured, and there remains debt capacity at some subsidiaries such as in Hong Kong and New Zealand. In our opinion the business is worth approximately 60p per share, a valuation contingent upon modest levels of debt repayment and no growth in the UK operations. This compares with Nomad's purchase price of 14p (in late November), and the current market price of 33p (early JANUARY). Souter's sacred dividend (with his sister he continues to own around 25% of the equity) is being maintained and implies a gross yield of over 12% at Nomad's purchase price. Having analysed many complicated and highly indebted businesses especially in the US recently, Stagecoach's problems are relatively simple, and we have made the firm our largest investment to date.

Case Study #6

Costco (2002)

From the Partnership Letters

DECEMBER 31st, 2002

At Costco Wholesale there is no need to fix the business which is performing well already. Costco is one half of the wholesale club warehouse duopoly (with Sam's Club) and had annual revenues of U$35bn in 2001. The retail concept is as follows: customers pay an annual membership fee (standard U$45) which provides entry to the stores for a year, and in exchange Costco operates an every-day-low-pricing strategy (EDLP) by marking up 14% on branded goods and 15% on private label with the result that prices are very, very low. This is a very simple and honest consumer proposition in the sense that the membership fee buys the customer's loyalty (and is almost all profit) and Costco in exchange sells goods whilst just covering operating costs. In addition by sticking to a standard mark up savings achieved through purchasing or scale are returned to the customer in the form of lower prices, which in turn encourages growth and extends scale advantages. This is retail's version of perpetual motion and has been widely employed by Wal-Mart among others. To understand how important EDLP is to Jim Sinegal, the firm's founder, consider the following story which was recounted to us by a company director. Costco bought 2m designer jeans from an exporter and shipped them into international waters and re-imported the jeans for an all in price of U$22 or so per pair. This was U$10 less than the firm had sold the jeans for in the past (offering the potential for a 50% mark up) and half the cost of most other retailers. One buyer recommended taking a higher gross margin than was usual (i.e. more than the usual 14% mark up) as no one would know. Apparently Sinegal insisted on the standard mark up, arguing that if "I let you do it this time, you will do it again". The contract with the customer (very low prices) must not be broken.

Many retailers do not operate in such a way, and instead employ high-low price strategies, that is to say they take prices up and down in an attempt to influence store traffic. The consumer goods companies then add to the confusion through running their own promotional campaigns. Although many of us are used to this behaviour, consider for a moment how confusing a proposition to the consumer it is. For example, is a bottle of shampoo worth US$2 if it is periodically available through a couponing campaign for US$1? The high-low strategy may even backfire: do consumers feel taken advantage of when paying US$5 for tissues that were available last week for US$4? They should. At Costco the consumer knows the price is 14 or 15% above wholesale, period.

Costco management describe the strategy as "easy to understand and hard to operate" perhaps because the temptation is to mark up the goods and break the contract with the customer. Costco is profitable enough to self fund growth of around 14% per annum and not to have to resort to leases for expansion (The Gap's mistake). This means that growth will be more measured (none of the 30% per annum purges that populate the retail industry) and should be more sustainable. As to the potential for growth the firm has 21 stores in Washington State which houses just 2% of the US population. This density coast to coast implies room for around 1,000 US stores (currently 284) and 200 stores in the UK (currently 14) although planning regulations may not allow for this. Even then Home Depot, the largest DIY store in the US currently has 1,500 stores. At 10% growth per annum, this implies the firm has another 13 years of growth ahead. The share price has declined from a year 2000 high of US$55 to US$30 (Nomad's purchase price) as margins declined slightly (they are measured in basis points at this firm) with the cost of several new distribution centers which will support the next few year's growth. For example in the UK the firm has warehousing and logistics capacity for 40 locations but only has 14 stores. At US$30 the firm is valued as a cash cow, with higher levels of profitability (as capacity utilisation increases) and modest levels of growth justifying a valuation over U$50 per share. Costco is as perfect a growth stock as we have analysed and is available in the stock market at a close to half price.

Case Study #7

Weetabix (2003)

From the Partnership Letters

JUNE 30th, 2003

Weetabix was established by the George family in 1932 as Britain's answer to the growing popularity of imported cereals, notably from the Kellogg Company. The firm was initially capitalised by the family and, as may have been common at the time, by a group of local farmers to secure their supply of commodities. The company has required no further equity capital and the share count is essentially unchanged since the 1930s although some farmers have chosen to sell their shares and it is these that form the free float that trades on Ofex. Weetabix manufactures and markets Weetabix, Alpen, Ready Brek and Weetos and has a total market share of around 22% of UK breakfast cereals. The company spends heavily behind its brands through advertising and marketing, a cost the Chairman refers to as "investment in the future". This has been in contrast to some of Weetabix's competitors who have cut spending in order to meet Wall Street's short-term earnings expectations. The effect is that Weetabix's share of voice (share of industry marketing spend) has exceeded the firm's share of market. For a consumer goods company this is often a powerful combination, as market share tends to rise or fall in the direction of share of voice. The high marketing spend also has the effect of creating a direct relationship with the customer which retailers find hard to break. In a recent test of the strength of the franchise a large UK supermarket suspended Weetabix in favour of own branded goods only to change their minds after disappointing own-brand sales and resume stocking

Weetabix cereals. We particularly enjoyed this Weetabix advert run in the 1940s that could be applied to the firm's negotiating stance with retailers today.

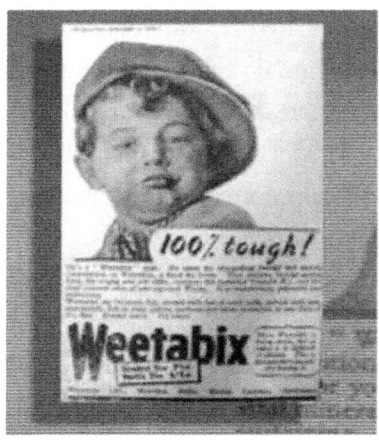

Source: Weetabix Limited

The firm does not skip on capex either and runs its factories with fifty percent capacity redundancy in an effort to maintain standards of production and delivery reliability. This belt and braces approach lowers short-term returns on capital, something the City would also frown upon, but builds the reputation of the firm in the long-run. Value creation is often most sustainable when it is built slowly, and notably last year Weetabix became the largest selling breakfast cereal, overtaking Corn Flakes seventy years after the company's foundation.

The investment case is sealed, as the shares are ludicrously cheap. If one assumes modest levels of growth in free cash flow as the advertising spend bears fruit then the firm might be worth around £70 per share compared to Nomad's purchase price around £20. In a rare indiscretion, Sir Richard George, Chairman, let slip that on his death a search of his wallet will reveal a multitude of rejected offers for the business over the last thirty years from a host of international food groups. And what might these prices be? At the price PepsiCo paid for Quaker Oats (ex Gatorade) or Hershey was bid for more recently, the implied private market value of Weetabix is around £75 per share. Both valuations are depressed by the weight of cash on the balance sheet, which amounts to £5 per share, and ignores the value of property, which is in the books at 1988 prices.

So the real issue is, why is the business so cheap? The answer may be found in the firm's listing status, that is to say it does not have one, as the firm's shares trade on Ofex (similar to the pink sheets in the US) rather than on the London Stock Exchange. Big institutions are often not permitted by their mandates to invest via Ofex, and the shares remain relatively illiquid and the market capitalisation modest, further depressing City interest. And whilst the free float may have been an accident of history, management do care enough about the share price to have included it as a component of incentive compensation. In other words, Weetabix is just our sort of company.

Case Study #8

Lucent Technologies (2003)

From the Partnership Letters

JUNE 30th, 2003

In the autumn of 2002 Nomad purchased a sizeable investment in 8% Redeemable, Convertible Preferred stock issued by Lucent Technologies. The prefs, purchased for U$350 per share, are an unusual security as they can be put back to the company at par (U$1,000 per share) in August 2004 for payment in cash or a variable number of common shares. As at the time the market capitalisation of the firm was so low, the put risked (from a common equity holder's perspective) delivering half of the common shares to the pref holders if the share price failed to rise. The put also made the prefs the first of Lucent's fixed liabilities to come due (so they were at the top of management's to do list) and just as important pref holders would receive almost half of their investment back through cumulative dividends before the put became due! In effect, one half of Lucent's proforma common equity could be purchased for U$500m (the market value of the prefs) a figure equivalent to only a few months' research and development spending. The capital markets had all but given up on the company even though they had enough cash on deposit to redeem the prefs and all outstanding debt entirely.

The investment controversy was how would management respond to the dire prognosis delivered by the market? Management presented two choices: (a) continue as before and hope that operating cash flow would turn positive with further cost savings and perhaps an upturn in orders. This had been management's preferred route since the bubble burst. Or (b) dilute the existing shareholders whose investment had already fallen 98% from the peak three years earlier and issue more equity to fund redemption of the prefs. Management's assessment might have been something like Woody Allen's prognosis:

> *"More than any time in history mankind is at a crossroads. One path leads to despair and utter hopelessness, the other to total extinction. Let us pray we have the wisdom to choose correctly".*

But there was a third choice which, as common shareholders, Marathon was urging the company to pursue: (c) conclude the market was wrong and buy back the prefs and common shares and repay debt with cash on hand and return the firm to an un-leveraged balance sheet. This would have preserved the upside for existing common shareholders and restored value for the pref holders but would have left management without a cash cushion, but this, we argued, could be restored through a rights issue if necessary. Management chose (b) the sleep-at-night choice. In short, management marked their emotions and the company's balance sheet to market at the weakest point in the cycle, and although time will tell this is likely to be a huge source of value foregone for the common equity holder. For the pref holders issuance of new common shares has provided the resources to meet the put (which is now covered many times with cash on hand) and the prefs have risen three-fold to trade at a premium to par, as the 8% yield is deemed attractive by fixed income investors. The investment has reached full value and will be sold as new investments become available.

Case Study #9

Weetabix Update (2003)

From the Partnership Letters

DECEMBER 31st, 2003

Weetabix

Many of you will have read that Hicks, Muse, Tate and Furst Inc., a private equity firm, bid £53.75 for each Weetabix share at the end of last year. We have received several e-mails from Partners offering congratulations. As detailed in the June 2002 Partnership letter your broadminded approach to investing and approval of the amendment to the investment objectives facilitated this investment and so you too should be congratulated. Freud might conclude that that is why the e-mails were sent. However, may we caution against euphoria?

Take the structure of the transaction, which is a Scheme of Arrangement rather than General Offer. The threshold of approval under a Scheme of Arrangement is 75% of the shareholders rather than 90% in the case of a General Offer. Proponents favour the lower threshold as it makes it harder for minority shareholders to block the transaction – but why be so defensive? The George family have signed irrevocable undertakings to sell to Hicks, Muse which would only be broken in the event of a bid at greater than a 25% premium to the Hicks, Muse offer. Why are the irrevocables necessary if the business has been properly auctioned, as the bankers claim? The family and board have a deal that is not available to shareholders through their continued employment with the firm post sale. It strikes us as odd that the highest bid for the company should come from a private equity firm who have an eye on selling the business at a profit, rather than a natural competitor who would enjoy the benefits of removing duplicate costs over many years. All this reinforces the notion that the price is low, in our opinion by around 25%, and note that Hicks, Muse will no doubt feel they have a good deal too.

We have written to Sir Richard George, Weetabix's Chairman, met the investment bankers who purportedly represent our interests, listened to their responses and voted against the deal. This is a cry in the dark, as even the largest non-family shareholder publicly supports the deal. Our shareholding is too small to make a difference to the outcome and although our preference is to retain the shares, in private unlisted form alongside Hicks, Muse, that option is not available under a Scheme of Arrangement and the Court will require us to sell our shares.

The Weetabix offer is only one of many privatisations of cheap, small and mid capitalisation businesses in the UK. Institutional shareholders have abandoned these firms in favor of mega-caps, and the shareholder base is left dominated by one or two inside interests and a tail of small holders. Our view is that the discount that the shares trade at in the market is an asset to be harvested for the benefit of all shareholders through share repurchase. But human nature being as it is, insiders will be incented by the low valuation to buy the shares for themselves. A Scheme of Arrangement is the most ruthless method of asserting one party's will over a fragmented and non- professional shareholder base and, coupled with irrevocable acceptances allows take-over offers to be presented as a fait accompli to shareholders. Please note: bad practice spreads. Despite this, and the almost daily occurrence of privatization proposals in the UK, there has been almost no criticism by shareholders, the authorities or in the media. In no other sphere of capitalism can your property be seized in exchange for cents on the dollar (except compulsory purchase on the grounds of national interest). But fund managers, who in their private capacity would be insulted if someone offered less than their house was worth, happily sell shares in their professional capacity at discounted prices to smart buyers. And no one cries foul.

The indifference shown by those in positions of influence reminds us of Horatio Nelson who, when ordered by semaphore to withdraw from the Battle of Copenhagen, placed a spyglass to his blind eye and said, "I really do not see the signal!" Whilst we have a profit on our investment in Weetabix, shareholders should be careful what they wish for. Before congratulations are in order, Partners need to weigh in their minds short-term profits against value forgone in the discounted offer price and the incentive provided by the success of seizure for potentially more of the same in the future.

So, what is to be done? The best defense is to own enough of the company to influence the outcome. In most cases in excess of 10% of the shares outstanding would suffice. Those that advocate market liquidity of their investments over other considerations might like to bear in mind an investor's inability to influence outcomes whilst owning a deminimus proportion of a company. Should Nomad continue to grow in size, we intend not to make this mistake.

Case Study #10

Union Cement (2004)

From the Partnership Letters

JUNE 30th, 2004

We have holdings ranging from almost 7% to 0.3% of assets. At the time of writing, Jardine Matheson/Strategic and Costco Wholesale are around 6.5% of Partnership assets each, Xerox 3.1%, but Union Cement around 1% and Velcro 0.6%. Why? A consequence of price discipline is that one cannot be certain of the size of the investment opportunity in advance. We simply cannot be sure how many people will be prepared to sell to us at our price: it may be 20 shares or 20% of the company. We hope for the latter but more recently have found it to be the former. An extreme example has been our attempt to purchase shares in Union Cement. This is the Philippines' largest cement company and has been priced in the market at around one quarter of the replacement cost of its assets. The assets are world scale and reasonably new, or at least were constructed during the Asian tiger boom of the early 1990s. The low valuation of the company in the markets had the desired effect in reducing capital investment (why spend discretionary resources on shiny new assets when the market valued them at 25% of cost?) and free cash flow was instead used to repay debt. Despite the turnaround in strategy, investors barely seemed to notice and the shares, which had already fallen from U$0.30, bounced around between 1 and 2c a share. We started buying and in doing so raised the price over a six-month period from 1.5c to 2.5c and despite being almost the only buyer of shares we managed to purchase just U$1m worth of stock. This is remarkably little when one considers that Union Cement is a large company with a market value of U$200m and around U$700m in gross assets. The shares simply would not trade, indeed the average holding period indicated by share turnover during much of this period implied a 40+ year outlook by investors, coincidentally comparable to the life of a cement plant. Of course, the more undervalued the company became the less the shares traded, as more holders understood the under-valuation. But still we plugged along in the hope that as the price rose, we would be able to secure some more stock. This was not to be. By the time Holcim, one of the world's largest cement companies, purchased a control block in the firm at an effective price for Union Cement of close to 10c (US) a share, five times our average purchase price, we had secured only a small holding. It is possible that we could have made Union Cement a meaningful ten percent investment in the Partnership. As it was, and despite our best efforts, we managed to achieve a miserable 1% investment. Charlie Munger is right when he says, "it is aggravating to just buy a bit".

Case Study #11

Costco (2004)
The Perpetual Growth Machine
From the Partnership Letters

DECEMBER 31st, 2004

Deconstructing the Business Case For Costco Wholesale

We have written about Costco before (December 2002) but make no apologies for its inclusion again. The reason is that it is important to us that you understand not only what we do, but why we do what we do. This is not easily done, as I am sure I will now demonstrate. In our experience very few investors understand what their managers really do. We know this because fund managers are often sacked at the trough of their relative performance, and invariably just as performance is about to turn. Clients that sacked Marathon at the end of 1999 (you know who you are) have missed out on a 12% annual gain compared to the index since, a gain which far outstrips any deficit against the benchmark during previous years. So education is important. It helps both parties make rational decisions. Costco is also an important investment for the Partnership at close to 10% of assets. I am also conscious that in the September issue of the Global Investment Review, your manager wrote an article explaining the risks of doing precisely what he is about to do. That is, by publicly committing to an investment it may become harder subsequently to change one's mind. A copy of the essay is contained in the appendix. However, on the basis that fore-warned is fore-armed, I shall continue. You will understand if we don't sell our shares just yet!

Costco Wholesale is a member-only wholesaler of consumer goods. Membership is available to the public at a price of U$45 per annum. The act of purchasing membership has the effect of raising the company's share of mind with the customer in the same way that consumer goods companies hope to achieve with conventional advertising. At Costco, the consumer has chosen to commit to the retailer. In other words people shop at Costco because it is Costco, not because Costco stocks Coke. And the reason they shop is that goods are priced at a fixed maximum 14% mark up over cost. The fixed mark up is referred to in the industry as "every-day-low-pricing" or EDLP, in order to differentiate it from normal industry practice of changing prices in an attempt to influence traffic, or so called high-low pricing. At Costco the consumer pays no more than 14% over what the company paid, period. In the December 2002 letter to shareholders we wrote:

"To understand how important EDLP is to Jim Sinegal, the firm's founder, consider the following story which was recounted to us by a company director. Costco bought 2m designer jeans from an exporter and shipped them into international waters and re-imported the jeans for an all in price of U$22 or so per pair. This was U$10 less than the firm had sold the jeans for in the past (offering the potential for a 50% mark up) and half the cost of most other retailers. One buyer recommended taking a higher gross margin than was usual (i.e. more than the usual 14% mark up) as no one would know. Apparently Sinegal insisted on the standard mark up, arguing that if "I let you do it this time, you will do it again". "

Most supermarkets mark up goods in aggregate by twice as much (in margin terms) as Costco and even the mighty Wal-Mart marks up by half as much again as Costco. In order to make money at such low (gross) margins Costco must ensure that: (1) Operating costs are low, indeed very low. It is indicative of the paranoia with which the company is run that costs are measured in basis points (there are 100 basis points in one percentage point). This makes life difficult for Wal-Mart and the hypermarkets who cannot price at aggregate Costco levels and make money as their cost bases (approximately 15% and 25% of revenues respectively) are too high. (2) That the wholesale price is as competitive as can be. The key to negotiating terms is that the number of items in a store (stock keeping units) are fixed at 4,000, and the right to fill one of these spaces is auctioned, with the supplier that provides the best value proposition to the consumer winning space on the shop floor! Contrast this to normal industry practice whereby the supermarket assumes the role of landlord, auctions space to the highest bidder and pockets the rents ("slotting fees" in industry parlance). Many supermarkets make their money from buying from the supplier. Costco makes money from selling to the consumer. The firm publishes the criteria required to become a Costco supplier on its UK web site. After setting out the definitions of quality, pricing, packaging and gratuities ("expressly prohibited" for reasons we can all understand) there is the following statement about purchasing quotes:

> *"We expect all vendors to consistently and voluntarily quote the lowest possible acquisition price available on all items. A vendor who does not consistently and voluntarily quote its lowest prices to our buyers will be permanently discontinued as a purchasing source for Costco."*
>
> Source: Costco.co.uk

Grief. One strike and you're out!

(3) Revenues need to be very high. This last factor is partly a self fulfilling prophesy – revenues will be high if the other factors, (1) and (2), are favorable. The issue is what the company then does with this revenue advantage. In the case of Costco scale efficiency gains are passed back to the consumer in order to drive further revenue growth. That way customers at one of the first Costco stores (outside Seattle) benefit from the firm's expansion (into say Ohio) as they also gain from the decline in supplier prices. This keeps the old stores growing too. The point is that having shared the cost savings, the customer reciprocates, with the result that revenues per foot of retailing space at Costco exceed that at the next highest rival (Wal-Mart's Sam's Club) by about fifty percent.

The stores are mainly owned rather than leased. This makes sense in terms of controlling costs (no greedy landlords putting up rents) but also means that growth is measured and predictable, if slower than Wall Street might like. But this is fine with us if it means that the probability of continued success is higher than under a going- for-broke expansion plan.

In the office we have a white board on which we have listed the (very few) investment models that work and that we can understand. Costco is the best example we can find of one of them: scale efficiencies shared. Most companies pursue scale efficiencies, but few share them. It's the sharing that makes the model so powerful. But in the center of the model is a paradox: the company grows through giving more back. We often ask companies what they would do with windfall profits, and most spend it on something or other, or return the cash to shareholders. Almost no one replies give it back to customers – how would that go down with Wall Street? That is why competing with Costco is so hard to do. The firm is not interested in today's static assessment of performance. It is managing the business as if to raise the probability of long term success.

Deconstructing the Investment Case for Costco Wholesale
What is it about growth stocks that dooms them to failure? In other words, why is Michael Goldstein's growth stock failure rate, and our shunning of Dell, normally right? The answer is that success encourages competition, and capital flows into an industry to compete away the excess returns. Like all heuristics, this works most of the time, and we can all think of businesses that were super profitable for a while before the competition caught on. But what of those that don't fail? Michael Dell succeeded by keeping costs low and passing back his scale benefits to the buyer of his PCs. By the time the competition had matched him in pricing he had moved on. And on and on. (Perhaps someone could slip this letter into Carly Fiorina, Chairman and CEO of Hewlett Packard's suggestion box). Amazon.com may be following this path as well. So, the first point is that whilst Costco continues to recycle cost savings to the consumer, it is lowering the probability of failure.

So what heuristics do investors incorrectly apply to Costco (why might the shares be mis-priced?). Heuristic One: "the company has low margins" (net profit margin is 1.7%, compared to Wal Mart at 3.6% and Target at 4.2%). True, but that's the point. The firm is deferring profits today in order to extend the life of the franchise. Of course Wall Street would love profits today but that's just Wall Street's obsession with short term outcomes. Heuristic Two: "its expensive at 24x earnings". Really? Net income is a small residual, as discussed above. The firm could earn Wal-Mart margins by taking pricing up a little, in which case the firm would be on 11x earnings, but would it be a better business as a result? We think not, if it allowed the competition to catch up. Heuristic Three: "Costco has a cost problem". Costs have risen as a percentage of revenues in the last few years due to the expense of a warehouse and distribution system associated with the next phase of the firm's growth and the cost of employee benefits and insurance, especially in California. This has people fooled who really should not be. At the annual general meeting for an investment company that we hugely admire, the investment firm's founder (and industry hero) was asked by an client why their holding in Costco was just 1% of the fund, especially when they have a reputation for portfolio concentration. The answer given was that of the firm's three constituencies (labour, customers and shareholders) the first two had been ascendant. This sounds nice and neat, but the phenomenon is cyclical: labour are "happy" according to Sinegal, Costco's founder and CEO, incremental stores will leverage fixed costs, and in the letter to shareholders Sinegal describes costs as "unacceptable". In short, they are on to it. Our investment hero was mistaken, by about U$20 per share so far, or a gain of 65%.

Is it perfect?
No. But that suggests an interesting question: What characteristics could one bestow on a company that would make it the most valuable in the world? What would it look like? Such a firm would have a huge market place (offering size), high barriers to entry (offering longevity) and very low levels of capital employed (offering free cash flow). Costco has some of these attributes. The range of products is as wide as any retailer, and by passing savings back it is building a formidable moat. It is also more asset light than its peers, but it is not the lightest of them all. For that one must turn to the Internet. In our opinion a business such as eBay could be the most valuable in the world. It has a huge market place, the biggest, an auction marketplace naturally aggregates to one player, offering high market share and high barriers to entry to the winner.

Product pricing may be supported by the incumbent local newspapers and publishing businesses which have expensive machinery to replace and usually unionised labour, and may provide a price umbrella for eBay. Better still eBay makes the customer pay for a high proportion of the assets used in the transaction such as PCs, modems, phone lines and so forth. But best of all, the incremental assets required to grow are so small. At Costco the firm will spend around US$15m per incremental store which will serve a radius of perhaps thirty miles. US$15m is a lot of servers for eBay, and whilst we are not experts, that may be enough to serve some countries. So no, Costco is not perfect. Perhaps we should own eBay as well.

What are the economics of our purchase of shares in Costco?
Readers that don't enjoy sweating the maths can resume at the next paragraph. Those that like a work out, read on. Analysis of the annual report (disgraceful lack of colour pictures) reveals that revenues of US$47.2bn (year to August 2004) represented a 12% mark up on "merchandising costs" and left enough to pay for operating costs (SG&A) of 9.8% of sales (one third of the hi-lo supermarkets). Profits from retailing are therefore around US$456m per annum to which one should add the membership fees of US$961m = US$1.41bn pre taxes. Taxes approximate depreciation most years, so pre- tax income equates to gross cash flow before maintenance capex which at around US$250m per annum implies around US$1.17bn in free cash flow as a cash cow. This compares to a fixed asset base of company owned real estate of US$9.6bn (depreciated value US$7.3bn). Working capital is "supplier funded" and means that the US$1.17bn free cash flow represents a yield of around 12% on fixed assets. A bear argument is that if the real estate was leased, free cash flow would be nought: this looks right but may miss two things: (1) Rents provide a return to their owners, not just break even on the cost of capital and (2) The store base is under-earning, perhaps significantly. Evidence for this is as follows: revenue per store at the oldest stores is twice this year's new openings, revenues per store at the oldest stores are still rising at 3 to 4% per annum, costs per new store suffer from low capacity utilisation of warehouses, and penetration in California is six times US State average. Store growth will be around 5% per annum and management confess to "always under-estimating saturation": in LA post the merger with Price Club in

1993 they thought 31 stores were too many for the market, but today there are 36. Likewise, in Seattle and Alaska the penetration of cards (membership) is 65% of households (gosh) but in most markets it is below 10%. Note also that one third of the store base remains in California, and almost half on the West Coast. This is a very young franchise. Half of the store base is over ten years old and earns 65% of the revenues whilst using approximately 40% of the asset base. What this means is that the oldest stores earn around 16.5% on assets and the youngest earn 6%. In other words there is an approximate 50% rise in aggregate profits to come as the store base matures (4% growth per annum), plus same store sales growth at the mature stores (approx 4% per annum) implying 8% growth before new store openings, which will add 5% to the store base and can easily be funded through free cash flow. This suggests normalised growth of 13%, and I don't think it is a stretch.

How do we think about valuation? There is a range of possible outcomes for the business, some are more likely than others, and in our mind they have various probabilities attached. What we present below is our assessment of central value for Costco, but you should bear in mind that it is not the only value for Costco. Our average purchase price of U$39 per share (a blend of U$30 per share when the Partnership was small, and U$40 per share following the draw down of the Nomad subscription queue in the summer) discounts modest growth of 5 to 6% per annum, and is too low for a business that will be pushed not to grow earnings 10% per annum. A price of U$43 per share discounts 7% growth and U$85 to U$90 per share 15% growth. There is a very real possibility that the business could be priced to discount growth of 10% which would imply a price of U$62 per share today (and that price should rise by our 10% discount rate per annum). If it takes five years for the shares to converge on a price which discounts 10% growth per annum then the shares would need to rise by 20% per annum from our average purchase price of U$39 per share.

Such a gain would add around 2% per annum to Partnership assets. And it is this that makes me think the weighting in the portfolio is too small. If Dell is the appropriate model for Costco, then the probability of failure is lower than for most growth stocks. It is lower again when one considers self funded, as opposed to, rented growth. And lower again when one considers the fixity of mark up. To a far greater extent than for many businesses the company controls its own destiny. So what attracted us to Costco is the predictability of outcome: we don't think it is going to fail for many years. But is a 2% gain per annum optimal? If one applies the Kelly criterion (discussed in the last letter) the weighting should be much higher. So already your manager may have made his first mistake investing in Costco. From not buying enough. Perhaps I will get my opportunity to make amends.

So, the consensus has it that Costco is a low margin, expensive retailer with a cost problem. That is certainly one description. In our judgement it is a cost disciplined, intellectually honest, high product integrity, perpetual motion machine trading at a discount to value. The weighting in the Partnership may be too small, but even so as the description of the business migrates in the minds of the average investor from the former to the latter I think we will do quite well.

Case Study #12

Zimbabwe (2005)

From the Partnership Letters

JUNE 30th, 2005

Zimbabwe as an Example of a Second Investment Model
We have begun making some investments in Zimbabwe and wrote about the background to these in a recent Global Investment Review (also contained in the appendix). The investment case relies upon extreme undervaluation compared to normalised values, so much so that a wait of ten years for normalisation would still yield wonderful results. It makes little sense to discuss stocks we may or are buying (Costco is likely to be a rare exception in this regard) but I can illustrate the investment case by describing Zimcem. This is the country's largest cement producer (after the local division of Pretoria Portland Cement), with around 700,000 tons of cement capacity and a replacement cost of around U$70 to U$100m. The firm has no debt and business conditions are awful (general inflation exceeds cement price inflation and product demand is low) but the company is priced on the Harare stock exchange at one seventieth (1/70th!) of its replacement cost.

Why is this relevant? So far we have only discussed one model we use to pick good investments which we call "scale efficiencies shared" as evidenced by Costco (and to a lesser extent Amazon.com). We have little more than a handful of distinct investment models, which overlap to some extent, and Zimcem is a good example of a second model namely, "deep discount to replacement cost with latent pricing power". Indeed these two models combined can be used to describe around 45% of total Partnership assets. It was this model that led to many investments during the Asian crisis (such as Siam Cement which has risen twenty fold from the trough in eight years) and to neighbouring South Africa where Pretoria Portland Cement could be bought at a price of U$20 per ton of capacity in 1998 and is now valued at U$180 per ton. The model is premised upon the observation that the business needs to replace its assets and will require prices which 1. fund the capex, and 2. economically justify the spending. Either that or Zimbabwe will have to go without cement, or import from abroad (tricky for this land locked country). In any event, provided discretionary capital is not invested to exacerbate the situation, the supply side remains muted (industry capex is zero) and the business is not nationalised, then the shares ought to do well, in time.

This last point, along with other confiscation events, does not have a zero probability, and is the main reason our investments in the country will be modest in size. Even if we were able to secure all the shares we desire (which we seem incapable of doing) it is unlikely that the total investment would be much more than a few percent of the Partnership at cost. There is no a priori reason why Zimbabwean businesses should not trade at a premium to replacement cost. Just over the northern border Zambia's dominant cement company is now valued at a premium to replacement cost following recovery in the economy after years of mismanagement. In Zimbabwe this may require "regime change", or even regime changes. Perhaps the investment case rests in your manager being fifty years younger than Bob Mugabe.

The Pricing of Shares in Zimbabwe

The official exchange rate at the time of writing is Z$9,100 to the U$1. The unofficial, street rate is around Z$17,000 to the U$1. In other words the Central Bank values its own currency at over twice the price set by the public with the effect that money entering the country via the Central Bank buys approximately half as much as at the street rate. Fortunately there is an alternative to the Central Bank for foreign investors, which is to purchase Old Mutual shares in

Johannesburg, re-register the same shares in Harare and then sell the shares in Harare. This we have done. But it creates a problem in valuing our Zimbabwean shares as Bloomberg, Reuters and the other main sources of currency prices use feeds from the Central Bank. In other words if we solely relied upon the official rate of exchange our investments would immediately show an 86% gain. This gain is entirely illusory. Were we to reverse the process by re-registering the shares in Johannesburg and selling our stock there, the proceeds would approximate the money we first put in (minus frictional costs and any change in the price of Old Mutual shares). The only way we could realise the 86% gain would be to present our Zim dollars to the Central Bank and ask for US dollars at a rate of Z$9,100. And we would be waiting for Godot. There are almost no transactions taking place at the Central Bank and priority is given to trade and working capital requirements, not foreign investment portfolios. So we could try, but I don't think it is prudent to value the portfolio on the basis of a warm response from the Zimbabwean Central Bank. So our solution has been to value the Zimbabwean investments at the rate of exchange implied by the Old Mutual share price in Harare divided by the price of exactly the same share in Johannesburg (note that the shares are fungible in both directions). The effect is to approximate the street rate of exchange and remove the artificial book gain implied by the official exchange rate, and hopefully the worst of any pricing distortions should be minimised as a result. This is a somewhat unusual solution, but one that I think is fair, and the auditors, board and administrators have decided to agree with my methodology. Please do call however, if all is not clear.

Appendix 2: "Zimbabwe". Global Investment Review, February 2005.

"That's what brothers are for, brother."
Gil Scott-Heron, "Small Talk at 125th and Lenox"

Some commentators believe that the current condition of stock markets is now more dangerous than the bubble of the late 1990s. Then at least there was the anti-bubble formed from cheap low growth companies. Today there is no Zen-like symmetry to stock prices; and there are few obvious pockets of undervaluation for the contrarian. A cheer all round then for Zimbabwe. The clients will hate it. Compliance will hate it. The consultants will hate it. Marketing will hate it. The size of the investment opportunity is tiny. It is not part of the benchmark. It is not even part of the Commonwealth. It's perfect.

Not that it is exactly risk free. Not "risky" in a tracking error, index relative, transient stock price quotation, quarterly reporting sense. The real risk comes in the form of a sleepy, quick to smile, want to get on with people apathy that pervades the population. The financial pages of Harare's Daily Mirror newspaper continue to publish the exchange rates for the deutschmark, French franc, Spanish peseta and Italian lira. Presumably it is someone's daily task to take one number and multiply it by another for the purpose of completing the next day's currency table. No one has noticed that the currencies no longer exist. This is not a good precedent for reform. Neither was the paper's headline which read – "Officials Grab Cell Phone Lines". First, there is the physical impossibility of the act; one could in theory grab a land line, but a wireless phone line? Secondly the problem is few people in Zimbabwe appear politically active, let alone angry. The editorial was not angry. And if no one is angry then what is the prospect of the Meikles Hotel occupancy exceeding its current 30%, except during the occasional English cricket team tour, which was controversial in England but locally ignored.

The most valuable company in the country as measured by the price of traded shares at the stock exchange is worth US$150m at the official exchange rate, and US$100m at the unofficial. That is less than one tenth of the quarterly dividend payment from the ExxonMobil Corporation. The price earnings ratio of the index constituent stocks is less than three. Most industrial concerns are valued at less than the replacement cost of their assets, not that anyone is replacing assets. And that's bullish. The ungeared Lafarge cement subsidiary has a market capitalisation of US$2.5m. There is some difficulty precisely assessing the size of plant capacity but bearing in mind that replacement cost for a cement plant is around US$120m per ton, we don't need to be too accurate.

Zimbabwe is not a good advert for black capitalism. But it is not a good advert for white capitalism either. The occupation of white-owned farms looks racially motivated but note, it has been followed with the intimidation of black bankers as well. Zimbabwe can be described as a fascist state, in denial. Not only is not encouraging, but it is also not sustainable. Destroying the agricultural sector because it is white-controlled is stupid to the point of evil, when agriculture makes up 65% of the economy. It's the poor blacks that will be affected the most. The closest parallel may be that of Indonesia where the minority Chinese population control a large share of the economy. That is not necessarily a disproportionate share of the economy, as one likes to think they earned it. But the point is that the majority resent the rich minority, black or white, and the politicians feed on the distrust when their own policies have failed.

But unlike Indonesia, there was no boom to precede the bust. Zimbabwe has never been a tiger economy. This bust is political not economic. It is not predicated upon over-investment, over-borrowing or over-enthusiasm. But that means there is almost no bad debt in the economy. A visit to the publicly listed Barclays Zimbabwe revealed bad debts at 4% of the loan book. So, there is no recapitalisation needed here, no Argentinean default situation. One reason is that the dispossessed white farmers have repaid their mortgages and working capital loans in order to take title to their land. In most cases their farms have not been compulsorily purchased by the government, although the government has tried. Most farms have been occupied by mobs whose interest has been to loot, not produce. One farmer we spoke to had been given twenty-four hours to collect his belongings and arrange his affairs before occupation. The looters then looted, taking the 2,000 head of cattle to market in the nearby villages and apparently feasting on the cattle not sold. Yet the agricultural equipment was left untouched. There is no market for the kit with few productive outlets for its use domestically, and so it is left idle, waiting for its owner's return. In the meantime, the farm lies fallow, the equipment sits in storage, the economy is denied its exports and the currency spirals downward to reflect the country's new worth. When and if the regime changes some farmers will return, armed with their title certificates and reclaim their property – just as the Chinese have in Indonesia, and the West Germans in East Germany. Meikles Financial Services, a retail credit operation, claim bad debts of just 1% of receivables. Their loan book is lent to those that are staying in Zimbabwe. With debts this low, the economy could recover quickly when confidence returns. But what is to be done about the apathy?

In the early 1970s the black American poet and musician Gil Scott-Heron was an angry man. Unlike his fellow activists he was not just angry at the white establishment, he was also angry at the insincerity of his fellow black men: especially "those that hung out on street corners in Harlem with a 'blacker-than-thou' attitude" who felt that everyone-else owed them a living. This is the attitude of the political class in Zimbabwe. These are Ayn Rand's "looters". In contrast to some of his fellow activists, Scott-Heron wanted his black peers to have integrity, be sincere, and be capitalists. Zimbabwe could do with a few Scott-Herons right now. Perhaps the lyrics to Scott-Heron's song "Brother" could be slipped into Robert Mugabe's suggestion box.

"We deal in too many externals, brother
Always afros, handshakes and dashikis
Never can a man build a working structure for black capitalism,
Always does the man rebound off a known.
I think I know you would-be black revolutionaries too well
Standing on a box, on the corner, talking about blowing the white boy away,
But that's not where it is at yet, brother.
...You need to get your memory banks organised, brother
Show that man you call an Uncle Tom just where he is wrong
Show that woman you are a sincere black man
All we need to do is see you shut up and be black
Help that woman!
Help that man!
That's what brothers are for, brother."

Case Study #13

AirAsia (2008)

From the Partnership Letters

JUNE 30th, 2008

AirAsia is Asia's largest low cost airline, and is probably the lowest cost airline in the world. The firm has borrowed heavily from Southwest Airline's model of operations (a point to point network configuration, on-line ticket sales, no reserved seating, one plane type). The effect is that costs including fuel are around 3c (US) per seat per kilometre (as of December 2007). Costs are very important when the product is, more or less, an undifferentiated commodity, and 3c compares with around 4.5c at Ryanair, 5.5c at Southwest or more importantly 4.5c at rival Malaysian Airlines. This cost advantage is shared with the customers in the form of low fares, although the firm has borrowed from Ryanair as well who extended the Southwest model to include revenue enhancements such as sales incentives for cabin staff, ancillary products and charging for complexity such as multiple bags. Even after allowing for these add-ons average revenue per seat kilometre at AirAsia is less than costs per seat kilometre at Malaysian Airlines! For example, our first enquiry on-line revealed that a flight between Kuala Lumpur and Bangkok, a distance of 730 miles (roughly the same as New York to Chicago), one way, booked a few months in advance can be had for M$75, or U$22. That's U$8 per ticket cheaper than Malaysian Airline's super discounted fare, or U$120 cheaper than the normal Malaysian fare. The product is relaxed and cheerful and the image is not unlike the early days of Southwest Airlines when "Southwest's low fares and service were as outrageous as its uniforms", (source: "Nuts! Southwest Airline's Crazy Recipe for Business and Personal success" by Freiberg and Freiberg), although Zak tells me the knee-length, high-heeled boots worn by 1970s Southwest cabin staff were not evident when we visited AirAsia (and boy, did he look!). The customer, unsurprisingly, reciprocates, and the planes run (in airline terms) full.

AirAsia is an example of scale-economics shared, which like Amazon, Costco, Carpetright and elements of other businesses in the portfolio (Geico, Nebraska Furniture Mart) have come to dominate Nomad (around 45% of the portfolio). AirAsia is the first sizeable, professional, entrepreneur owned and run low cost airline to operate in Asia and as the firm began operations in 2002 these are pioneering days. For example, we do not know how big the market for low cost travel is in Asia, although U$22 to Bangkok strikes us as market stimulating. Joint venture operations in Thailand and Indonesia offer a population base seven times the domestic Malaysian market and it is for this reason that the firm has 175 A320 aircraft on order. The negotiated price of the A320s is, as far as we can tell, the lowest price paid by anybody for A320s and the firm has secured a guaranteed lowest price for an Asian carrier from Airbus for its planes. On paper then, AirAsia could be the most fantastic business.

But there are wrinkles: funding for the new planes is not entirely secured, and lenders are twitchy. 175 aircraft is a huge amount of capacity (one third the size of Southwest which has been in operation for 40 years). Asian nations all feel they must have a flag, a song, a national car and a flag carrier. Malaysian Airline Systems, long the government supported inefficient flag carrier is resurgent and is leading a price war. Oil is U$140 a barrel.

Even so, the firm earns a reasonable spread over the cost of capital on its aircraft, whilst forcing pricing on other airlines which leaves them operating at sub economic returns. This is a powerful combination and implies that the business will win in the marketplace in the end. We have no ego invested our analysis (at least, I don't think we do: if you want to make rational decisions leave your ego behind), outcomes are leveraged and perfectly reasonable people could come to different conclusions as to the firms investment merits. However, we do struggle with the price of the shares in the stock market today, which appears to value the firm at a meaningful discount to the value of the company owned fleet of planes. In short, the market has concluded that AirAsia, despite the potential outlined above, should not exist. This is nonsense; as such a valuation would imply that Southeast Asians, who are some of the most price conscious people on the planet, don't want cheap airfares!

Case Study #14

Games Workshop (2008)

From the Partnership Letters

JUNE 30th, 2008

Games Workshop makes, distributes, retails and fosters the Warhammer family of tabletop games, think: modern equivalent of tin military soldiers. It is the largest firm of its kind in the world, although this is a small, but growing market. The customers are mainly boys between the age of 11 and 14 (no longer children, but before an interest in girls takes over!) and growth comes, in part, from word of mouth. Hobbyists must have the same soldiers as each other to comply with the stories that surround the battle scenes (otherwise, why are these sides fighting?) and so Warhammer is a standard and, if you want to play with your friends, you have to come to our shops. The firm grew steadily and profitably, if unspectacularly for many years until, that is, the Lord of the Rings line of models. These were very successful from the perspective of revenues and cash flow. However, windfall Lord of the Rings profits were invested in huge manufacturing facilities (that now run at 30% utilisation), funded new shops in marginal geographies, and a general complacency with the business set in, as the following excerpt from the Chairman's preamble to the 2007 accounts makes clear:

"So who was the enemy?

Is the world turning in such a way that mankind no longer wants or needs hobbies? No. All the evidence I see, with growing prosperity and increasing leisure time, is an increase in hobbies. Perhaps it is just collecting, painting and wargaming with miniatures that is passé? The evidence again says no. Too many of our stores around the world and their neighbouring independent accounts are in good healthy growth for that to be true. Have computer games, and especially these new online role- playing games, finally bitten Games Workshop? We have lived in happy harmony with computer games for our entire business life, our customers play computer games (they also eat meals and watch movies) but not at the expense of their hobby. The recent extraordinarily popular MMORPGs [massively multiplayer on-line role- playing games] would not, I think, have trimmed a little from us at the edges had they been in direct competition, they would have wiped us out. Are our overheads killing us? Well, yes, they could have, but they don't stop us selling things. Is it a change in society? No. Demographics? No. World recession? No, no, no. It was us.

We grew fat and lazy on the back of easy success. We forgot about customer service and forgot that hard work is and always has been the route to success. We forgot that we are a company which pursues profit and likes paying surplus cash to its owners. What was not expected was that it would take two poor years and a management reorganisation to get the problems taken seriously. Somewhere along the line too many of us thought that selling, sweating and saving were someone else's job. Well they aren't. That's my job and the job of all of us here at Games Workshop."

If the problems are self-inflicted they are usually within the powers of the firm to fix. According to the Chairman the firm is "seriously well funded" and this implies that free cash flow will be meaningfully in excess of net profits and will rise faster than revenues: all good then, for prospective profitability. Even so, the current valuation implies that the firm is worth little more than its investment in plant and equipment. To put it another way, like AirAsia, the market is saying that the company should not exist. We will leave it to the parents to break that news to their Warhammer-playing sons.

Case Study #15

MBIA (2008)

From the Partnership Letters

JUNE 30th, 2008

The Municipal Bond Insurance Association (MBIA) is the largest bond insurance company in the world. Insurance is provided against the principal and interest payments of a bond in the event of non-payment by the bond issuer. The recent problem has been that when premium prices declined, the Municipal Bond Insurance Association did not stick to municipal bonds and began underwriting the losses of other types of credit, most notoriously bonds issued against, not the tax raising powers of a municipality, but the static value of securitized mortgages. Well, it has been a perfect disaster. We purchased shares after the firm took a sizeable write down on its equity value, raised capital twice, changed management and after new management bought shares themselves, and that has been a disaster too (as judged by the subsequent decline in the share price). Much of the debate has centered on the size of the credit losses, whether they are U$2bn as indicated by the firm, or U$6 to U$8bn as indicated by some skeptics, or U$13.6bn as implied by Moody's worst case scenario, or greater than that as implied by the stock price discount to the firm's claims paying resources. There would appear to be considerable leverage to the upside considering the current market value, however we question our, indeed anybody's, ability to so finely judge the losses on U$680bn of insured assets. Both sides (longs and shorts) will think they are right, and it is perhaps the insecurity of their own positions that leads both to assert their cases so vocally in the media, at investment conferences and on the internet.

Whilst our interest was peaked by the stock's apparent discount to anything but the worst-case loss scenarios, in other words the odds looked attractive, the investment case from our perspective was somewhat different. The market value of the firm approximated the capital retained at the holding company and readily distributed from the insurance subsidiaries and attributes de-minimus value to the in place insurance contracts written by the subsidiaries. The possibility exists therefore for a new insurance firm to be set up separate from the old. The old can be left in runoff with any eventual surpluses used to fund share repurchase at the holding company or new business at a subsidiary level. So, at first blush there appear to be lots of options open to the firm, but to understand why we sold our MBIA, one must first discuss dilution risk.

Case Study #16

A Word on Zimbabwe (2008)

From the Partnership Letters

DECEMBER 31st, 2008

Richard Zeckhauser, at his brilliant behavioural finance course at Harvard, asks attendees to answer various questions to which they are not likely to know the answer, for example, the surface area of Norway. The answer is to be expressed in five numbers: a median best guess, two numbers which represent the 25 the and 75th percentile of what you think the answer may be, and two more representing the 99th and 1st percentile of what the number may be. The more confident one is of the answer the more bunched the figures would be. The less confident the wider the distribution. So, for the size of Norway a student's line of thinking may be as follows: I'm not sure how big Norway is but it looks kind of smallish (first mistake, our minds may picture a globe as if we were looking from above the equator, this has the effect of visually squashing the landmasses toward the poles. If we visualised the world as if we were hovering above the poles, on the other hand, we may form quite a different impression), so, I think Norway may be 250 miles long by 75 miles wide say, or 18,250 sq miles. I cannot be out by that much (oh yes you can) so I'll double and halve my best guess and that will be my range, so Norway is no bigger than say 40,000 miles and no smaller than 10,000 square miles, and I'll halve and double those answers for the 99th and 1st percentile. Turn to the end of this letter for the actual answer (but watch out, even the fact that I have led you through a worked example may affect your thinking!). It is a great test, and what it reveals is that, in aggregate, we tend to be far too confident that we know the answer to something that we don't.

If you had asked us for the range of possible outcomes to events in Zimbabwe, we would have given you a very wide distribution indeed, from immediate international rehabilitation to, well, continued looting, and I do not think our distribution would have been wide enough (Zak now tells me he forecast events exactly!) Most recently, the factor that effects Nomad is the suspension of trading on the Harare Stock Exchange. The market is not suspended as such, but as all the stockbrokers have failed to meet the minimum regulatory capital required by their licenses, this applies even to the international banks, the exchange might as well be suspended. The reason for the sudden impasse is that the settlement period for transactions in the banking system as a whole has been extended enormously as investigators, responding to the alleged presence of fraudulent cheques, have chosen to, perhaps personally we don't know, check the cheques in the banking system themselves. Nothing is settling or clearing in a hurry. As a concession to the stock exchange, the authorities have allowed the brokers to trade, but only if the Chairman of the custodian bank, in our case Barclays Plc., personally underwrites settlement in the event Nomad fails to deliver. Hmmm. We have not placed a call to Mr. Agius yet, or his CEO, John Varley, but we are not optimistic of a favourable response. As you may imagine, the financial system has stopped. And if there are no prices on the stock market, we cannot price our shares, nor price the unofficial exchange rate for the Zimbabwean dollar. We have no idea when trading will resume, it could be quite a long haul, and so the independent directors of Nomad's General Partner have taken the view that our Zimbabwean holdings should be valued at zero, as compared to 0.28% of Nomad at the end of November. Zak and I don't think our businesses are worth nought, indeed we know they are not but, then again, we cannot give you anything for your Zim shares either. So, for the meantime, zero it.

DECEMBER 31st, 2013

In the mid noughties, economic conditions were almost uniformly favourable around the world, and equity market prices reflected the prevailing conditions. In a perfect world, Zimbabwe was a glaring anomaly. In Zimbabwe one could purchase industrial assets, often monopoly or near monopoly operations, for much less than the cost of those assets: cement plants for ten cents on the dollar and breweries for one quarter of the cost of the stills and lorries.

So, we rolled up our sleeves, crossed the border from South Africa, and set about our work. We identified some reasonable investment candidates but the first wrinkle to overcome were exchange controls that artificially over-valued the Zimbabwean dollar. These controls could be legally side stepped through buying shares in firms listed on the Johannesburg (South Africa) stock exchange that also had a listing in Harare (Zimbabwe), re-registering the Jo'berg shares in Harare, and then selling the shares on the Harare stock exchange. The process took some time, but the uplift in purchasing power was many fold above the rate offered by the central bank for cash transactions. With Zimbabwean dollars we could then make investments. We chose three sectors in an attempt to diversify from nationalisation risk, and to invest in businesses with large, powerful, major shareholders who could protect their/our business interests. At least we hoped. To this end we purchased shares in a cement company, brewery and construction/engineering firm.

In the years that followed, the country has lived through: a decline in economic activity of, at one stage, perhaps as much as one half; hyperinflation; the abandonment of the local currency by the central bank as a means of exchange; the suspension of the stock market (and associated zero value attributed to our investments); violent, forced nationalisation of privately owned farms; the attempted assassination of political opponents; and a coalition government which included, and continues to include, the incumbent President Mugabe. Even though Zimbabwe is far from normalised, Nomad's investments have risen in price between three and eight-fold in US dollars and, following the sale of our final Zimbabwean investments last year, the dollars have been remitted to Nomad's bank accounts in London. It is quite a story but, not one we would repeat in a hurry (we can do better with the compounding businesses these days

– and they are much less stressful). Enclosed with (the analogue version of) this letter is a one hundred trillion Zimbabwean dollar bank note issued at the peak in hyperinflation (we have a limited number, and so only one note has been enclosed per limited partner. If your letter did not contain a note it is because we may have multiple addressees per limited partner interest, and so the note will be with one of your colleagues). Today the note is worthless (absent an eBay novelty value). But we thought you might like a hundred trillion dollar bill (and who wouldn't?) as a souvenir of Nomad's adventures in capitalism (frame it for the study/boardroom?). (Partners who are more digital in their reading habits may claim their note with an email to Amanda at Galactic HQ – we only have so many, so one application per limited partner, please.)

Case Study #17

Black Arrow PLC (2011)

From the Partnership Letters

DECEMBER 31st, 2011

Black Arrow and Accounting

Eagle-eyed investors may have noticed that Black Arrow Group plc, a firm valued at nil in the Partnership, has recently declared a dividend of one pence per share. A one- penny dividend from a worthless holding means that, in accounting terms, we have created money out of nothing! The Alchemists were not that good, so what has been going on? Black Arrow was founded and continues to be run by the octogenarian Arnold brothers, who own or control around eighty-eight percent of the shares outstanding. The shares were de-listed from AIM (a UK stock exchange) in February 2010. At the time, book value approximated one pound per share, although the last traded share price was fifty-two pence. There is no market for the shares, and no prospect of a market for the shares as the brothers do not wish to own more (we have tried), and so the investment has been valued at nil in the Partnership (with a paper loss of around one tenth of one percent of net asset value). Zak and I know the business is troubled but it is also not worth nothing; then again to assign a positive value would be just as arbitrary as we could not give you cash for your shares either - so zero it is. Almost all valuations are wrong, in effect, and in the case of Black Arrow, although de-listed and in poor health, the firm has continued to operate with the resultant one pence dividend. Enjoy it whilst it lasts. We remain hopeful, but not optimistic, that the dividend alchemy will continue.

Case Study #18

Amazon

From the Partnership Letters

JUNE 30th, 2005

Why is this relevant? So far, we have only discussed one model we use to pick good investments which we call "scale efficiencies shared" as evidenced by Costco (and to a lesser extent Amazon.com).

DECEMBER 31st, 2006

How should we think about the price givebacks? Here is what Jeff Bezos, Amazon's founder, had to say in last year's annual report:

"As our shareholders know, we have made a decision to continuously and significantly lower prices for customers year after year as our efficiency and scale make it possible. This is an example of a very important decision that cannot be made in a math-based way. In fact, when we lower prices, we go against the math that we can do, which always says that the smart move is to raise prices. We have significant data related to price elasticity. With fair accuracy, we can predict that a price reduction of a certain percentage will result in an increase in units sold of a certain percentage. With rare exceptions, the volume increase in the short-term is never enough to pay for the price decease. However, our quantitative understanding of elasticity is short-term. We

can estimate what a price reduction will do this week and this quarter. But we cannot numerically estimate the effect that consistently lowering prices will have on our business over five years or ten years. Our judgment is that relentlessly returning efficiency improvements and scale economies to customers in the form of lower prices creates a virtuous cycle that leads over the long-term to a much larger dollar amount of free cash flow, and thereby to a much more valuable Amazon.com. We have made similar judgments around Free Super Saver Shipping and Amazon Prime, both of which are expensive in the short term and – we believe – important and valuable in the long term."

This is a précis of the scale efficiencies shared model that we dealt with in some detail in our analysis of Costco (Nomad Letter to Investors, December 2004, please ask Amanda for reprints) and is deployed by companies which have now come to dominate Nomad: Costco, Dell, Amazon and Berkshire (Geico, Nebraska Furniture Mart). The controversy is in the first four words "As our shareholders know", judging by the share volumes - they don't! And that's the opportunity. If the share price is being set by those with an eye on the next data point, then they can't also be looking out for long-term value. There are few traders that disagree with Bezos' value creation process, but they don't think it will show up in the numbers just yet. And if you only own shares for a month or two then you may get away with several trades before Amazon's success becomes apparent. In short, the traders have many small ideas, and we have one big idea. Good luck to them. Picking up pennies in front of a juggernaut is just not how we behave.

Notice also that the decision to lower free cash flow this year through sharing scale benefits with customers through price givebacks is based on a subjective judgment of future returns and their timing. It is not a strictly maths based equation and there is no guarantee that investment spending will always work. Bezos again:

"Math-based decisions command wide agreement, whereas judgment-based decisions are rightly debated and often controversial, at least until put into practice and demonstrated. Any institution unwilling to endure controversy must

limit itself to decisions of the first type. In our view, doing so would not only limit controversy – it would also significantly limit innovation and long-term value creation". Amen.

I think Bezos would run a good investment fund: but that is the point, good investing and good business decisions are synonymous. Mr. Bezos does not control the timing of the payback, just as we do not control the timing of Nomad's performance but, in our judgment, the ever widening of the moat surrounding Amazon largely determines whether our investment will be a success. We must now have the patience to wait.

JUNE 30th, 2007

After the doubling in the share price and the weighty resultant position in the Partnership it would be easy for Zak and me to claim victory, high five, and sell our shares in Amazon. However, the high weighting makes sense given our understanding of the destination of the businesses and the probability of reaching that destination. In previous Nomad letters we have argued that the biggest error an investor can make is the sale of a Wal-Mart or a Microsoft in the early stages of the company's growth. Mathematically this error is far greater than the equivalent sum invested in a firm that goes bankrupt. The industry tends to gloss over this fact, perhaps because opportunity costs go unrecorded in performance records. For example, our greatest error was the sale of Stagecoach (which has risen ever since sold), not the purchase of Conseco! We wonder, would selling Amazon today would be the equivalent mistake of selling Wal-Mart in 1980 (a similar time period after both companies' IPOs)?

Short-term result volatility and stock weighting

It is commonplace for overall portfolio construction to be as a result of stock weightings built up from one to two to three percent of a portfolio and so on up to a target holding. This means that weightings are anchored at a small number with only outliers reaching double digits. There is another way to construct a portfolio, which is to invert and start at a hundred percent weighting and work down! If fund managers did this, I am sure they would end up with completely different portfolios. Now we are not advocating all the fund in Amazon (well, not just yet at least), but in allowing past habits to anchor portfolio construction we have probably made the mistake of a starting holding that was almost certainly too low. Be that as it may, one effect of having one sixth of the Partnership invested in a volatile stock, such as Amazon, is that our results will also be more variable over the short term. Please bear that in mind in future performance. The volatility does not bother Zak and me one jot.

Our results since inception have been large, out-sized multi-year gains during periods of market distress (2001 to 2004) and reasonable, index matching/bettering multi-year results during stock market boom periods (2005 to 2007). This follows the predicted path outlined in the June 2002 Nomad letter when we quoted a Buffett Partnership letter from 1960:

"I have pointed out that any superior record which we might accomplish should not be expected to be evidenced by a relatively constant advantage in performance compared to the Average. Rather it is likely that if such an advantage is achieved, it will be through better-than-average performance in stable or declining markets and average, or perhaps even poorer-than-average performance in rising markets."

And we certainly do not have a relatively constant advantage compared to the index!

JUNE 30th, 2008

AirAsia is an example of scale-economics shared, which like Amazon, Costco, Carpetright and elements of other businesses in the portfolio (Geico, Nebraska Furniture Mart) have come to dominate Nomad (around 45% of the portfolio).

DECEMBER 31st, 2008

Scale economics shared works across industries too with the effect that load factors at the low-price Malaysian airline, AirAsia, are superior to high-low flag carrying airlines. And it works online: Amazon have deployed it so well that Amazon's operating costs (per dollar of sales) plus its operating margin are less than some of its high street peers' costs (per dollar of sales). This offers the prospect that, in theory, Amazon's high street peers could price their products at net income breakeven and still not undercut Amazon's prices or profitability. For these high street competitors the game is over. They will leak revenues to more efficient rivals as customers respond to the incentive of consistently low prices and convenience. Over time high street rivals, and less successful online rivals, will need to restructure, change their product, or go out of business. We estimate Amazon's immediate hinterland of high street rivals have combined revenues of U$150bn in the US alone. If these firms go away over the next ten years, as Circuit City, Woolworths, Zavvi and others have recently, and Amazon picks up one dollar in ten of their sales, then this alone would be enough to quadruple Amazon's US revenues over the next decade.

JUNE 30th, 2009

Upon reflection, it is curious that this quiet attitude extends, in its own way, to the companies in which we have entrusted your dollars: Amazon and Costco do not advertise (no shouting here); Berkshire Hathaway and Games Workshop do not provide earnings guidance (popular with baying fund managers and stockbrokers); Amazon, Costco, AirAsia, Carpetright, and parts of Berkshire give back margin to the customer, we would argue that is a pretty humble strategy too. In other words, around two thirds of the portfolio is invested in firms that in some major way shun commonplace promotional activity and they are no less successful as a result. If one steps outside of stock market listed companies to instead observe private firms run by proprietors and founders, it is the quiet approach that is far closer to the norm. Let's invert: why are publicly listed companies so promotional about their affairs? Are these companies shouting to inform shareholders and customers or convince themselves?

Nomad's investments may be in publicly listed firms but these firms are also overwhelmingly run by proprietors who think and behave as if they ran private firms. Amazon for example struggles with institutional investor relations so much so that the good people that man the IR department do so knowing that the firm's founder, Jeff Bezos, thinks their role is all but a waste of time! Poor souls. Bezos was also quite forthright on the subject of product promotion and advertising at this year's annual general meeting:

"Advertising is the price you pay for having an unremarkable product or service".

It is interesting to note that the other end of the promotional scale is exemplified by the pop star razzle of General Motors which had the largest advertising budget of any company whose annual report we read this year (actually that title went to GM last year, and the year before, and the year before...). The advertising spend was U$5.3bn in 2008, or U$630 per car delivered. It is fun to muse that had the company made cars that required little advertising support, then the firm's last five-years' advertising spend may have been sufficient to retire half of the company's debt, at par, instead! But, it seems, it was easier to call Madison Avenue than build cars that sold themselves. In our opinion, GM is very much the empty vessel making the most noise, in this regard. Our portfolio takes a different path. The whispered voice of price givebacks is economically fruitful but only if the customer reciprocates in the form of more spending, even in the face of more promotional approaches by competitors. For evidence that this is the case with our whisperers look no further than the average revenue growth rate of the largest investments in Nomad (including some of the companies mentioned above, err, not GM!) which, in the most recent reporting period, was in excess of ten percent!

Why? In a word, price. It is in times like these that the hyper-efficient low-cost providers, who share the benefits with their customers, often take permanent market share. This fact rather reminded us of a quip by Wal-Mart founder, Sam Walton, who, when asked about the recession of the early 1990s, stated:

"I've thought about it and decided not to participate".

Amazon, for example, is choosing "not to participate" in as much as trailing twelve- month revenues have risen by over sixty percent since the onset of the credit crisis, say mid 2007. Not that the steady growth in revenues has always been apparent in its stock price, as the chart below describes. As a youthful analyst I used to have a notice on my desk that read, *"share prices are more volatile than corporate cash flow, which is more volatile than asset replacement cost"*. It was reminder to concentrate on non-transitory items. Today I would update such a notice to read, "share prices are more volatile than business values", but the gist is the same: a reminder to focus on lasting value, not transitory prices. More on this subject later in this letter.

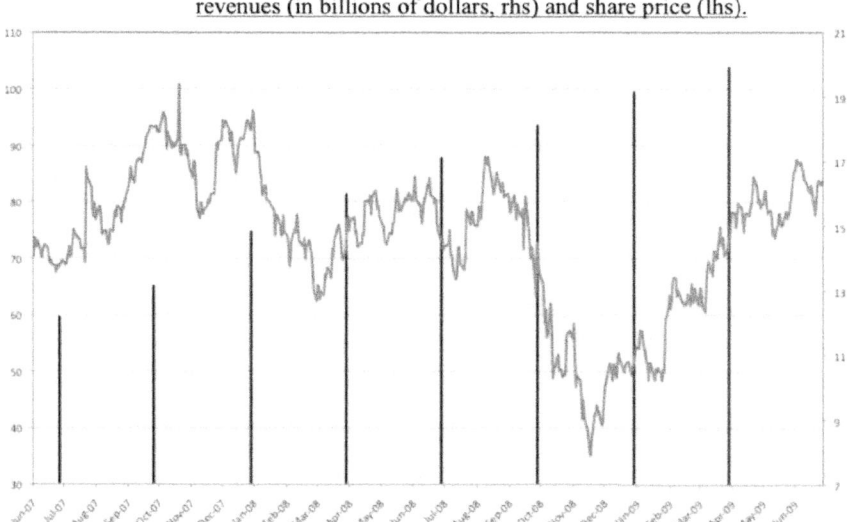

Chart 1: Make up your mind, U$100 or U$40? Amazon.com trailing twelve month revenues (in billions of dollars, rhs) and share price (lhs).

Source: Company accounts, Bloomberg, Sleep, Zakaria and Company, Ltd.

JUNE 30th, 2010

Forty-three years later, almost to the day, and Costco is the most valuable retailer of its type in the world. Cultures that care about the little things all the time are very hard to create and, in the opinion of Amazon.com founder Jeff Bezos, almost impossible to create if not put in place at the firm's genesis. (It may be worth noting that, in contrast, most businesses cut costs sporadically, often-in response to a crisis, as part of plan B as it were. With their backs to the wall, good costs (investment spending) may be cut as well as bad costs (bloat), with the result that the savings prove counter- productive in the long run). The Welsh insurance company was founded by a man who cared passionately about the little savings, and he institutionalised this orientation into the culture of the firm from the beginning. It was the way they lived; it was part of their raison d'être: it was plan A. And they shared that saving with their customers. Although I was slow to grasp the point, the insurance firm's advantage was very similar to that which had built Costco and builds Amazon today.

My mistake in not recognising that these businesses share similar roots ("D'oh!" as Homer Simpson might say) might be termed by psychologists as a "framing" error. When looking for an explanation to a situation the brain tends to latch on to what can be easily found to "frame" the situation, and if what is easily found is also vivid, then the brain stops looking for another explanation. I had gone looking for what I thought ought to be there, a vivid smoking gun such as a brand name, a location, a clever re- insurance contract, or a patent. However, there is no a priori reason why a comparative advantage should be one big thing, any more than many smaller things. Indeed, an interlocking, self-reinforcing network of small actions may be more successful than one big thing. Let me explain.

Take a one-big-thing-firm, such as a drug company, for example. A successful drug firm does not need to be particularly good at marketing, manufacturing, or research and development for that matter if, through a patent, it has a legal monopoly on a drug. But just look, if you will, at how fragile the drug company ecosystem is. A rival could displace it at any time with a better chemical and the firm would be left with little to fall back on, certainly not marketing, R&D, and manufacturing. Its period of exceptional profitability may therefore be quite finite and the big drug firms wrestle with this issue today.

Contrast this with a scale economics business: To better an incumbent's cost base a rival would have to be superior at, not one thing, but a million little actions – a far harder task. Amazon's letter to shareholders this year contains the following section:

"...We believe that focusing our energy on the controllable inputs to our business is the most effective way to maximise our financial outputs over time...we've been using this same annual [goal setting] process for many years. For 2010, we have 452 detailed goals, with owners, deliverables and targeted completion dates".

At Amazon one employee initiative to remove the light bulbs from the vending machines (really!) saves the firm U$20,000 per annum! At the Welsh insurance company the penny dropped: firms that have a process to do many things a little better than their rivals may be less risky than firms that do one thing right because their future success is more predictable. They are simply harder to beat. And if they are harder to beat then they may be very valuable businesses indeed.

DECEMBER 31st, 2011

The simple deep reality for many of our firms is the virtuous spiral established when companies keep costs down, margins low and in doing so share their growing scale with their customers. In the long run this will be more important in determining the destination for our firms than the distractions of the day. Jeff Bezos, founder of Amazon, made the following point in a recent interview in Wired magazine:

"There are two ways to build a successful company. One is to work very, very hard to convince customers to pay high margins [the Colgate, Nike, Coca-Cola model alluded to above]. *The other is to work very, very hard to be able to offer customers low margins* [the Wal-Mart, Costco, AirAsia, Amazon, Asos model]. *They both work. We're firmly in the second camp. It's difficult – you have to eliminate defects and be very efficient. But it's also a point of view. We'd rather*

have a very large customer base and low margins than a small customer base and higher margins."

Although Mr. Bezos does not mention it, one reason he prefers Amazon to be a large company with small margins is that if he shares the efficiency benefits that come with growth with his customers, he turns size, frequently an anchor on business performance, into an asset. In other words, the moat surrounding the firm deepens as the firm grows. So, having shared low costs with their customers, how are our firms' relationships with their customers going? One way to look at this is revenue growth. The weighted average revenue growth of Nomad's firms is currently over thirty percent per annum. Note: this is organic growth with, if anything, falling prices and no acquisitions in a time of austerity and little economic growth. It would appear to us that the company – customer relationship is in rude health. That's the cash-in. And the cash-out? Keeping it simple again: return on capital at Nomad's firms is over twice that of competing businesses.

The Postamble

From the Partnership Letters: The Postamble

SPRING 2021

We may be flattering ourselves to think that anyone will get this far but, for those that struggled through, congratulations are probably in order. And there they are, the Nomad Letters, our magnum opus (or, having read them, some might prefer "magnificent octopus" as Baldrick's malapropism goes in Rowan Atkinson's Black Adder series). Those that wish to read more (we are definitely flattering ourselves) can do so in William Green's book "Richer, Wiser, Happier". William has written the kind of book that we would love to have written but know that we lack the requisite skills. We are sure you will enjoy the read.

When we wrote the December 2013 letter, we did not know that it would be our last but, a few months later, the portfolio had been liquidated, funds returned to our partners and on we go. We did not like that final phase one bit: selling stakes built up over years felt wrong, the clients were grace itself but, even so, it is still an awkward conversation to take something away from someone, especially people that you like, and there was the administrative headaches of winding up an operation. Psychologically it all felt wrong.

So, why did we close? With big decisions like that there is often a mixture of forces pushing and pulling: The direction of regulation was certainly irksome and the tools of regulation unnecessarily blunt but, also, we wanted to feel that we did not have to justify actions, and inactions, on an ongoing basis to a revolving door of interested parties. We also felt we had wrung all that we could out of the investment process and to continue would have been to rinse and repeat, as it were. After all, we had what we needed, just a few superb businesses and we were unlikely to sell any of those to fund the purchase of another cigar butt, Philippine cement company, were we? The pull was the prospect of independence and a new adventure, this time working out how to recycle the funds for others to benefit. We wound up at an age (mid 40s) when it forced us to build something new (you can't sit on the beach forever) and, hopefully, we would live long enough to also see the consequences of our actions; we would have to eat our own cooking, as it were. Previous generations that retired in old age and died soon after, have not always had that opportunity. And, as we said in the preamble, we have not entirely left investing behind either.

Many of the successful and wealthy people we know are a little mystified by what the money really means. Investors can think their way to success without seeming to work in the traditional sense and the payoff in capitalism from stock picking can be extraordinary. It is one thing for capital allocators to be rewarded for their efforts but, in our opinion, taking personal identity in everything above X-amount is not a route to building a better world. We suspect that if you made it to the end of our letters, then you are one of the good guys and know that already. If good investing is a minority sport, then good philanthropy is a minority sport for those that do minority sports. Our band could do with moving from the fringes of society to becoming the norm. We hope you will join us on the journey.

Nick Sleep and Qais Zakaria, Spring 2021.

Printed in Great Britain
by Amazon